PlayStation.2

THE THIRD PLACE

A high-performance assault on your senses

rallyxs

The World Rally Championship magazine with attitude

Coming to rallyxs in 2002!

- **Exclusive Carlos Sainz column**
- **Hands-on tests of works rally cars**
- **Brilliant 'money can't buy' competitions**
- **Inside stories on the sport's biggest stars**

RALLY YEARBOOK
World Rally Championship
2001/02

Performance Clothing

The Pocket Polo
Code: SWRT-PS-POC
£19.95

The Baseball Cap
Code: SWRT-TBC £10.95

The Heavyweight Jacket
Code: SWRT-HW £149.95

The 1:43 Model Car £27.95

RALLY YEARBOOK
World Rally Championship
2001/02

Photography
Pascal Huit

Words
Philippe Joubin
Jean-Philippe Vennin "Rallyes Magazine"

Layout
Cyril Davillerd, Nicolas Bonardot

Coordination
Vincent Souchaud, Solange Amara

ISBN 2-940125-84-8
© 2001, Chronosports S.A.
Jordils Park, Chemin des Jordils 40, CH-1025 St-Sulpice, Suisse.
Tél. : (++41 21) 694 24 44. Fax : (++41 21) 694 24 46.
e-mail: info@chronosports.com   internet: www.chronosports.com

Printed in France by Imprimerie Sézanne,
11 rue du 35e Régiment d'Aviation, F-69500 Bron.
Relié par la SIRC, Zone Industrielle, F-10350 Marigny-le-Châtel.

It is a great privilege for me to write the preface to a book, which will take you on an incredible journey to all the countries, visited on the World Rally Championship. It is also my pleasure, as this year I have won the title.

The season was very closely fought and several drivers were in the running and there were still four of us capable of winning as we came to the final round, the Rally of Great Britain. For all those involved, it was a very exciting end to a hard fought season.

It has always been my dream to win the World Championship. I am glad that Robert and I had the opportunity to win it at home and I hope that there will be another Championship title in the near future.

I look forward to next year's Championship and hope to be writing to you again.

See you soon.

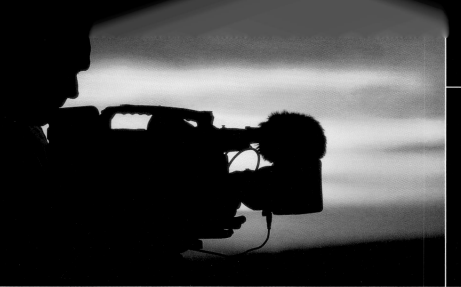

Contents

World Champions... And they,re getting together!

Richard Burns for the first time and Peugeot for the second year in a row have won the world championships at the end of a close fought season full of twists and turns. And for 2002, they will be fighting out of the same corner.

In twelve years of an assiduous presence at the highest level of on-road motorsport, a Subaru-Prodrive driver had only once won the world title. That was back in 1995 and the happy man in question was Colin McRae. The team took the Constructors, that same year and went on to repeat the feat over the next two seasons, but the Drivers, title continued to elude them.

Joining in 1999, or rather, returning, as he had left the team in 1996, as a replacement for McRae, Richard Burns got into his stride too late to challenge Tommi Makinen and finished second. In 2000, his season started well and then went downhill and he crumbled in the face of Marcus Gronholm,

when at one point he had enjoyed a 14-point lead.

In 2001, Richard finally found the back of the net, to become the second ever Subaru driver to be crowned World Champion. This time, it all came good in the last part of the season, rapidly making up the gap to the leaders.

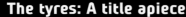

The tyres: A title apiece

In short, and it is nothing new, Michelin can be considered as the tarmac specialist, (unbeaten since 1998), while Pirelli has the rights to loose surface events.

With Ford joining Subaru on the books, the Italian firm could now count on two top teams, but it was not enough to defeat the Peugeot-Bibendum duo. On the other hand, thanks to the efforts of Richard Burns, Pirelli also picked up a title in 2001; its, first since 1997, when it took the Constructors, Championship with Subaru.

A really crazy championship

It was not a very big gap. Because while this season saw the usual changes of fortune, it was different to past years. In 2000, from the mid-point on, it turned into a duel between Gronholm and Burns, but this time it was not a question of a duel or even a three-way fight. No one really stood out and there seemed to be more pretenders to the crown, the further the season developed. Proof of that comes from the fact that no less than four drivers could have taken the title on the eve of the final round. And if there had been one extra round on the calendar, six drivers might have won it, as Gronholm and Rovanpera would have joined the quartet of Burns, McRae, Makinen and Sainz.

In truth, all these drivers had a funny old season, all of them experiencing more highs than lows. But not at the same time. For Tommi Makinen, everything went fine at first, but then took a downturn and he failed to score points in the second half of the season. Colin McRae,s score went from zero after four rallies to thirty after seven. That included three wins, so that for a long time, these two guys thought they were fighting for the title, ending up with 42 and 41 points respectively, scored in five events, including three wins. The peaks and troughs for these two were of truly Himalayan proportions!

Carlos Sainz was more consistent, but he lacked panache. For a while, it looked as though he could take the title without a single win. But he made too many mistakes in the final two rounds.

Finally, Richard Burns himself was not particularly outstanding until the second half. He only won once, but took the title in Great Britain, pretty much as he pleased, while his rivals all dropped out one by one.

Eight different winners

No one in this championship really managed to make a break for it. Gronholm,s return to the front end proves that. Indeed, it would not have taken much for the Finnish Peugeot driver, with three wins to his name as well, to retain his crown. Just think that, with two rallies remaining, the tarmac specialist, Gilles Panizzi still had a mathematical chance of taking it, after winning once and coming second twice. But, it was just a mathematical possibility. Didier Auriol, Harri Rovanpera and Jesus Puras also wrote their name on the winner,s trophy this year. That makes eight different winners for fourteen rallies. It is yet further proof, if proof is needed, that the World Rally Championship is the most hotly contested and keenly fought of all the motor sport disciplines.

Peugeot the recidivists

Peugeot and Ford out in front, ahead of another duo made up of Subaru and Mitsubishi and finally a third tandem comprising Skoda and Hyundai. The constructors, hierarchy hardly changed in 2001, when compared with the previous year.

If one includes Citroen, who were ineligible for points as they did not take part in every round, there were five constructors out of the seven present, who were in the running at every round of the series. It,s an impressive number, but there were really only two in the fight for the championship. Yet again they were Peugeot and Ford. They are the two „generalists‰ and clearly the two most powerful, even if it would seem hard for anyone to come close to Peugeot,s resources.

For a long time, it looked as though Ford would get its revenge for last year. The Focus was running away with it, even if the points, score was not so big, as Colin McRae was taking forever to finish a rally. For its part, Peugeot was proving adept at tripping itself up and went home from most of its excursions in sulky mood. It looked as though Malcolm Wilson and his men would bring home the title to the Ford men, who had been chasing it since their last success in 1979. And yet, it was not to be.

The first half of the season was a complete shambles for Peugeot: a triple disaster for its drivers on the Monte, a loss of reliability on the 2000 model and later with the 2001 evolution of the 206 not being ready on time and too many distractions in the form of trying to service the needs of too many customer teams. The times were good though, which was reassuring, but what was the good of that on its own? And this time, there

was no hope of doing well in the drivers, category as the men at the wheel split all the points between them. But the Lion was not dead yet. He had just gone to sleep. When he woke up, it was with even more of an appetite than in 2000. It was impressive and Ford was powerless against it. In 2002, Peugeot,s rivals, their nerves now stripped to the bone, will not be able to say they had not been warned..

And already favourites

If Peugeot had lost the title in Wales, it would have been pointless for the team members to cry over the ten points missing from the Swedish Rally. While Harri Rovanpera duly won, it had brought home absolutely sweet nothing in the way of points, as he was not nominated to score points for the team.

However, Ford also made the same mistake. Francois Delecour finished in the top six on the first four rallies, while Colin McRae failed to finish, but the French driver had not been nominated by the blue oval and could offer no comfort to his employer. This situation will not be repeated in 2002, as the rules have changed and from now on, teams will be able to pick three crews to score their points, with the results of the best two finishers from this trio, counting towards the classification. It is a positive move.

It will be the only change to the regulations, which might actually benefit Peugeot. Strengthened by the arrival of the man himself, Richard Burns, the French team actually looks even harder to beat than ever before. Unless Tommi Makinen, who replaces the Englishman at Subaru, manages to restore the balance. It,s one title apiece, unless of course Ford....

They should all make hay while the sun shines, because Citroen arrives as a full time competitor in 2003! ■

WORLD RALLY CHAMPIONS 2001.

Richard

the lionheart!

Maybe the man is no longer quite as accessible as in the early days of his career and the driver was not as impressive this season as in the previous two. Nevertheless, in the year he turned thirty, he quite logically became the World Rally Champion.

The carrot top is shorter, the look a bit darker and the man himself a bit more distant. But the laid-back kind of guy is still the same, while his driving has picked up some polish.

For a long time, he seemed to be following in the footsteps of that other lofty Brit, Colin McRae. Apparently, they were even friends in the early days, that is until the younger man started to put the older one in the shade. Bit by bit, Burns became the equal of McRae, before outdoing him at a time that is hard to pinpoint, but probably came along during the 1999 season. The success of one began to destabilise the other and relations between them got tense.

McRae-Burns, Burns-McRae. The world of rallying grew obsessed with comparing the two of them and as their performances grew to match one another, in the end it set one against the other. However, the image of the easy going Burns and the sulky McRae soon changed. Because today, Richard seems to have become more introverted and locked away in his own ivory tower.

You can't blame them, it is the price of success in a sport which has entered the big league. Richard and Colin have occasionally crossed verbal swords, but there has always been a little bit of finesse in Burns' barbs. Before the Rally of Great Britain, he compared his alter ego with Lara Croft, suggesting he was a virtual being in the minds of many, in the same mould as the muscled computer maiden. All this of course was a reference to the computer game which the Scotsman has endorsed. It was a subtle little dig.

In truth, it seems the two men need one another in a sort of love-hate relationship. It is understandable, given they are two of only three British drivers to have won a world rally and the only two to have been crowned world champion. That creates ties.

Having won what used to be called the RAC, three times in a row from 1998 to 2000, Burns had thus taken the upper ground over the McRae, but only in terms of results. Because, standing out in the Welsh forests at night, the hordes of fans who braved the fog always reserved the biggest explosion of fire crackers and the noisiest signs of encouragement for McRae, while Burns only merited the sort of polite reception the fans gave the likes of Gronholm, Delecour or whoever.

Maybe that will change now that Richard has won the title. He was happy to miss out on the fourth win to ensure he took the crown, which Colin handed to him virtually within sight of the start.

With this title in his pocket, Burns is now completely liberated from his rival. He is definitely his equal and maybe even better. He took the title through consistency rather than brilliance, and it does not really matter that he seemed less probing than in previous years. This consistency has paid off before, as in 1998 when it helped Mitsubishi to claim its one and only Constructors' championship, his points being added to Makinen's wins. Is there a weakness in his armoury? When the on-board cameras are on him in the cockpit, he always looks the picture of calm at the wheel, but he can still prove fragile under pressure, especially when things are not going his way. Several times this year, he appeared to lose concentration when something out of the ordinary occurred.

From now on, Richard should be stronger in the head. He will need to be as he has chosen to fly the Subaru nest to join a Peugeot team already built around another driver.

Is it a risk? Maybe. But Burns wants it too much and it has been a long time since he felt he wanted to drive the 206. If he succeeds in this new adventure, his nickname of Richard the Lionheart will suit him better than ever. ■

WRC

1. The famous London-Mexico Rally was not part of the world championship and was more of a rally-raid. It is probably the toughest and longest event of its type ever organised. Hannu Mikkola won in 1970. Rauno Aaltonen and Timo Makinen were in the same team.
2. 1969 marked the debut of the Escort Twin Cam 1.8l and the Mk.1 V6, a year before the RS1600. A prototype GT70, derived from the race car, also ran in 1970. In 1971, the two-litre RS1600 appeared and then the famous RS1800 came along in 1975, here in the hands of Waldegaard in the 1979 Rally of Quebec.
3. Recognise them? In 1988, Didier Auriol and Carlos Sainz are the two young hopefuls on the world stage and they are Ford team-mates. Unfortunately for the constructor, they switched to Lancia and Toyota, on their way to the top.
4. The 1998 RAC was the Escort's last rally. The WRC, in the hands of Kankkunen and Thiry, failed to win a single event that year. The Finn, who joined Subaru the following year, never won in a Ford.

Words: Jean-Philippe Vennin

Ford

a century of motor sport

In 2001, Ford celebrated a hundred years of motor sport participation. Throughout the season, Francois Delecour, the French driver, carried a discrete sticker to this effect on his Focus. Here we take a trip down rallying's memory lane to look at the men and machines which contributed to Ford's achievements.

In 1953, rallies were hardly the sprint events we know today, but the car constructors were already taking an interest. Maurice Gastonides won the Monte Carlo in a Ford Zephyr 6. In this remarkable shot, the winning crew are cooling the brakes with buckets of water!

The Cortina, in various versions, was the cornerstone of Ford's rally programme in the early Sixties. The Swede, Bengt Soderstrom won several events with this model, including the 1966 RAC.

The RS200 was a purpose-built rally car and Ford's only Group B machine. Aesthetically, it was easily the best looking car in the category. But its career ended prematurely, when Group B stopped at the end of 1986, before it had managed to hold its own against the likes of Peugeot, Lancia and Audi.

Two years after his terrible accident in the Argentinian Rally, at the wheel of a 205 T16, Ari Vatanen made his World Rally Championship comeback at the 1987 Finnish event, driving a Group A Escort Cosworth. He finished third.

François Delecour, with co-driver Anne-Chantal Pauwels. Alongside them, Peter Ashcroft, Ford's rally boss, who that year had chosen a trio of promising young drivers: Delecour, Wilson and Alessandro Fiorio.

A young English driver called Malcolm Wilson joined the Ford team in 1990, along with fuel supplier Q8. His co-driver was called Nicky Grist. Eleven years later, they are Colin McRae's boss and co-driver respectively. What goes around comes around!

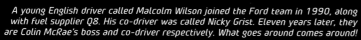

Having missed out on victory, giving away a few seconds to Didier Auriol in 1994, Delecour finally won the event the following year. A few weeks later, a road traffic accident would keep him off the world rally stage for several months, robbing him and Ford of the chance of the title.

During 1997, four-times world champion, Juha Kankkunen took over from Schwarz in the Ford team. With Sainz, they formed a formidable duo, but it was not enough to stop Subaru taking the title.

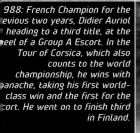

Shrugging off the image of a driver who could not stay on the road, Ari Vatanen became world champion in 1981, at the wheel of an RS1800 after a great duel with Guy Frequelin and his Talbot). The Finn's co-driver was a certain David Richards, who put an end to his career as a navigator at the end of the RAC.

The Swede, Bjorn Waldegaard won the world title with Ford in 1979, also the last time the company won the constructors' series.

1988: French Champion for the previous two years, Didier Auriol heading to a third title, at the wheel of a Group A Escort. In the Tour of Corsica, which also counts to the world championship, he wins with panache, taking his first world-class win and the first for the Escort. He went on to finish third in Finland.

In 1997, the new Escort World Rally Car, developed from the Group A version, bore Repsol colours, following the return to the team of Carlos Sainz the year before. The Spaniard won two events, including here on the Acropolis

1993 sees the debut of the Escort RS Cosworth. Delecour establishes himself as the undoubted team leader, despite the presence of double world champion, Miki Biasion. The Frenchman (here on the RAC) won in Portugal, Corsica and Spain

Ford took a second win in 1994, in Finland with Tommi Makinen. Driving a big Group A car for the first time, the new "Flying Finn" dominated his rivals. He joined Mitsubishi the next year and his career took off.

The new Focus WRC took its first win at its third attempt, on one of the toughest rallies from a mechanical point of view, the Safari. It is 1999 and Colin McRae is at the wheel. By the end of 2001, the Focus had won eight times thanks to McRae and Sainz.

TELLY VISION

The televisual revolution

This is the catch-phrase chosen by International Sportsworld Communicators (ISC) to promote the World Rally Championship on television. It is true that, looking at the way the sport has been broadcast over the past few years, one can talk about a revolutionary change to come in the next few years.

"The World Rally Championship can become as important as Formula 1." So says FIA President Max Mosley. Eighteen months ago, the Federation handed over the TV rights for the series to ISC, the company headed up by David Richards and since then, things have moved fast. We have never had so much rallying on our screens, filmed in such a spectacular fashion. At the moment, most of these images are to be found on satellite or cable channels, but moves are afoot to show them on terrestrial channels in several countries.

ISC has been unstinting in its efforts to put on a good show, with no less than three different types of camera positions. Some are located on the stages themselves, with others at the end of the stage, while a helicopter camera provides the sort of shots which give an idea of the fantastic backdrop to be found on most rallies. On top of that, there are twenty-two small on-board cameras fitted to the cars; looking to the front, or at the driver, the co-driver, the driver's feet and even the brake discs which glow red with the effort of stopping the cars. Every evening, all the film material is edited on-site in the service area. A round-up, lasting twenty-six minutes is provided to the contracted companies running from Thursday to Sunday night. A further fifty-two minute show is available on the Monday after the rally. The companies who have signed up with ISC can also use their equipment to provide further footage of their own.

The aim is that by 2003, rallying will be shown live on television. "Our aim is to have a presenter front a one-hour live show, for example, following the best drivers through the seventeenth stage of the Catalunya Rally, just as they would pick up Tiger Woods as he approaches the eighteenth hole in the Ryder Cup in golf," explains David Richards.

There is a body of opinion that rallying is best served as a television show, with a well put together segment of highlights, as the live event is hard to follow, with a series of cars coming through the same piece of road. But skiing has proved that it is possible to make a sport exciting, even when competitors are not running head to head. One possible solution for rallying is the use of fibre optics and mobile cameras. "As you change direction, you look towards the corner," continues Richards. "We would like to have cameras that do the same thing."

That's not all. Soon we will have split screen images, showing two cars at the same time at the same place, as we have already seen in F1 during qualifying. That will allow the viewer to see where and how one driver has an edge over another. There will also be interviews coming right from the cars as they run on the link sections between stages. Graphics will also be run over the images, showing speed, engine revs, the stop watch and distance covered, as well as which gear is being used. In the future, the sport will go interactive and the viewer will be able to chose the images to fill his screen. The future is here today. ■

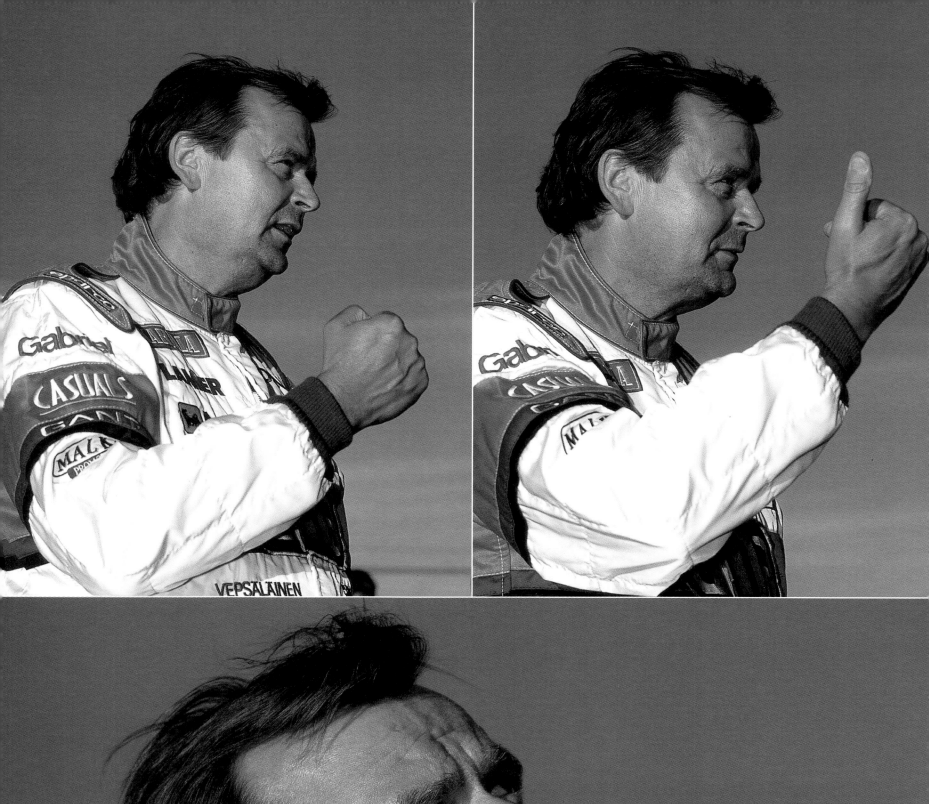

Markku Alen

the original "Maximum attack"!

Markku Alen turned fifty in 2001. To celebrate, he entered the Rally of Finland and he also took time to talk to "Rally Yearbook" about the highlights of his career.

Markku ended his world championship career with Toyota. Here, he drives the Celica GT4 in the 1993 Safari.

Markku's two sons were his biggest fans on this year's Rally of Finland. There were plenty of others!

Markku (here on the 1981 San Remo) took many of his victories at the wheel of a Fiat 131 Abarth, including the 1978 FIA Drivers' Cup.

To be honest, the Rally of Finland outing was not a great success, with a first generation Ford Focus WRC, which was two years old. "It was an old car with an old driver," he suggested.
Markku Alen is one of the greats in the history of rallying. In spring 2001, the magazine RallyXS listed him as the fourth greatest driver of all time. The list was headed by another name from the past, Bjorn Waldegaard, with two more recent talents, Tommi Makinen and Carlos Sainz, slotted in between them.
A driver of this calibre and long time holder of the record for the greatest number of wins (20, but 19 official), has naturally got plenty of memories, most of them good ones.

With the Group A Delta, Alen was always a front runner in 1987 and '88, taking six wins and only just missing out on the title.

In Finland this year, Markku Alen relived the days of "maximum attack." Who could forget them?

"The best moment of my career was my first rally in 1968," he recalls, speaking with that typically Finnish staccato version of the English language. "It was a little rally in Finland, which took place the day after I got my driving license. I'd had the car for six months. As far as I can remember, everything was going well, until I had some mechanical problems, when I was in second place. But it was a great moment."
And in the World Championship? "My first win in Portugal in 1975. I had already had some wins outside Finland, notably the Welsh International, but, well, I have too many good memories to only pick out one. All the wins were important, even if the first one was extra special. Portugal is a rally and a country which I like a lot, and actually I think it's a real shame it's not on the 2002 calendar. I won it six times, the first time with a Fiat Spider, just like my first win in Finland. Of course, my two wins in Corsica stand out, especially the first one in 1983. We fought like mad with Walter Rohrl. We were flat all the time!" Indeed, his duels with the German are now the stuff of legend.
Although he won the last ever FIA Drivers' Cup in 1978, he was never crowned world champion. It is one of his main regrets, especially when he thinks about the way he lost

the title in 1986. "I was world champion for ten days. So at least I know what it feels like. But it is not a pleasant memory. "It was a difficult time, for Lancia and for the world of rallying. We lost Henri Toivonen and his co-driver Sergio Cresto in Corsica, just as we did Attilio Bettega a year earlier. Then, everything was changed. Myself and Juha Kankkunen, who was driving for Peugeot and was my rival for the title, both took a lot of risks in the last rally, the Olympus in the United States. It was in December, there was a lot of snow, rain and fog on the hills. If I won, I was champion. I won the rally and the title."

The facts are as follows. After the Peugeots were disqualified in San Remo, Alen and Lancia were in a strong position for the title. But later, the results of the Italian event were simply annulled. That was Alen's famous twentieth win, the "unofficial" one. "Ten days after we got back from the States, we lost everything. We were in the middle of testing with the Delta and we were asked to rush back to Turin. I immediately understood what had happened. But that's all in the past."

It was not the only time Alen lost the title at the wire. A year later, it was the same scenario. "In 1987, I again lost to Juha, who had joined me at Lancia and again it happened on the last event, the RAC. But this time, it was my fault as I rolled. I finished third and Juha won."

Alen was part of the fabulous, but tragic time that was the Group B era. He has mixed feelings about those days. "I really liked the Group B cars, they were very beautiful and high tech. But, it's true that on tarmac they were too much. The power came in very quickly and we had up to five hundred, six hundred horsepower. On the loose, it was different. They were fantastic to drive." Known as the "Latin Finn" because he spent most of his career driving Fiat group products, he is still keen on Italy - his second home - and still casts an expert eye on the current rallying scene. He does not agree

that having to run flat out from start to finish on an event is a recent development. "In my day, it was also flat all the time. At least, it was for me. Sure, we might lift off a bit towards the end of an event, depending on the situation. But apart from that, it was flat out from day one." Alen refuses to single out a driver from the current crop. "As in every period, there are three or four who are better than the others, who are quick everywhere. That's always been the case." And of those he raced against? "I was the best, all the time!" he says before even waiting for the end of the question. And with that, he takes off laughing to himself. ∎

In 1987, he lost the title on the last event, the RAC. "But this time, it was my fault."

The association between Alen and the Lancia Delta S4 Group B car kicked off in 1986 with a second place in Sweden. At the end of the season, Alen was world champion, but only for ten days.

Having left the Fiat Group, Alen was part of Subaru's rallying debut, in 1991 with the Legacy.

In the 1975 Monte Carlo, Alen was third at the wheel of the Fiat 124 Abarth. A few weeks later, he would take his first win in Portugal.

An unexpected moment in 1987, which did not stop him scoring his fifth win in Finland, a feat later repeated by Tommi Makinen.

There are several reasons why Tommi Makinen is a worthy successor to Alen. Both men won their home event in Finland five times. Both of them were able to beat the Latin drivers on tarmac.

Alen was the first Scandinavian driver to win in Corsica. He did it twice, in 1983 and '84, with the Lancia Rally 037.

Markku Alen
Date of birth: 15th February 1951
Place of birth: Helsinki (Finland)
First rally: 1968
First world rally: 1973

His 20 wins:
1975 (Fiat 124 Abarth) Portugal
1976 (Fiat 124 Abarth) Thousand Lakes
1977 (Fiat 131 Abarth) Portugal
1978 Portugal, Thousand Lakes, San Remo
Winner of the FIA Drivers' Cup
1979 (Fiat 131 Abarth) Thousand Lakes
1980 (Fiat 131 Abarth) Thousand Lakes
1981 (Fiat 131 Abarth) Portugal
1983 (Lancia Rally 037) Tour of Corsica
1984 (Lancia Rally 037) Tour of Corsica
1986 (Lancia Delta S4) San Remo (annulled) , Olympus
1987 (Lancia Delta 4WD) Portugal, Acropolis,
                                  Thousand Lakes
1988 (Lancia Delta Integrale) Sweden, Thousand Lakes,
                                  RAC

World Championship
1st in FIA Drivers' Cup in 1978
2nd in Championship in 1986 and 1988
3rd in 1979, '83, '84 and '87

Sebastien Loeb, Daniel Elena and the Saxo quickly put an end to any suspense in the championship. They quite logically took the title despite missing the San Remo. "Seb" and Daniel will drive a Xsara WRC in 2002.

LOEB
takes inaugural title

2001 saw the first ever staging of the Super 1600 World Championship, now re-christened the "Juniors Championship". Here we look back at this debut season and the first man to claim the victor's laurels, Sebastien Loeb.

It certainly seemed like an attractive proposition as the idea was to introduce young drivers to the delights of the World Rally Championship. If possible they were to be integrated into factory teams, so it was a well-intentioned project.

This was the aim of the Super 1600 series. It attracted a field of around twenty runners, with no age limit, although in 2002, the maximum age allowed will be 29. There were a handful of well-known names in the pack: Sebastien Loeb from France, Andrea Dallavilla from Italy - a past winner of his home championship, and Manfred Stohl from Austria, the 2000 Group N World Cup winner. They would compete at the wheel of not so small kit cars; 1.6 litre capacity, two-wheel drive, on six rounds of the World Championship: Catalunya, Acropolis, Finland, San Remo, Corsica and Great Britain. Citroen, Ford, Fiat and Peugeot all joined the party and Renault, Opel and MG are expected to join in the future.

The season was not all plain sailing. Most of the time, only about one third of the cars made it to the finish. There was not much suspense to speak of either, as Citroen's rivals fielded cars that were too new to offer much of a challenge to the well-sorted and battle-hardened Saxo. It took

An experienced and acknowledged driver, the former Italian champion, Andrea Dallavilla hoped to relaunch his career via the Super 1600. The Fiat Punto's lack of development quickly saw that hope evaporate, but the end of the season went better. He finished runner-up to Loeb in the classification.

until the Tour of Corsica for Dallavilla and his Punto to give Sebastien Loeb a hard time, but mechanical gremlins intervened, allowing the Citroen driver, who won three of the first four rounds - all those in which he took part in fact - to walk off with the title.

"It's true that, at the start, we had a slight advantage because of the Saxo's better reliability, because the other cars were newer and lacked development," explained the category's first world champion. "Often, there was not such a big gap in the early part of the rally, but then the others ran into mechanical problems. Later in the season, life got more difficult. Especially in Corsica, where Dallavilla had a car which had evolved considerably. It had improved quite a bit on the engine side and it was around 50 kilos lighter than in San Remo."

A disappointing season for Manfred Stohl, the 2000 Group N champion, who had failed to find a WRC drive. His Punto was never really on the pace and he was dominated by Dallavilla.

The young Italian, Giandomenico Basso proved to be very quick at the wheel of a Fiat Punto. He should be among the ones to watch in 2002.

The Saxo was not immune to the occasional mechanical mishap itself. "We had problems every time, which cost us a bit of time, but we always managed to sort it out. That meant we always had to attack to get back on top and that's no bad thing."

Generally, Loeb reckoned the Super 1600 class was a good thing and that it's first season had worked well. "The championship gave young drivers a chance to be in the spotlight, because not everyone can afford to run a WRC. It also provides experience. That was the main reason I was interested in taking part. The fact that I was dominant this year has been enough for Citroen to have the confidence to give me a drive for next year. It's the same thing for Francois Duval. That was after all the aim of the Super 1600, and it seems to have worked."

From a driving point of view, one would assume there is a big difference between a Super 1600 and a World Rally Car. According to Loeb, there is not much in it. "Of course, it's not the same. A WRC is driven with a much more sliding style at the rear. But coming from the kit car, I did not have much of a problem adapting to the WRC. So I don't think the difference is that big. You can go quickly with a Super 1600. When you can master a car like that, it proves you have got what it takes."

It was an up and down year for the rapid Scotsman, Niall McShea. He had to wait until he traded in his Ford for a Citroen to show what he could do.

The young 20-year-old Belgian, Francois Duval was the revelation of the series. He was the only driver capable of doing good times at the wheel of the Ford Puma. He had no major results because of the car's lack of reliability. However, he ended up with a Ford contract for 2002 to do the Juniors Championship and five world championship events.

With two podium finishes, Belgium's Larry Cols finished third in the championship.

A season to forget for Frenchmen Patrick Magaud and Benoit Rousselot. They suffered an incredible string of mechanical failures with their Ford Pumas and could never mount an effective challenge.

The Peugeot 206 was never quick or reliable enough to challenge the Saxo. It was a shame for Cedric Robert, who was often one of the quickest. His team-mate, Nicolas Bernardi was crippled with bad luck and made too many mistakes. Peugeot will not take part in the championship in 2002.

It was a dream season for Loeb and it seemed as though his career had recently been overseen by a guiding star. "I'm not complaining! The season was really great, apart from going off the road twice in the French Championship. On the mechanical side, we hardly had any serious bothers all season. In France, I learned to work with a factory team, to drive a powerful car (Xsara kit-car) and to drive it quickly. The Super 1600 gave me experience on the world stage and I added the Monte and Sweden with a private programme."

In 2002, Seb will join the "big boys" in the seven rallies which Citroen plans to enter, with the likelihood of a full season the following year. Does he owe it to his results in Super 1600, or to his impeccable performance on the San Remo (2nd in the Xsara WRC?) "The San Remo was the key to Guy Frequelin's decision to give me a drive next year. But it was the Super 1600 and the French Championship together, which meant I was ready for San Remo." ■

THE STARS

RICHARD BURNS
SUBARU

IDENTITY CARD
- Nationality: British
- Date of birth: January, 17 1971
- Place of birth: Reading (England)
- Resident: Reading (England)
- Marital status: Single
- Hobbies: Motorbikes, Moutain-bikes
- Co-driver: Robert Reid, British

CAREER
- First Rally: 1990
- Number of Rallies: 76
- Number of victories: 10

1994 - 19th in championship
1995 - 9th in championship
1996 - 9th in championship
1997 - 7th in championship
1998 - 6th in championship
1999 - 2nd in championship
2000 - 2nd in championship
2001 - WORLD CHAMPION

All things considered, Richard Burns was something of a surprise guest at the end of season decider. After the Finnish Rally, having just crossed the line in second place at the end of a fantastic performance, where he had been lucky to benefit Rovanpera's troubles, he still was not seen as a title contender. He was nineteen points down on Tommi Makinen, after the gap had peaked at twenty-five and fifteen behind Colin McRae. However, no one could have predicted that the Finn would then hit a terrible barren spell and the money would have been on the Scot having the best chance of chasing him home.
But then came victory in New Zealand and the whole situation was turned on its head. That win was a tactical masterpiece.
However, this was the only victory of the season, whereas McRae and Makinen had three. It does not mean that much, when you consider that in 2000, Burns was not in contention for the title, even after winning four rallies to Gronholm's three.
Burns made more serious mistakes than McRae (in Sweden, in Greece and San Remo), but fewer than Makinen. The first part of the season was fairly anonymous and he won the title through his consistency rather than scoring the big points. Until this year, he had never been champion, having finished runner-up for the past two years. Having won the greatest number of events in that period, this title was well deserved.

COLIN McRAE
FORD

Colin McRae was crowned world champion back in 1995 and he had never looked closer to repeating that feat than he did in 2001. For four years, from 1996 to 1999, like everyone else, he had to contend with being a loyal subject of King Tommi Makinen. During the first three of those years, he made too many mistakes at the wheel of his Subaru, to do any better than scrape into the top three at the end of the season. This despite picking up several wins and showing a sense of panache and a permanent attacking spirit. Having then switched to Ford, he had to contend with a new and underdeveloped Focus WRC. After two surprise wins at the start of the year, the car proved dramatically fragile and unreliable. Almost inevitably, the Scotsman drifted back into his bad old ways towards the end of the season.

In 2000, after a chaotic start, Colin picked up two wins and several good finishes, which put him back in the hunt for the title. But then came Corsica and that accident, which led to an inevitable loss of confidence, prior to suffering a blown engine in Australia.

For all these reasons, McRae really did not want the 2001 championship to slip from his grasp, as he lined up at the start of the Rally of Great Britain. After another terrible start to the season, with no points on his scoreboard after four rallies, he was back in the hunt, taking three wins on the trot. All year long, he had avoided the sort of accident that usually blotted his copybook. Right up to the last event of the year, when his huge crash could not have come at a worse time.

IDENTITY CARD
- Nationality: British
- Date of birth: August, 5 1968
- Place of birth: Lanark (Scotland)
- Resident: Scotland, Monaco
- Marital status: Married
- Children: 1 daughter
- Hobbies: Water-skiing, motocross
- Co-driver: Nicky Grist (British)

CAREER
- First Rally: 1986
- Number of Rallies: 115
- Number of victories: 23

1992 - 8th in championship
1993 - 5th in championship
1994 - 4th in championship
1995 - WORLD CHAMPION
1996 - 2nd in championship
1997 - 2nd in championship
1998 - 3rd in championship
1999 - 6th in championship
2000 - 4th in championship
2001 - 2nd in championship

TOMMI MÄKINEN
MITSUBISHI

This was, by a long way, the great Makinen's most inconsistent season. The 2000 season had already seen him slip from the spotlight and back into the pack. What had happened to the man who had taken four consecutive titles, averaging around four wins a year? In 2000, his Lancer was past it and he could nothing against Gronholm, not to mention Burns, Sainz or even McRae.

But if he started this season in the unexpected role of an underdog, he soon reminded everyone what he was made of. He set off at supersonic pace, winning three rallies from seven starts! While some of the credit had to go to the driver, who had obviously not mysteriously lost his skills at the wheel, much of it had to do with the rejuvenated Mitsubishi. The fact that many of Makinen's rival drivers and teams were busy getting things wrong on their own account, also helped of course.

Sadly, after the pride came the fall and it was a hard one. This time, Makinen really was relegated to the role of spear carrier. The new Lancer World Rally Car, which arrived in the autumn, was not as competitive. Disarmed, Tommi resorted to throwing himself off the road, no less than six times! Even the elements joined forces against him in New Zealand. Although he was handily placed at the start of the final event of the season, his name was never mentioned in any list of possible winners. Sadly, with good cause.

IDENTITY CARD
- Nationality: Finnish
- Date of birth: June, 26 1964
- Place of birth: Puupola (Finland)
- Resident: Puupola and Monaco
- Marital status: Single
- Children: 1 son (Henry)
- Hobbies: Golf, skiing, hiking
- Co-driver: Risto Mannisenmaki (Finnish)

CAREER
- First Rally: 1984
- Number of Rallies: 111
- Number of victories: 23

1990 - 20th in championship
1991 - 29th in championship
1993 - 10th in championship
1994 - 10th in championship
1995 - 5th in championship
1996 - WORLD CHAMPION
1997 - WORLD CHAMPION
1998 - WORLD CHAMPION
1999 - WORLD CHAMPION
2000 - 5th in championship
2001 - 3rd in championship

ALISTER McRAE
HYUNDAI

Just looking at the results sheets reveals a less than brilliant season for the younger McRae brother. It adds fuel to the fire for those who maintain he is not a patch on Colin, in terms of ability. But closer inspection of the facts shows that McRae junior was a worthy competitor who did not waste his time. Whatever the terrain, he equalled or bettered the performance of his so-called "specialist" team-mates - Erikkson on the loose, and Liatti on tarmac. He also gained plenty of useful experience for the future. 2002 will be an important step forward for Alister as he joins the top ranks, driving for the factory Mitsubishi team.

IDENTITY CARD
- Nationality: British
- Date of birth: December, 20 1970
- Place of birth: Lanark (Scotland)
- Resident: Lanark
- Marital status: Single
- Hobbies: Moto-cross, Moutain-bike
- Co-driver: David Senior (British)

CAREER
- First Rally: 1988
- Number of Rallies: 55
- Number of victories: 0

1995 - 10th in championship
2000 - Not classified
2001 - 16th in championship

MARCUS GRÖNHOLM
PEUGEOT

The "surprise" world champion of the 2000 season was never in a position to repeat that performance. He had a disastrous start to the year, with a string of mechanical failures and driver errors. Marcus returned to form with his home event, the Finnish Rally. But, by then, it was much too late to think in terms of a second Drivers' title. On top of that, some cracks began to appear in his relationship with Peugeot, which previously had been all sweetness and light. It stemmed from those early season problems, as well as rumours of Richard Burns lining himself up for some preferential treatment, when he joins the team in 2002. Rivalry between these two should be one of the features of next year.

IDENTITY CARD
- Nationality: Finnish
- Date of birth: February, 5 1968
- Place of birth: Espoo (Finnish)
- Resident: Inkoo (Finland)
- Marital status: Married
- Children: 3 (Jessica, Johanna and Niclas)
- Co-driver: Timo Rautiainen (Finnish)

CAREER
- First Rally: 1989
- Number of Rallies: 57
- Number of victories: 6

1996 - 10th in championship
1997 - 12th in championship
1998 - 16th in championship
1999 - 15th in championship
2000 - WORLD CHAMPION
2001 - 4th in championship

CARLOS SAINZ
FORD

Once again, the highly-experienced Spaniard was in the hunt for the title right up to the end of the season, as he still had a very slight mathematical possibility of taking the crown, going into the final round, the Rally of Great Britain. It was a repeat of the scenarios of 1989, '91, '94, '95 and '98, not to mention 1990 and '92, when he took the World Championship title. But his score, in terms of rally wins, has not moved forward. The Matador has only won twice in the last four seasons: once in 1998 and the other time in 2000. It is therefore consistency which has paid off this year, even if Carlos was usually running in the shadow of team-mate Colin McRae. Rumour has it that 2002 will be his final year.

IDENTITY CARD
- Nationality: Spanish
- Date of birth: April, 12 1962
- Place of birth: Spain
- Resident: Madrid (Spain)
- Marital status: Married
- Children: 3 (Bianca, Carlos and Ana)
- Hobbies: Football, squash, tennis
- Co-driver: Luis Moya (Spanish)

CAREER
- First Rally: 1987
- Number of Rallies: 151
- Number of victories: 23

1988 - 11th in championship
1989 - 8th in championship
1990 - WORLD CHAMPION
1991 - 2nd in championship
1992 - WORLD CHAMPION
1993 - 8th in championship
1994 - 2nd in championship
1995 - 2nd in championship
1996 - 3rd in championship
1997 - 3rd in championship
1998 - 2nd in championship
1999 - 4th in championship
2000 - 3rd in championship
2001 - 5th in championship

DIDIER AURIOL
PEUGEOT

There is no point in mincing words; much was expected of Didier Auriol's year with Peugeot, in the way of miracles and marvels, but it simply did not happen. It was a terrible waste. The waste was all the harder to understand as the driver still had the speed, and results for the other 206s proved the car was on the pace. Yes, there was a win in the Catalan event, second places in Italy and Corsica, and some very good stage times in Finland and Australia. But there were also plenty of mistakes scattered around. However, above all, there was a major lack of understanding and empathy between driver and team, and a lack of dialogue with the technical crew. The crisis rumbled on throughout the year until the inevitable divorce.

IDENTITY CARD
- Nationality: French
- Date of birth: August, 18 1958
- Place of birth: Montpellier (France)
- Resident: Millau (France)
- Marital status: Married
- Children: 2 (Robin and Diane)
- Hobbies: Golf, Moutain-bike
- Co-driver: Denis Giraudet (french)

CAREER
- First Rally: 1984
- Number of Rallies: 136
- Number of victories: 20

1988 - 6th in championship
1989 - 4th in championship
1990 - 2nd in championship
1991 - 3rd in championship
1992 - 3rd in championship
1993 - 3rd in championship
1994 - WORLD CHAMPION
1995 - Excluded (Toyota)
1996 - 25th in championship
1997 - 11th in championship
1998 - 5th in championship
1999 - 3rd in championship
2000 - 12th in championship
2001 - 6th in championship

ARMIN SCHWARZ
SKODA

This was Armin's third season with the Skoda outfit, which had ensured he maintained a presence in the world championship. The season got underway with an exceptional performance on the Monte Carlo event, which was run in the most treacherous conditions we have seen in a long time. He narrowly missed out on a podium finish, after a thrilling duel on the last day with Delecour. Then, there was the Safari. In Kenya, a combination of the driver's experience and the car's strength worked wonders and this time he ended up in third place. But after that, came nothing but disappointment for the German, as his car stagnated in performance terms and seemed to become more and more fragile. In the end, Schwarz had enough of all the pain and misery, and so he embarks on a new adventure with Hyundai in 2002.

IDENTITY CARD
- Nationality: German
- Date of birth: July, 16 1963
- Place of birth: Oberreichenbach (Germany)
- Resident: Monaco
- Marital status: Married
- Hobbies: Water-skiing, music
- Co-driver: Manfred Hiemer (German)

CAREER
- First Rally: 1988
- Number of Rallies: 76
- Number of victories: 1

1991 - 6th in championship
1994 - 7th in championship
1995 - Excluded (Toyota)
1997 - 8th in championship
1999 - Not classified
2000 - 17th in championship
2001 - 11th in championship

PETTER SOLBERG
SUBARU

The Norwegian seemed to be facing a hard task, "nominated" pretty much for the year by the Subaru team, after just two incomplete seasons with Ford, and a stormy divorce with the team which had given him his initial opportunity to race on the world stage. The early part of the season provided a backdrop for a series of accidents for young Petter, despite the best efforts of his bosses to calm him down. He started to lose some self-confidence, before getting his act together from Greece onwards, where he scored his best ever result to date, finishing second. He was also very quick on tarmac. Undoubtedly talented and a pleasant sort of chap, Petter Solberg has all the requisite talent to make it to the big time in the sport, both as a driver and a personality.

IDENTITY CARD
- Nationality: Norwegian
- Date of birth: November, 18 1974
- Place of birth: Spydeberg (Norway)
- Marital status: Single
- Children: 1
- Co-driver: Phil Mills (British)

CAREER
- First Rally: 1996
- Number of Rallies: 32
- Number of victories: 0
1999 - 18th in championship
2000 - 10th in championship
2001 - 9th in championship

HARRI ROVANPERÄ
PEUGEOT

Just as they did with Gronholm, Peugeot went and plucked Harri Rovanpera out of the pack, when his career appeared to be in the doldrums, or even worse. Just like Gronholm, it did not take Harri long to repay the team for its kindness and he repeated Marcus' 2000 performance by winning in Sweden. There was one big difference though, as this was his first ever rally behind the wheel of a 206! He used all the experience gained from 1997 to '99 with Seat, to become the most consistent element of the French team's line-up. He was actually the most reliable, which led the team to nominate him more often than originally planned to score its points in the Constructors' Championship. 2001 saw Rovanpera move from unfuldaughterd promise to a sure thing.

IDENTITY CARD
- Nationality: Finnish
- Date of birth: April, 8 1966
- Place of birth: Jÿvaskÿla (Finland)
- Resident: Jÿvaskÿla
- Marital status: married, 1 children
- Co-driver: Risto Pietiläinen (Finnish)

CAREER
- First Rally: 1989
- Number of Rallies: 54
- Number of victories: 1

1999 - 9th in championship
2000 - 9th in championship
2001 - 4th in championship

PHILIPPE BUGALSKI
CITROËN

"Bug" was a big loser. His hopes of building a career in the World Rally Championship were already limited by his lack of brio on the loose - a common fault with a number of French drivers. Sixth place in Greece, although satisfying in itself, came at the end of a rather anonymous performance. But it was on tarmac, his surface of choice, where he is one of the best drivers in the world, that bad luck really struck. He retired towards the end in Spain, having dominated the event. That was followed by one mistake after another in San Remo and Corsica, even though he was blameless on the latter. No doubt, the uncertainty surrounding his future was an alien experience and contributed to the mistakes. In 2002, he will be relegated to the role of third driver, competing in just three rallies.

IDENTITY CARD
- Nationality: French
- Date of birth: June, 12 1963
- Place of birth: Busset (France)
- Resident: Busset
- Marital status: married, 2 children
- Co-driver: Jean-Paul "Coco" Chiaroni (French)

CAREER
- First Rally: 1982
- Number of Rallies: 26
- Number of victories: 2

1998 - 16th in championship
1999 - 7th in championship
2000 - Not classified
2001 - 20th in championship

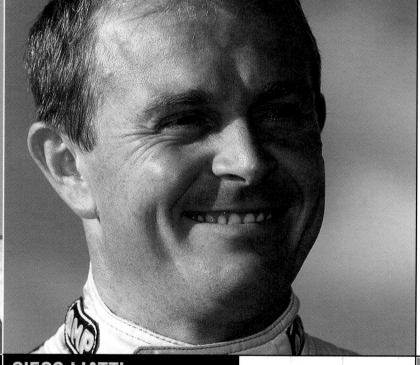

PIERO LIATTI
HYUNDAI

He won the Monte Carlo rally in 1997 and then took a moral victory in that year's San Remo, when he was deprived of winning his home event, having been asked to move over for Colin McRae. Piero Liatti had given Subaru something to smile about on tarmac events. But he had also picked up the tag of being a specialist in this discipline, something he tried to shake off by joining Seat two years later, without any success. With no plans for 2000, he had to maintain a low profile and accept the offer from Hyundai, who proposed four tarmac rallies, and two on the loose as a bonus. Sadly, the Accent underwent virtually no development on tarmac and Piero just racked up mistakes in Monte Carlo and in Italy. But he did manage to thank his team with two points in Corsica.

IDENTITY CARD
- Nationality: Italian
- Date of birth: May, 7 1962
- Place of birth: Biella (Italy)
- Resident: Monaco, Biella
- Marital status: married, 1 children
- Hobbies: ski, motorbike, Mountain bike
- Co-driver: Carlo Cassina (Italien)

CAREER
- First Rally: 1985
- Number of Rallies: 42
- Number of victories: 1

1995 - 8th in championship
1996 - 5th in championship
1997 - 6th in championship
1998 - 7th in championship
1999 - 22th in championship
2000 - Not classified
2001 - Not classified

JESUS PURAS
CITROËN

IDENTITY CARD
- Nationality: Spanish
- Date of birth: March, 16 1963
- Place of birth: Santander (Spain)
- Resident: Santander
- Marital status: married, 3 children.
- Co-driver: Marc Marti (spanish)

CAREER
- First Rally: 1982
- Number of Rallies: 33
- Number of victories: 1

1998 - Not classified
1999 - 10th in championship
2000 - Not classified
2001 - 10th in championship

"Chus" finally hit the target, winning the Corsica Rally. He also had the honour of being the first driver to take the Xsara WRC to a world championship victory. In the past, he had not been as quick as Bugalski and was slowed by mechanical worries on his home event in Catalunya. He then smacked a wall at full pelt in San Remo, when victory had seemed to be within his grasp. Success in Corsica therefore came at just the right time, but it was not enough to patch things up between him and Citroen. For 2002, the French team is only offering Puras, the multiple Spanish champion, a three-tarmac rally programme, when he had been hoping for a full season on the world stage. Jesus is still saddled with the reputation for being a tarmac specialist, despite competing in the Spanish loose surface championship in 2001.

MARKKO MÄRTIN
SUBARU

IDENTITY CARD
- Nationality: Estonian
- Date of birth: November, 10 1975
- Place of birth: Tartu (Estonia)
- Resident: Tartu
- Marital status: Single
- Hobbies: basket-ball, Mountain-bike
- Copilote: Michael Park (British)

CAREER
- First Rally: 1994
- Number of Rallies: 23
- Number of victories: 0

1998 - Not classified
1999 - 18th in championship
2000 - 21th in championship
2001 - 17th in championship

A fascinating tussle had been expected between Solberg and Martin, the two most promising drivers signed up by Subaru, in search of a replacement for Kankkunen. But the match did not last very long at all. Chosen to score constructors' points in Monte Carlo, Markko never even made it to the start of the first stage, because of electrical gremlins. Was it a sign? The young Estonian had been promised a twelve-rally programme, but he only took part in eight. Strangely enough, he only shone after announcing his plans to move, in Finland and Corsica. With Subaru unable to offer him much for 2002, he finally opted to hitch his wagon to the Ford team.

FRANÇOIS DELECOUR
FORD

At the time when last year's edition of this annual was heading for the printers, Francois Delecour's career did not seem to hold much promise. But today, it has been relaunched. Sacked without ceremony by Peugeot after the Rally of Great Britain, as a thank you for services rendered and points scored, he was pulled from the water by Malcolm Wilson. With Ford, Francois did not set the world alight, but still delivered a remarkable performance given the circumstances. As third driver, most of the time he was at the wheel of Ford Focus which had taken a serious pasting in endless test sessions and on several occasions, he had to work for his team-mates. With Mitsubishi, he will find a team devoted to his cause.

IDENTITY CARD
- Nationality: French
- Date of birth: August, 30 1962
- Place of birth: Cassel (France)
- Resident: Plan de la Tour (France)
- Marital status: Single
- Children: 2 (Anne-Lise, Gabriel)
- Hobbies: Jet-ski, mountain-bike
- Co-driver: Daniel Grataloup (French)

CAREER
- First Rally: 1984
- Number of Rallies: 84
- Number of victories: 4

1991 - 7th in championship
1992 - 6th in championship
1993 - 2nd in championship
1994 - 8th in championship
1995 - 4th in championship
1997 - 17th in championship
1998 - 10th in championship
1999 - 16th in championship
2000 - 6th in championship
2001 - 8th in championship

TOSHIHIRO ARAI
SUBARU

"Toshi" was brought into the factory team for ten rallies and, through the mysteries of marketing, he was often preferred to Martin as nominated driver. However, he was less effective and reliable than the previous year at the wheel of the satellite team Allstars' Impreza. It did nothing to spoil his good humour, because Arai is a guy who is always laughing. He has reason to do so as a nice seat with Subaru is always on the cards.

IDENTITY CARD
- Nationality: Japanese
- Date of birth: December, 25 1970
- Place of birth: Gumma Ken
- Marital status: married, 2children

2001 - 17th in championship

GILLES PANIZZI
PEUGEOT

Peugeot had done everything to hang on to its tarmac expert, even giving him some loose surface events in a private 206 run by Grifone. And Peugeot had been right to do so. Caught out early on the Monte, where he went off the road, and then unable to match the Citroens and Auriol in Catalunya, he was perfect in Italy, where he won. He drove sensibly in Corsica too, refraining from chasing Puras, when it was obviously futile. As in 2000, Puras delivered his fair share of points for Peugeot and finished respectably in the Drivers' Championship. Of course, he secured a new deal and a better one at that: five tarmac rallies (the same as this year, plus Germany) in a factory car and the nine other events with a private team.

IDENTITY CARD
- Nationality: French
- Date of birth: Sept, 19. 1975
- Place of birth: Roquebrune Cap Martin (France)
- Resident: Monaco
- Marital status: Married, 1 daughter
- Co-driver: Hervé Panizzi (French)

CAREER
- First Rally: 1990
- Number of Rallies: 33
- Number of victories: 3
1997 - 9th in championship
1998 - 12th in championship
1999 - 10th in championship
2000 - 7th in championship
2001 - 7th in championship

BRUNO THIRY
SKODA

Before 2001, Thiry's only rally with Skoda had resulted in a good fourth place. It was the 1999 British event. After a year on the European Championship trail with Citroen, the likeable Belgian returned to the world stage with the little Czech team. As he had expected, it proved a difficult season. In 2002, he is due to drive a privately entered 206 WRC.

IDENTITY CARD
- Nationality: Belgian
- Date of birth: October, 8 1962
- Place of birth: Saint-Vith (Belgium)
- Resident: Les Awirs
- Marital status: married, 2children
- Co-driver: Stéphane Prévot (Belgium)

CAREER
- First Rally: 1981
- Number of Rallies mondiaux: 67
- Number of victories: 0

1994 - 5th in championship
1995 - 6th in championship
1996 - 6th in championship
1997 - not classified
1998 - 9th in championship
1999 - Not classified
2000 - 17th in championship
2001 - Not classified

KENNETH ERIKSSON
HYUNDAI

He might have a baby face, but at the age of 43, he is the oldest driver in the circus and in 1999, he had opted to concentrate on tarmac with the Hyundai coupe. He persevered with it the following year at the wheel of the Accent WRC. But his best performance came on the loose, especially in the Antipodes, where he was very successful in his heyday with Mitsubishi and Subaru. So, his boss decided to push him into this type of event. He did not shine as much as in 2000, failing to stand up well in comparison with Alister McRae. Having lost his drive, in preference to Kankkunen, he refused to contemplate retirement and the genial Swede has signed up with Skoda for 14 events, including tarmac rallies in 2002.

IDENTITY CARD
- Nationality: Swedish
- Date of birth: May, 13 1956
- Place of birth: Appelbo (Sweden)
- Resident: Appelbo, Monaco
- Marital status: Single
- Hobbies: fishing, hunting, plane
- Co-driver: Staffan Parmander (Sweden)

CAREER
- First Rally: 1977
- Number of Rallies: 116
- Number of victories: 6

1986 - 10th in championship
1987 - 4th in championship
1989 - 6th in championship
1991 - 5th in championship
1993 - 7th in championship
1995 - 3rd in championship
1996 - 4th in championship
1997 - 5th in championship
2000 - 11th in championship
2001 - 20th in championship

THOMAS RADSTRÖM
MITSUBISHI / CITROËN

Under contract to Citroen, Thomas Radstrom moonlighted for Mitsubishi on his home event in Sweden, where victory still eludes him. He drove impeccably, finishing second, steering clear of the pitfalls, unlike team-mate Makinen. In Greece, this time at the wheel of the Xsara WRX, he retired very early, having failed to live up to Guy Frequelin's expectations. He did not manage to click with his team and his future did not look bright. But with no top-class driver having succumbed to Citroen's charms, he will be dusted off again for seven rallies in 2002, partnered by Denis Giraudet, who replaces Tina Thorner. We will see what happens on the Monte. And then there's Sweden of course.

IDENTITY CARD
- Nationality: Swedish
- Date of birth: July, 22 1966

CAREER
- First Rally: 1984
- Number of Rallies: 32
- Number of victories: 0

1998 - 19th in championship
1999 - 10th in championship
2000 - 16th in championship
2001 - 13th in championship

Ole Pozzo !

Team Cordoba, from Argentina, as one can guess from its name, conclusively dominated the Group N category. The 23-year-old Gabriel Pozzo was very much the star of its driver line-up. He rapidly built up a solid track record to inherit Manfred Stohl's crown, the Austrian having opted to try his luck in the Super 1600 class. He did not always have to fight that hard for his wins. He dominated on home turf and in Spain, he picked up the win after Legato went out. Mind you, he had to fight tooth and nail to beat Trelles on the Acropolis, while in Kenya, his team-mate was ordered to move over for him. On top of that, he scored some other good results on varied and difficult terrain, finishing third on the Monte and second in Finland. Towards the end of the season, his team manager, Martin Christie, who is also his personal manager, tried to secure him a WRC drive, but at the time of writing, it had proved a fruitless quest.

Marco Ligato, the team's second driver was less successful, but enjoyed his moment of glory in Finland, after no less than three Finns were forced to retire close to the line while leading! Gustavo Trelles, a four-times Group N champion, finished runner-up to Pozzo. He won in Cyprus and then again in Corsica, where he celebrated his one hundredth world championship start. As in the past, several rally wins went to local heroes: Walfridsson in Sweden as usual, Dias da Solva in Portugal, after Stohl and Ligato were disqualified, Fiorio, making a comeback in Italy and Ordynski in Australia, for the eighth time. Finally, a mention for Switzerland's Gillet, who won in Monaco and the fact that the great Stig Blomqvist did part of the series, but did not have much success.

Pozzo

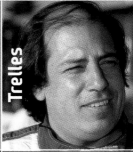

Trelles

Ligato

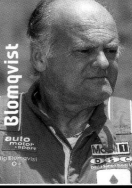

Blomqvist

Lundgaard the last one

The third and final year of the "Privateers' Cup" never really made the headlines. It came down to an anonymous battle between two Nordic drivers, both at the wheel of a Toyota Corolla WRC: the reigning European Champion, the Dane, Henrik Lundgaard and the Finnish champion, Pasi Hagstrom. The decision went down to the wire at the last event, with Lundgaard taking the title. The winner of this event in Australia, Oman Hamed Al Wahaibi, driving a Subaru Impreza WRC, finished third in the championship.

Lundgaard (Toyota)

FREDDY LOIX
MITSUBISHI

Over the past three seasons, Freddy Loix has never managed to adjust his style to the Mitsubishi Lancer/Carisma, be it the Evolution V, VI or WRC. It has to be said that this car, which is much bigger than the Toyota Corolla, had been set up by Finland's Lampi to suit fellow countryman Makinen. But even Freddy admitted that the team had made a special effort to help him out in 2000. It changed nothing and it was something of a mystery, as the driver had shown so much promise with Toyota. This season, patience on both sides was stretched to breaking point and there was no more room for polite discussion. It ended in divorce and the Belgian now finds himself in the Hyundai camp.

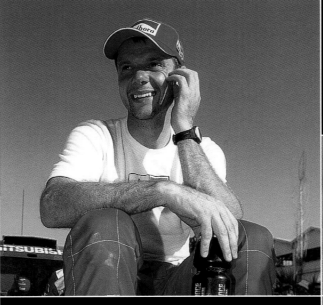

IDENTITY CARD
- Nationality: Belgian
- Date of birth: November 10, 1970
- Place of birth: Tongres (Belgium)
- Resident: Millen (Belgium)
- Marital status: Single
- Hobbies: Squash, mountain-bike
- Co-driver: Sven Smeets (Belgium)

CAREER
- First Rally: 1993
- Number of Rallies: 64
- Number of victories: 0

1996 - 8th in championship
1997 - 9th in championship
1998 - 8th in championship
1999 - 8th in championship
2000 - 12th in championship
2001 - 11th in championship

Al Wahaibi (Subaru)

THE TEAMS

PEUGEOT
206 WRC

Engine
- Type: XU9J4
- Layout: front transverse
- Number of cylinders: 4
- Capacity: 1,998 cc
- Bore x stroke: 85 x 88 mm
- Power: 300 bhp > 5,250 rpm
- Maximum torque: 535 kgs/m > 3,500 rpm
- Cylinder head: aluminium
- Valves: 4 per cylinder
- Cylinder block: aluminium
- Camshaft: double overhead
- Engine management system: Magneti Marelli Step 9
- Turbo: Garrett Allied Signal
- Lubrification: carbon wet sump

Transmission
- Clutch: 5.5" or 6" AP carbon tri-disc
- Gearbox: longitudinal 6-speed X-Trac sequential
- Differentials: programmable

Suspension
- Front and rear: McPherson-type
- Dampers: Peugeot

Steering
- Power-assisted rack and pinion

Brakes
- Front: ventilated discs, 355 mm diametre, 6-piston calipers
- Rear: ventilated discs, 300 mm diametre, 4-piston calipers

Tyres
- Michelin

Dimensions
- Wheelbase: 2,468 mm
- Length: 4,005 mm
- Width: 1,770 mm
- Rims: OZ 8 x 18"
- Weight: 1,230 kgs
- Fuel tank capacity: 85 litres

Do miracles happen in rallying? It might seem a far-fetched concept, except that the fact Peugeot managed to retain the Constructors' title had something of the miraculous about it. It fell short of being a faultless performance. There were shortcomings in all areas; performance, reliability, management, decisions and organisation. The drivers were not blameless either. But, at the end of the day, Peugeot repeated its 2000 trick of exploiting the series' diversity in terms of the terrain which hosted the events. They did this by picking up over half their points' total on tarmac rallies. It juggled its four driver line-up, designating different men to score their points at different rallies, as a function of their abilities or their current form. The French team had the means to do this and it did not need to be asked twice to make the most of it.

POSITION

- 1973 - 3rd
- 1973 - 15th
- 1974 - 13th
- 1975 - 5th
- 1976 - 8th
- 1977 - 13th
- 1978 - 8th
- 1979 - 11th
- 1980 - 8th
- 1981 - 9th
- 1983 - 10th
- 1984 - 3rd
- 1985 - 1st
- 1986 - 1st
- 1988 - 10th
- 1993* - 3rd
- 1994* - 5th
- 1995* - 1st
- 1996* - 4th
- 1997* - 3rd
- 1998* - 2nd
- 1999 - 6th
- 2000 - 1st
- 2001 - 1st

Position (*= 2 liters)

FORD FOCUS RS WRC

POSITION

- 1973 - 3rd
- 1974 - 3rd
- 1975 - 6th
- 1976 - 3rd
- 1977 - 2nd
- 1978 - 2nd
- 1979 - 1st
- 1980 - 3rd
- 1980 - 8th
- 1981 - 3rd
- 1982 - 4th
- 1984 - 12th
- 1985 - 11th
- 1986 - 5th
- 1987 - 5th
- 1988 - 2nd
- 1989 - 13th
- 1990 - 8th
- 1991 - 4th
- 1992 - 3rd
- 1993 - 2nd
- 1994 - 3rd
- 1995 - 3rd
- 1996 - 3rd
- 1997 - 2nd
- 1998 - 4th
- 1999 - 4th
- 2000 - 2nd
- 2001 - 2nd

Engine
- Type: Ford Zetec E
- Number of cylinders: 4
- Capacity: 1,995 cc
- Bore x stroke: 84.8 x 88 mm
- Power: 300 bhp > 6,500 rpm
- Maximun torque: 550 kgs/m > 4,000 rpm
- Engine management system: M-Sport
- Turbo: Garrett
- Lubrification: wet sump

Transmission:
- Clutch: Sachs
- Gearbox: 6-speed X-Trac sequential
- Differentials: M-Sport

Suspension
- Front and rear: McPherson
- Dampers: Reiger

Steering
- Power-assisted rack and pinion

Brakes
- Front and rear: ventilated discs, 4- piston calipers

Tyres
- Pirelli

Dimensions
- Wheelbase: 2,635 mm
- Length: 4,152 mm
- Width: 1,770 mm
- Weight: 1,230 kgs

How on earth did the Ford team manage to lose the Constructors' Championship? It's a complete mystery. The 2001 version of the Focus was rather more reliable than its competitors, and its two "nominated" drivers made less mistakes than the others. To cap it all, with two rallies to go to the end of the series, Ford enjoyed a comfortable forty-point lead over Peugeot, the only other team in the running for the title, given that Subaru and Mitsubishi were concentrating on the Drivers' crown.

But Ford lost as the season came to an untidy end. It seemed that the further down the road they went, the less competitive they were and the team was unable to maintain its early season pace. It was the same story we had seen before in 2000 and just like last year, Peugeot had started off poorly and improved during the year.

SUBARU IMPREZA WRC 2001

Engine
- Type: 4 cylindres à plat Number of cylinders: 4
- Capacity: 1,994 cc
- Bore x stroke: 92 x 75 mm
- Power: 300 bhp > 5,500 rpm
- Maximun torque: 48 kgs/m > 4,000 rpm
- Turbo: IHI

Transmission
- Gearbox: 6-speed Prodrive manual/semi-automatic
- Differentials: electro-hydraulically controlled

Suspension
- Front: McPherson strut
- Rear: McPherson strut, longitudinal and transversal rod
- Dampers: Bilstein

Steering
- Power-assisted rack and pinion

Brakes
- Front and rear: ventilated discs, 305 mm diametre, 4-piston calipe
- For tarmac: 366 mm discs, 6-piston calipers

Tyres
- Pirelli

Dimensions
- Wheelbase: 2,520 m
- Length: 4,340 m
- Width: 1,770 m
- Rims: OZ 8 x 18"
- Weight: 1,230 kgs
- Fuel tank capacity: 75 litres

Contrary to appearances, the new Subaru, code-named the S44, was not really new at all. While the bodywork was totally new, it was only the result of a restyling demanded by the arrival of a new Impreza road car. Compare this with the car which made its debut in Portugal in the spring of 2000, and was eighty percent new. Having employed the relatively inexperienced Solberg and Martin alongside Burns, Subaru was obviously targeting the Drivers' Championship. Despite respectable reliability, Richard Burns had a disastrous start to the year and only fought back in the latter stages. In the end, reliability proved to be his strongest weapon.

POSITION

- 1983 - 7th
- 1984 - 9th
- 1985 - 12th
- 1986 - 8th
- 1987 - 10th
- 1988 - 9th
- 1989 - 12th
- 1990 - 4th
- 1991 - 6th
- 1992 - 4th
- 1993 - 3rd
- 1994 - 2nd
- 1995 - 1st
- 1996 - 1st
- 1997 - 1st
- 1998 - 3rd
- 1999 - 2nd
- 2000 - 3rd
- 2001 - 3rd

MITSUBISHI
LANCER EVOLUTION WRC

Engine
- Type: 4G 63 - DOHC
- Number of cylinders: 4
- Capacity: 1,996 cc
- Bore x stroke: 85,5 x 86,9 mm
- Power: 300 bhp > 6000 rpm
- Maximun torque: 539 kgs/m > 3,500 rpm
- Valves: 4 per cylinder
- Turbo: Mitsubishi

Transmission
- Clutch: carbon
- Gearbox: 6-speed sequential (INVECS)
- Differentials: active control of anti-locking system

Suspension
- Front: independent, with McPherson strut with coil springs
- Rear: independent, with pullrods with coil springs
- Dampers: Ohlins with adjustable system

Steering
- Power-assisted rack and pinion

Brakes
- Front: ventilated discs, 4-pot calipers
- Rear: ventilated discs, 4-pot calipers

Tyres
- Michelin

Dimensions
- Wheelbase: 2,600 mm
- Length: 4,360 mm
- Width: 1,770 mm
- Rims: OZ 8 x 18"
- Front: 1,550 mm
- Rear: 1,550mm

The season got off to a pretty good start for Mitsubishi, with a hybrid Lancer, featuring a new rear suspension which made it a car which was half Group A and half WRC. It won three of the first seven rallies, before starting to run out of steam, which forced Makinen to over-drive and make mistakes. Sadly, the much awaited WRC, which was not really ready, when it made its debut on the San Remo, proved to be no help for the Finn. However, despite the fact that Loix was of little support, Mitsubishi still led the Constructors' classification up to the fifth rally of the year. That had not happened since 1998, the only time it took the title with Makinen and Burns.

POSITION			
	• 1977 - 10th	• 1984 - 14th	• 1995 - 2nd
	• 1978 - 13th	• 1988 - 14th	• 1996 - 2nd
• 1973 - 3rd	• 1979 - 13th	• 1989 - 4th	• 1997 - 1st
• 1973 - 16th	• 1980 - 15th	• 1990 - 3rd	• 1998 - 4th
• 1974 - 11th	• 1981 - 14th	• 1991 - 3rd	• 1999 - 3rd
• 1975 - 11th	• 1982 - 8th	• 1992 - 5th	• 2000 - 4th
• 1976 - 10th	• 1983 - 16th	• 1993 - 5th	• 2001 - 4th

SKODA
OCTAVIA WRC

The cumbersome Octavia also enjoyed a second coming in 2001. However, it did not really show in the results, as it also suffered a cruel lack of horsepower. On the Safari, its robust construction worked miracles. Schwarz finished on the podium and Thiry almost ended up in the points. The other good result of the season came on the Monte, when once again it was the German driver who shone, finishing fourth. In a season which, according to rumour, could be the last, before the team switches to the Super 1600 category with the smaller Fabia, Skoda will enter a new driver pairing next season, which makes equally impressive reading, with Erikkson and Gardemeister.

Engine
- Type: 4 cylindres
- Capacity: 1,999 cc
- Bore x stroke: 82.5 x 93.5 mm
- Power: 296 bhp > 6,000 rpm
- Maximum torque: 50.1 kgs/m > 3,250 rpm
- Valves: 5 per cylinder
- Turbo: Garrett

Transmission
- Gearbox: 6-speed sequential
- Differentials: programmable central diff

Suspension
- Front and rear: McPherson strut
- Dampers: Proflex

Steering
- Power-assisted rack and pinion

Brakes
- Front and rear: ventilated discs

Tyres
- Michelin

Dimensions
- Wheelbase: 2,512 mm
- Length: 4,511 mm
- Width: 1,770 mm
- Weight: 1,230 kgs

POSITION
• 1993* - 2nd
• 1994* - 1st
• 1995* - 3rd
• 1996* - 3rd
• 1997* - 2nd
• 1999 - 7th
• 2000 - 6th
• 2001 - 5th

HYUNDAÏ ACCENT WRC 2

The Korean company entrusts its rallying interests to the English preparation company MSD, just as Subaru does with Prodrive, Mitsubishi with Ralliart and Ford with M-Sport. In Portugal it turned up with the second evolution of the Accent WRC, which had made its debut a year earlier. All season long, the little Hyundai was handicapped by its engine and almost total lack of tarmac development. But it enjoyed its moment of glory in New Zealand, when Kenneth Erikkson emerged as the leader at the end of the first leg, even if he owed it all to a favourable start position on the road.

POSITION

- 1996* - 7th
- 1997* - 6th
- 1998* - 5th
- 1999* - 2nd
- 2000 - 6th
- 2001 - 6th

Engine
- Type: DOHC
- Number of cylinders : 4
- Capacity: 1,998 cc
- Bore x stroke: 84 x 90 mm
- Power: 300 bhp > 5,200 rpm
- Maximum torque: 520 kgs/m
- Valves: 4 per cylinder
- Turbo: Garrett
- Lubrification: wet sump

Transmission
- Clutch: tri-disc, 140 mm, carbon
- Gearbox: 6-speed X-Trac sequential
- Differentials: programmable central diff

Suspension
- Front and rear: McPherson strut
- Dampers: Ohlins

Brakes
- Front: ventilated discs, 304 mm diametre, 4-piston calipers
- For tarmac: 368 mm discs, 6-piston calipers
- Rear: ventilated discs, 304 mm diametre, 4-piston calipers

Tyres
- Michelin

Dimensions
- Wheelbase: 2,475 mm
- Length: 4,200 mm
- Width: 1,770 mm
- Rims: OZ 8 x 18'''
- Weight: 1,230 kgs

CITROËN XSARA WRC

Team boss Guy Frequelin had set out their objective: to win at least one of the four rallies entered with the new Xsara WRC, homologated on 1st March as a successor to the T4, built in 2000 especially for the French Championship. Everyone took him seriously, given that Citroen had the resources as well as an undoubted know-how on tarmac rallies. The objective was reached. Citroen dominated, but dropped out with mechanical bothers in Catalunya and again in San Remo, because of driver error. Then, in Corsica, the "other" French car in the PSA group, triumphed in style in the hands of Puras. In 2002, the second year of its progressive appearance on the world stage, Citroen will take part in seven rallies, four of them on the loose.

POSITION

- 1982 - 12th
- 1983 - 14th
- 1984 - 13th
- 1985 - 18th
- 1986 - 10th
- 2001 - Not classified

Engine
- Type: XU7JP4
- Layout: transverse, tilted at a 30° angle
- Number of cylinders: 4
- Capacity: 1,998 cc
- Bore x stroke: 85 x 88 mm
- Power: 300 bhp > 5500 rpm
- Maximun torque: 53 kg/m > 4000 rpm
- Valves: 4 per cylinder
- Camshaft: double overhead
- Engine management system: Magneti Marelli
- Turbo: Garrett

Transmission
- Clutch: carbon two-disc
- Gearbox: longitudinal 6-speed X-Trac sequential

Suspension
- Front and rear: McPherson with helicoidal springs
- Dampers: Extrem Tech

Steering
- Hydraulic, power-assisted rack and pinion

Brakes
- Front: ventilated discs, 376 mm diametre, 6-piston calipers
- Rear: ventilated discs, 318 mm diametre, 4-piston calipers

Tyres
- Michelin

Dimensions
- Wheelbase: 2,555 mm
- Length: 4,167 mm
- Width: 1,770 mm
- Rims: OZ 8 x 18"
- Weight: 1,230 kgs

Ultimate ꜱＴＩmulation.

Rally-bred 265 PS power, perfectly controlled through a 6 speed box and rally-tuned, ground gripping, All-Wheel Drive. A rally-honed 'Wow' from Subaru.

monte carlo

Once again, the Monte Carlo Rally lost much of its interest with a triple retirement for the Peugeot team. The event was run in tricky conditions and fell to a stunning Makinen, who was helped in part by McRae's retirement.

Second, Carlos Sainz was never able to threaten Makinen, unlike his team-mate, Colin McRae, who was forced to retire.

The Col du Turini – as Armin Schwarz comes through in the Skoda – is forever the symbol of the Monte, a true monument of the winter rally.

THE RALLY
MAKINEN, THE GIANT

The one thing Peugeot wanted to avoid at all costs was a replay of the 2000 event. If you recall, it happened in Gap. It was a chilly little morning which left three frozen little Peugeots refusing to fire up! They might have been waiting for a thaw, but instead they were left with a flood of recrimination. The French press had a field day attacking the 206.

A new century brought new hopes. The problems on the Monte, which had left the 206 stranded, had been put under the microscope, analysed and sorted from the very next event.

So there was absolutely no chance that the Lions would return to licking their wounds in despair. No, but, that wasn't the end of it. The car had changed little since the San Remo, the previous tarmac event, the drivers even going for the Delecour option of mechanical front and rear diffs, trusting electronics only to run the central diff. But Peugeot had come here determined to conquer all and win the most prestigious of all the rallies. Woe, thrice times woe, it all happened again. It was as if the Monte was cursed for them. The first round of the 2001 series would last a mere 330 kilometres for the French team, not quite seven hours, just three special stages or 20.40 percent

of the total timed distance of the rally. It was not a lot.

At least this time, the Peugeots did not suffer the ignominy of retiring, stranded in the parc ferme, as happened in 2000. This time, two of them fell with honour, steering wheel in hand, during the daunting section which went by the poetic name of "Bifurcation D5/D10 - Roquesteron." Better known to the fans as the "Le Mas to Aiglun" stage, it is a classic among classics, with the sublime run through the hamlet of Aiglun. Its chalky cliffs with vertiginous precipices, throws up a dream backdrop, unique in that its route is almost entirely downhill. The power of the engine is less important here

Three consecutive wins: after some difficult years, Tommi Makinen is crowned Prince of Monaco.

Faced with Makinen's supremacy, Freddy Loix can only opt for damage limitation in the same type of car as the master.

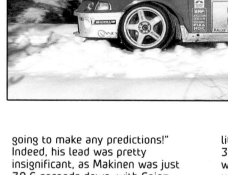

than the talent of the artists at the wheel and their immense courage in times of snow or black ice. Evidently, the Peugeot duet were trying just a little bit too hard as they tackled this stage for a second time on the first leg. Just over a kilometre after the start, Panizzi was the first to be caught out, getting his wheels out of the ice ruts. Ambulance, hospital, check-ups, a bruise to the soul, sent home...

"I am terribly disappointed, but it was 100% my fault," admitted the driver a few days later. "I took some risks because, in this place, if it had worked I could have picked up 20 seconds over the second place man. If I had to do it again, I would tackle it with the same approach."

A few minutes after he was eliminated from the rally, Auriol was attacking the mountain near the end of the stage. He even got a time, second behind Delecour, which allowed him to safeguard his lead overall. But the rock was stronger than the Lion, which had to hobble out of the stage, with its left rear wheel ripped off. "It all came to nothing," said Didier. "The only positive thing to come out of this negative, is that this was my first event in the 206 and I was leading at the time." He was bruised mentally, shipped back to Monaco and his hotel room. It was a shame all the same,

as Auriol had been leading and Panizzi was fifth. Their great performance had almost made up for the disappointment of Marcus Gronholm's premature retirement, with his water pump working as well as a sieve as early as the second stage. "Just like in 2000, my season will start in Sweden," said the world champion, trying a touch of self-consolation after his inaugural run with the Number 1 on his doors, came to nothing. Maybe he had a point and maybe Peugeot should consider simply missing the first event on the calendar in future. The French team was not alone in getting whitewashed, on this Monte, as white as the snow, which had fallen abundantly for the two days prior to the start. Getting back to the Principality each evening was not an easy task this year, as the event had a bite to it. In the Subaru camp, Martin (electrics) and then Solberg (accident) had both been flying as usual, but not for long enough, as usual. They never made it to the end of the first leg and neither did Liatti (engine). Once Auriol was out of the running, Colin McRae settled happily into the lead, thanks to a consistent run, during which he showed unusual prudence. "I was careful all through the leg and I made no mistakes. Even though I plan to do the same for the rest of the event, I am definitely not

going to make any predictions!" Indeed, his lead was pretty insignificant, as Makinen was just 30.6 seconds down, with Sainz trailing by only 33.9.

This meant that the second leg turned into a good old family feud between the Scotsman and the Finn. It was just like the old days, which had done so much to give the fans a fun time since 1996, usually refereed by the battling Spaniard. Makinen gave it his all to take the lead, making up 28.1 seconds in just two stages. He then pushed even harder, just to make sure. A master strategist, he pulled off a fantastic gamble at the end of the day on one stage, the one which tackled the Font-Belle col, running up to 1.304 metres, to be precise. Up there, at the end of the day, the five kilometres or so of snow and ice had compacted with the cold. The knot of the problem was there, with this final climb before attacking the dizzy descent to Thoard. Choosing the right tyres was the key.

With no studs in the tyres, these five

little kilometres, out of a total of 36.69 which made up the stage, were bound to be dangerous. Getting up the hill was not guaranteed, but these tyres had been perfect everywhere else on the cold, damp tarmac. On the other hand, starting on the same tyres, fitted with studs on the inside part of the tread, meant plenty of grip, with the downside of not much speed. Talking about the route that lay ahead, Juha Kankkunen was in the habit of saying: "it's for men, not for little boys." It was looking pretty exciting! After deep thought, Makinen finally chose to run without studs! "The artist has made his call," said an admiring Aime Chatard, in charge of Michelin's rally effort. He and his men would have preferred it if the quadruple world champion had played it safe. But the choice was made and there was no turning back and no room for doubt. Going for the other option, sticking to his game plan, McRae, second, five seconds down, opted for caution, as did fourth placed Delecour. In third place, Sainz made a late call and told his mechanics to change his wheels,

Burns is out of luck: not only is the new Subaru difficult to set up, but on top of that, it packed up halfway through the event, with electrical failure.

The ideal line: Tommi Makinen makes his car dance over the Alpine roads.

To see Markko Martin do his bit on snow, one had to attend the shakedown, a session designed to check out the cars before the rally. On the morning of the start, his Subaru stayed put in the Principality.

opting to run without studs, although they were designated a "mixed" tyre. In the end, the mountain proved the conservative choice to be the right one. "Well, there you go, no studs was not good," said Makinen. On top of that, the night frost came quicker and harder than I had expected and there were all sorts of unexpected traps. It was getting too risky to attack. But, I haven't lost much. 3.5 seconds behind Colin isn't bad going into the last leg. I like that." Sadly, the much expected duel never materialised, as the third leg rapidly sealed Highlander's fate and thus the outcome of the rally. The first climb up the Col de Turini had been fatal for the Focus and for its driver's hopes. Two kilometres before the pass, deep in snow, ice and spectators, the electronic accelerator refused to cooperate. The computer got its wires crossed and the engine was done for and there was nothing left to do but retire. Makinen could now take his time on the run to the Principality and the sunshine, ahead of Sainz and Delecour, who completed the podium. There it was, another success. Well done maestro. He was now, along with Munari and

Rohrl one of only three men to have won this event three times in a row. Not a bad reference... ■

SURPRISES
SUBARU TRIPS OVER THE RUG

Of course there was the Peugeot fiasco, but the new Monte Carlo was never short of surprises. Perhaps, the biggest came on the second stage, when the fastest time went to the German Gassner. Champion in his own village, unknown outside it, he was at the wheel of a mere Group N Proton! Of course, this is nothing more than a Malaysian Mitsubishi hiding behind a different label, but at least history will show that the constructor really did set a fastest stage time on a world championship event. In fact, the lucky German had set off a long time after the front runners had literally cleaned the slippery surface off the tarmac. Another happy surprise: the performances of Armin Schwarz and Toni Gardemeister. This German, a well known one and rightly so, likes the Monte Carlo and he proved it

again, by finishing fourth at the wheel of a big and solid Skoda. In fact, it was purely driver skill which overcame the car's generous proportions and less generous horsepower. It was a great show from Armin. As for the young Finn, he finished in Herr Schwarz's wake with a privately entered 206 WRC, belonging to the Grifone team. He was even the rally's first leader, as he set the fastest time on the opening stage. Finally, someone had salvaged some honour for the French car company. The bad surprise came from Subaru. As was the case for Peugeot, not a single works Impreza

made it to the finish and it was a pitiful showing. Sure, Solberg went off the road, but it was electrical problems which finished off Markko Martin on the run out of the Principality, before the very first stage. The next morning, it was Burns' car which refused to start with similar problems. Not only had the Englishman run an anonymous first leg, but it was exactly the same fault which had knocked him out of the previous year's event. In 2000, it was not only the 206s which refused to listen to the wake up call. It seemed that unlike the French, the English had not learnt their lesson. ■

While Auriol and Panizzi gave their 206s a pasting, Gronholm did not even make it to the end of the second stage, as his car's water pump gave up the ghost.

Armin Schwarz was breathtaking in his Skoda, finishing a remarkable fourth.

69ᵗʰ MONTE-CARLO RALLY

1ˢᵗ leg of the 2001 World Rally Championship for constructors and drivers.
1ˢᵗ leg of the Group N World Championship.

Date 19ᵗʰ to 21ˢᵗ January 2001

Route
1759,37 km divided into 3 legs
15 special stages on tarmac roads (372,06 km) one of which neutralized (351,53 km)

1ˢᵗ leg
Friday 19ᵗʰ January: Monaco - St-André-les Alpes - Monaco, 6 stages (141,74 km)

2ⁿᵈ leg
Saturday 20ᵗʰ January: Monaco - Digne - Monaco, 5 stages but 4 ran (112,25 km)

3ʳᵈ leg
Sunday 21ˢᵗ January: Monaco - Monaco, 4 stages (98,54 km)

Starters - Finishers: 56 - 27

Conditions: roads were dry, humid, damp, snow-covered and icy.

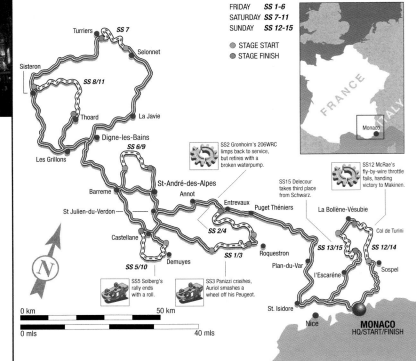

FRIDAY **SS 1-6**
SATURDAY **SS 7-11**
SUNDAY **SS 12-15**
● STAGE START
● STAGE FINISH

SS2 Gronholm's 206WRC limps back to service, but retires with a broken waterpump.

SS12 McRae's fly-by-wire throttle fails, handing victory to Makinen.

SS15 Delecour takes third place from Schwarz.

SS5 Solberg's rally ends with a roll.

SS3 Panizzi crashes, Auriol smashes a wheel off his Peugeot.

0 km ⸻ 50 km
0 mls ⸻ 40 mls

MONACO HQ/START/FINISH

TOP ENTRIES

1 Marcus Gronholm - Timo Rautiainen
   Peugeot 206 WRC

2 Didier Auriol - Denis Giraudet
   Peugeot 206 WRC

3 Carlos Sainz - Luis Moya
   Ford Focus RS WRC

4 Colin McRae - Nicky Grist
   Ford Focus RS WRC

5 Richard Burns - Robert Reid
   Subaru Impreza WRC

6 Markko Martin - Michael Park
   Subaru Impreza WRC

7 Tommi Makinen - Risto Mannisenmaki
   Mitsubishi Lancer Evo 6

8 Freddy Loix - Sven Smeets
   Mitsubishi Carisma GT

9 Piero Liatti - Carlo Cassina
   Hyundai Accent WRC

10 Alister McRae - David Senior
   Hyundai Accent WRC

11 Armin Schwarz - Manfred Hiemer
   Skoda Octavia WRC

12 Bruno Thiry - Stephane Prevot
   Skoda Octavia WRC

16 Gilles Panizzi - Herve Panizzi
   Peugeot 206 WRC

17 Francois Delecour - Daniel Grataloup
   Ford Focus RS WRC

18 Petter Solberg - Philip Mills
   Subaru Impreza WRC

19 Toni Gardemeister - Paavo Lukander
   Peugeot 206 WRC

20 Philippe Bugalski - Jean-Paul Chiaroni
   Citroen Saxo Kit Car

21 Jesus Puras - Marc Marti
   Citroen Saxo Kit Car

22 Piero Longhi - Lucio Baggio
   Toyota Corolla WRC

23 Manfred Stohl - Ilka Petrasko
   Mitsubishi Lancer Evo 6

24 Gustavo Trelles - Jorge Del Buono
   Mitsubishi Lancer Evo 6

26 Gabriel Pozzo - Edgardo Galindo
   Mitsubishi Lancer Evo 6

37 Sebastien Loeb - Daniel Elena
   Citroen Saxo Kit Car

54 Marcos Ligato - Ruben Garcia
   Mitsubishi Lancer Evo 6

60 Jurgen Barth -
   Jean-Claude Perramond
   Opel Astra

63 Gabriele Cadringher -
   Gianfranco Serembe
   Opel Astra

Special Stage Times

SS1 Roquesteron 1 22,89 km
1.Gardemeister 20'48"9; 2.Auriol 20'55"8; 3.Burri 21'03"5; 4.Liatti 21'05"2; 5.Schwarz 21'06"1; 6.Solberg 21'07"9; Gr.N Gillet 21'08"0

SS2 St Pierre - Entrevaux 1 30,34 km
1.Gassner 25'38"5; 2.Solberg 25'46"1; 3.Burri 25'49"7; 4.Auriol 25'53"5; 5.A.McRae 25'54"3; 6.McRae 25'55"3; Gr.N Gassner 25'38"5

ES3 Roquesteron 2 22,89 km
1.Delecour 18'32"7; 2.Auriol 18'41"9; 3.McRae 18'42"6; 4.Sainz 18'43"5; 5.Burns 18'57"4; 6.Makinen/Solberg 18'57"7; Gr.N Ligato 19'20"8

SS4 St Pierre - Entrevaux 2 30,34 km
1.McRae 22'10"4; 2.Burns 22'17"9; 3.Makinen 22'23"7; 4.Sainz 22'23"8; 5.Solberg 22'33"1; 6.Gardemeister 22'35"1; Gr.N Stohl 23'22"6

SS5 Comps - Castellane 1 20,53 km
1.Makinen 13'45"4; 2.Sainz 13'51"5; 3.McRae 13'51"9; 4.Gardemeister 13'58"7; 5.Schwarz 14'03"0; 6.Burns 14'06"4; Gr.N Stohl 14'23"3

SS6 Clumanc - Lambruisse 1 14,75 km
1.Sainz 10'32"5; 2.Delecour 10'35"2; 3.Burns 10'37"9; 4.McRae 10'40"0; 5.Schwarz 10'45"4; 6.Makinen / Gardemeister 10'57"1; Gr.N Galli 11'13"8

SS7 Turriers 24,12 km
1.Makinen 17'31"1; 2.McRae 17'39"1; 3.Schwarz 17'43"6; 4.Delecour 17'52"5; 5.Sainz 17'59"4; 6.A.McRae 18'02"2; Gr.N Galli 18'13"7

SS8 Sisteron - Thoard 1 36,69 km
1.Makinen 26'02"3; 2.Delecour 26'14"0; 3.Sainz 26'16"3; 4.McRae 26'22"4; 5.Schwarz 26'26"9; 6.Loix 26'28"5; Gr.N Galli 27'08"1

SS9 Clumanc - Lambruisse 2 14,75 km
1.Delecour 10'25"1; 2.Makinen 10'25"2; 3.Schwarz 10'27"8; 4.Gardemeister 10'31"4; 5.McRae 10'32"7; 6.Sainz 10'33"7; Gr.N Stohl 10'54"7

SS10 Comps - Castellane 2 20,53 km
Cancelled - too many spectators.

SS11 Sisteron - Thoard 2 36,69 km
1.McRae 26'22"1; 2.Sainz 26'28"7; 3.Makinen 26'30"6; 4.Schwarz 26'41"3; 5.Delecour 26'52"4; 6.A. McRae 27'13"8; Gr.N Stohl 27'50"9

SS12 Sospel - La Bollene 1 32,72 km
1.Loix 28'19"0; 2.Makinen 28'22"4; 3.Delecour 28'25"5; 4.Schwarz 28'31"9; 5.Sainz 28'39"1; 6.Gardemeister 29'03"0; Gr.N Gillet 29'18"0

SS13 Loda - Luceram 1 16,55 km
1.Makinen 14'57"6; 2.Sainz 14'58"4; 3.Schwarz 15'01"2; 4.Delecour 15'04"4; 5.Gardemeister 15'50"7; 6.Loix 15'22"2; Gr.N Trelles 15'30"8

SS14 Sospel - La Bollene 2 32,72 km
1.Delecour 26'24"6; 2.Gardemeister 26'28"4; 3.Sainz 26'40"0; 4.Loix 26'40"4; 5.Makinen 26'42"2; 6.Schwarz 26'44"2; Gr.N Stohl 27'43"0

SS15 Loda - Luceram 2 16,55 km
1.Sainz 14'09"5; 2.Gardemeister 14'15"1; 3.Delecour 14'15"5; 4.Makinen; 14'16"2; 5.Schwarz 14'18"0; 6.A. McRae 14'37"1; Gr.N Trelles 15'45"0

Results · WRC

	Driver/Navigator	Car	Gr.	Time
1	**Makinen - Mannisenmaki**	Mitsubishi Lancer Evo 6	A	4h38'04"3
2	Sainz - Moya	Ford Focus RS WRC		+ 1'00"8
3	Delecour - Grataloup	Ford Focus RS WRC		+ 2'05"3
4	Schwarz - Hiemer	Skoda Octavia WRC		+ 2'26"0
5	Gardemeister - Lukander	Peugeot 206 WRC		+ 5'52"1
6	Loix - Smeets	Mitsubishi Carisma GT		+ 6'25"9
7	A. McRae - Senior	Hyundai Accent WRC		+ 9'04"8
8	Thiry - Prévot	Skoda Octavia WRC		+ 13'55"0
9	**Gillet - Delorme**	**Mitsubishi Lancer Evo 6**	**N**	**+ 16'23"9**
10	Stohl - Petrasko	Mitsubishi Lancer Evo 6		+ 17'50"3

Leading Retirements

SS.12	C. McRae - Grist	Ford Focus WRC	Electronics
SS.6	Burns - Reid	Subaru Impreza WRC 2001	Engine
SS.5	Solberg - Mills	Subaru Impreza WRC 2001	Accident
SS.3	Auriol - Giraudet	Peugeot 206 WRC	Wheel torn off
SS.3	Panizzi - Panizzi	Peugeot 206 WRC	Accident
SS.1	Liatti - Cassina	Hyundai Accent WRC	Engine
SS.1	Gronholm - Rautiainen	Peugeot 206 WRC	Engine
SS.1	Martin - Park	Subaru Impreza WRC	Engine

Performers

	1	2	3	4	5	6
Makinen	4	2	2	1	1	2
Delecour	3	2	2	2	1	-
Sainz	2	3	2	2	2	1
C. McRae	2	1	2	2	1	1
Gardemeister	1	2	-	2	1	2
Loix	1	-	-	1	-	2
Gassner	1	-	-	-	-	-
Auriol	-	2	-	1	-	-
Burns	-	1	1	-	1	1
Solberg	-	1	-	-	1	1
Schwarz	-	-	3	2	5	1
Burri	-	-	2	-	-	-
Liatti	-	-	-	1	-	-
A. McRae	-	-	-	-	1	3

Event Leaders

SS.1	Gardemeister
SS.2 & SS.3	Auriol
After SS.3	Solberg
SS.4 > SS.8	C. McRae
SS.9	Makinen
SS.10	*canceled*
SS.11	C. McRae
SS.12 > SS.15	Makinen

Previous winners

1973	Andruet - "Biche" Alpine Renault A 110	1988	Saby - Fauchille Lancia Delta HF 4WD
1975	Munari - Mannucci Lancia Stratos	1989	Biasion - Siviero Lancia Delta Integrale
1976	Munari - Maiga Lancia Stratos	1990	Auriol - Occelli Lancia Delta Integrale
1977	Munari - Maiga Lancia Stratos	1991	Sainz - Moya Toyota Celica GT-Four
1978	Nicolas - Laverne Porsche 911 SC	1992	Auriol - Occelli Lancia Delta HF Integrale
1979	Darniche - Mahé Lancia Stratos	1993	Auriol - Occelli Toyota Celica Turbo 4WD
1980	Rohrl - Geistdorfer Fiat 131 Abarth	1994	Delecour - Grataloup Ford Escort RS Cosworth
1981	Ragnotti - Andrié Renault 5 Turbo	1995	Sainz - Moya Subaru Impreza 555
1982	Rohrl - Geistdorfer Opel Ascona 400	1996	Bernardini - Andrié Ford Escort Cosworth
1983	Rohrl - Geistdorfer Lancia rally 037	1997	Liatti - Pons Subaru Impreza WRC
1984	Rohrl - Geistdorfer Audi Quattro	1998	Sainz - Moya Toyota Corolla WRC
1985	Vatanen - Harryman Peugeot 205 T16	1999	Makinen - Mannisenmaki Mitsubishi Lancer Evo 6
1986	Toivonen - Cresto Lancia Delta S4	2000	Makinen - Mannisenmaki Mitsubishi Lancer Evo 6
1987	Biasion - Siviero Lancia Delta HF 4WD		

Championship Classifications

Drivers
1. Tommi Makinen — 10
2. Carlos Sainz — 6
3. François Delecour — 4
4. Armin Schwarz — 3
5. Toni Gardemeister — 2
6. Freddy Loix — 1

Group N
1. Olivier Gillet — 10
2. Manfred Stohl — 6
3. Gustavo Trelles — 4
4. Gabriel Pozzo — 3
5. Marcos Ligato — 2
6. David Truphemus — 1

Constructors
1. Mitsubishi — 13
2. Ford — 6
3. Skoda — 5
4. Hyundai — 2

Swedish

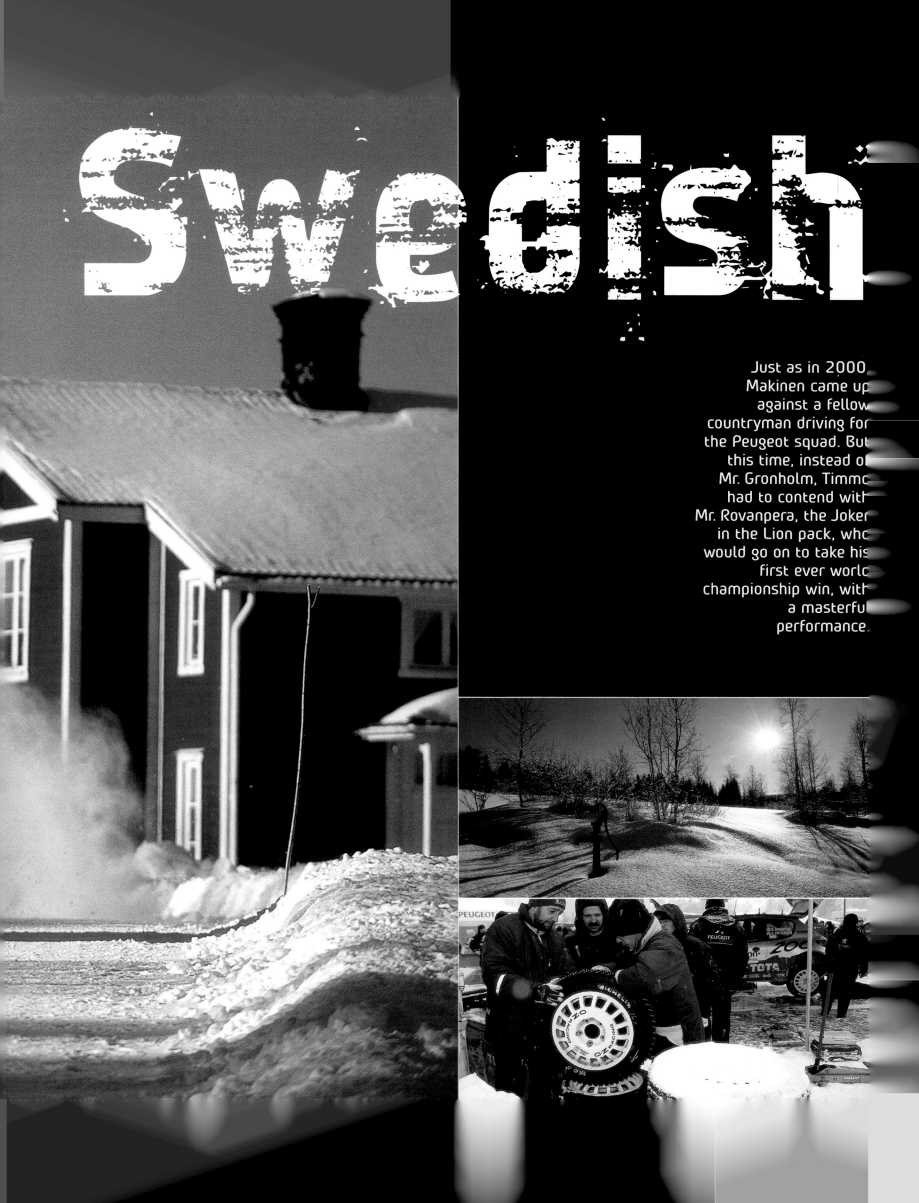

Just as in 2000, Makinen came up against a fellow countryman driving for the Peugeot squad. But this time, instead of Mr. Gronholm, Timmo had to contend with Mr. Rovanpera, the Joker in the Lion pack, who would go on to take his first ever world championship win, with a masterful performance.

THE RALLY
ROVANPERA TAMES THE BEAST

The first Swedish rally of the new century seemed to have taken its cues as to what sort of winter to lay on, from the previous rally in Monaco. The Principality weather gods had kindly layed on a fresh fall of snow in the days leading up to the event. It had made the Monegasque event one of the most complex and interesting in recent years. The same thing happened in Sweden. Yes, it was cold, glacial in fact, in the run up to the rally, with the mercury in the thermometer refusing to climb higher than minus 30 degrees. Recce cars would not start as their engines caught cold and the mechanics were forced to keep engines running all night. But then, a final flurry of fresh snow arrived on the eve of the event. All was set for a classic Swedish Rally, far removed from the ersatz versions of recent years when the event hung around the tracks of Varmland (literally "warm land,") near Karlstad. But poor old Marcus Gronholm would not get to see the Aurora Borealis. Having set a convincing fastest time on the opening stage, the engine of his 206 managed to overheat despite the polar cold, on the second stage. It turned out to be more than a minor moment of warmth and on the next stage, it gave up the ghost and its head-gasket. Rest in peace, four cylinders and thanks for the short trip. With much dignity and without

The Skodas – here we see Bruno Thiry, who finished tenth – ran a very anonymous rally.

showing signs of anger, the reigning world champion read his own car's obituary with a laconic, "no luck," before ending the reading with, "the same story as in Monte Carlo." This time it was for a different reason, as the water pump was no longer to blame. But for the Finn it was a dismal start to the season, with no points after two rounds. Maybe he could take some consolation from the fact that, once again, when it came to getting it wrong, the Brits were leading the way. Confusing speed with haste, Burns and then McRae both got it wrong shortly after the start. "I came to a fork too quickly, flat in sixth," related the Subaru driver. "I didn't brake in time and we got buried in a wall of snow." It

took him thirteen minutes to get out ; thirteen minutes which would cost him victory, despite a great fight back in the final stages of the event. All he could salvage was some honour. In the third stage, it was down to his fellow national, if not countryman to have a go at auditioning for Holiday On Ice. "Too quick," admitted the Ford Scotsman. "The car tipped into the side and luckily the spectators helped us out." If they had not, they might still be there today, near Valberget, which is well worth a visit in the depths of a Scandinavian winter. After a mere 52.34 kilometres, the Swedish Rally had lost three serious contenders for victory. Brilliant up until then, the Estonian, Markko Martin was the

leading Subaru up to the point when he joined the other victims. A puncture in the middle of the day led to a broken suspension, which called for a wheel change.
The order at the end of the first leg was conditioned by something approaching a Demolition Derby, with those most efficient at avoiding the hazards and pitfalls, finding their way to the top of the leaderboard. After Gronholm, his team-mate Harri Rovanpera hoisted his 206 to the top of the order, but just for a brief while. Brake caliper problems caused a loss of fluid which slowed him down. These difficulties allowed Thomas Radstrom into the lead. He had been taken on for one appearance only, by Mitsubishi,

First class locum for Mitsubishi, Thomas Radstrom posed a threat to Rovanpera right to the end of the event.

In 2001, the 1984 world champion, Stig Blomqvist, was back in harness for a full season of Group N.

who hoped he would pick up points that Loix could only dream of. It was an impressive showing, as the Swede had only acquainted himself with the Carisma GT five days before the start. Some of the big names were still hanging around though and Sainz actually led at the end of the opening leg. "Every thing was great; the cars and the tyres. There was just one scary moment when the anti-puncture foam caused some vibrations in the front end. But honestly, I am delighted with the performance of my Pirellis."
Indeed, tyres had been one of the big questions before the start. The answer was obvious. The Italian tyres were excellent on the snow. Not only was the Spaniard's Ford in the lead, but the

similarly mounted McRae had set three classy fastest stage times. As for the Monaco winner, he had been in the wars all day, complaining about his start number, as he had the "privilege" of running first on the road. On the radio to his team, the most frequently heard word to emanate from Makinen's lips was "perkele (Finnish for "shit") perkele, perkele! When asked to explain, Timmo said: "On some stages, the night before the start had left a sort of light crust of snow, hardened by the cold, but not enough. On these places, I did not have the same grip as those who were coming through later, like McRae or Burns."
As things turned out, Carlos Sainz

As in Monte Carlo, Toni Gardemeister, made the most of the 206 run by the Grifone team, to finish fourth.

suffered the same fate the following day. First at the end of Friday's leg, he therefore had the "honour" of leading the field on Saturday and quickly realised it was a lost cause. "I am going as quickly as I can, but it really is a big handicap. More than I thought." This meant that Rovanpera, Radstrom and Makinen were now able to devour the seconds, catching the Spaniard in the process as he made a mistake. A spin in that purest of stages, Fredriksberg, the Ford engine stalled, 14 seconds were lost and so too was the lead. As an immediate follow-up, his Eminence made another error, this time relating to tyre choice and could do no better than fourth. He had left the two Mitsubishi men to lead the dance, along with the sole Peugeot man. In the French team, following Gronholm's engine gremlins on Friday, Auriol was now finding it pretty hard to hang onto fourth place, which he had fought for, despite being crippled with a bad dose of flu. In the inter-Nordic battle, Makinen was getting

Alister McRae retired with engine failure.

back in the groove. "Once again, I have a car I have total confidence in. I can brake late and lengthen my lines through the corners." All of which he did without making any mistakes. On the other side of the coin, Radstrom admitted to having scared himself a few times, while Rovanpera continued

his apprenticeship at the wheel of the 206. "I am getting more confident with the car," he informed those who were interested. "But even though I am getting the hang of it, I still can't get the maximum out of it." There have been worse debut performances, given he pulled off the tour de force

of winning the second leg, with a 7.3 second lead over Makinen, 12.4 over Radstrom and 28.5 on Sainz. Nevertheless, the Monte winner had not pushed excessively at the end of the day, keen as he was not to lead off for the final leg. That night, a thin powdery snow fell, covering the pine trees with a lacy decoration. But then, much heavier snows arrived, even though, by this stage, there was no need for Sweden to justify its winter weather credentials. This icing on the cake was only waiting for its cherry. It would come at the very end of this splendid rally. In fact, after the first four stages of the final leg, Rovanpera had done more than enough, actually extending his lead. These sections did not suit the Mitsubishi's stocky architecture and they all came down to the infinitesimal detail of tyre stud length, with pain or glory going down to fractions of a millimetre!

But there was still one stage to go, the 22.21 km of Hagfors. Before the start, the Lucky Lad from Jyvaskyla led Makinen by 18.6 and Radstrom by 25.6. It was a lot on paper, but not so much on the road. All three men

chose different tyres to tackle the final run. With such a plethora of snow type tyres to choose from, and not knowing the Michelin range too well, Rovanperra decided to stick with those more suited to ice, while Makinen went for snow and Radstrom went for a mixed brew of ice in front and snow on the rears, just in case. Scenting a kill, the four times world champion set off, sure of what he was doing. He wanted the win and the ten championship points that came with it and second place was simply not worth considering. Sadly, it was not to be and the master tripped himself up, going off the road near the start of the stage. "My choice was the best," he admitted honestly enough afterwards. "I made a mistake. That's all. The car ended up in a snow bank and there was no way of getting it out again. It's very disappointing." Shoving both fists in the air, letting out a generous "Wow!" of satisfaction as he crossed the stage finish line, Harri Rovanpera could finally let his happiness overflow, unable to say anything more exciting than, "it's marvellous, it's marvellous." In the right-hand seat,

co-driver Risto Pietilainen was finding it hard to fight back the tears. They had pushed the great Makinen into making an error, thus beating the reference points for all Finnish rally drivers. It was no mean achievement for a first win, the 28th for Peugeot in the World Rally Championship. ■

THE DISAPPOINTMENT
THE PEUGEOT PARADOX

Rovanpera's win, coming on the heels of the Monte mishap, was met with cold indifference by the reigning world championship team. There was no one waiting for the winner at the final check-point, in contrast to Gronholm's 2000 success. The mechanics, irreproachable as ever, showed no sign of emotion. It was a non-win. Peugeot had won, but had failed to score a single constructors' point, a consequence of the rule regarding "nominated" drivers.

Rovanpera, unlike Gronholm and Auriol, who both retired, was not one of the chosen ones. The world champion suffered a failure that had never reared its head before. Until now, the head gasket had never given the slightest bother during a rally for the Peugeot camp. But his car was fitted with an engine that used a new type of gasket, which was due to be used on an evolution of the engine planned to make its debut later in the year. As for Auriol, who was suffering with some malady or other, his car broke its transmission two stages from the end. Nevertheless, he drove a very courageous race. His brother Gerard was impressed. "I've never seen him look so bad," he said at the end of the rally." Not even in the '94 San Remo, which he won using all his strength." Gronholm and Auriol were out and although Corrado Provera claimed "we are very happy with Harri's win," the boss' long face told a completely different story. "We must take reassurance from the fact the car has proved its potential," he continued. "But we can't be happy about coming

away without any points." For his part, Jean-Pierre Nicholas tried to create a diversion: "we are leading the Drivers' classification." It was a brave try to look on the bright side, but it fooled no one. Because, although Rovanpera was

indeed in the lead, Makinen and Sainz also had the same total of ten points and so the position of championship leader was somewhat devalued, being shared out between three drivers. One finds consolation where one can. ■

First World Championship win for Rovanpera and Pietilainen.

Ever consistent, Carlos Sainz picked up the four points for third place.

50th SWEDISH RALLY

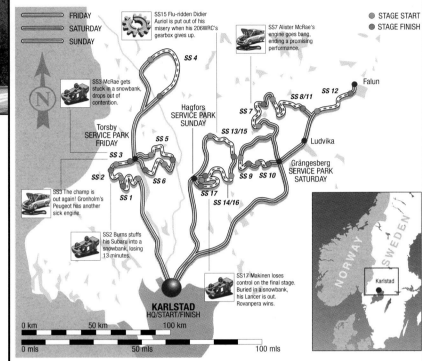

FRIDAY
SATURDAY
SUNDAY

● STAGE START
● STAGE FINISH

SS15 Flu-ridden Didier Auriol is put out of his misery when his 206WRC's gearbox gives up.

SS7 Alister McRae's engine goes bang, ending a promising performance.

SS4

SS3 McRae gets stuck in a snowbank, drops out of contention.

Falun

SS 8/11   SS 12

SS 7

Hagfors
SERVICE PARK
SUNDAY

Torsby
SERVICE PARK
FRIDAY

SS 13/15

Ludvika

SS 5

SS 3

SS 2

SS 6

SS 9   SS 10

Grängesberg
SERVICE PARK
SATURDAY

SS 1

SS 17

SS3 The champ is out again! Gronholm's Peugeot has another sick engine.

SS 14/16

SS2 Burns stuffs his Subaru into a snowbank, losing 13 minutes.

SS17 Makinen loses control on the final stage. Buried in a snowbank, his Lancer is out. Rovanpera wins.

KARLSTAD
HQ/START/FINISH

0 km   50 km   100 km
0 mls   50 mls   100 mls

NORWAY   SWEDEN

Karlstad

2nd leg of the 2001 World Rally Championship for constructors and drivers. **2nd leg** of the Group N World Championship . **1st leg** of the Team's cup.

Date 8th – 11th February 2001

Route
1924,97 km divided into 3 legs
17 special stages on snow covered tracks (380,62 km)

Start
Thursday 8th February: Karlstad, 0 stages
1st leg
Friday 9th February: Karlstad-Torby-Karlstad, 6 spéciales (148,56 km)
2nd leg
Saturday 10th February: Karlstad-Grangesberg-Karlstad, 6 stages (134,05 km)
3rd leg
Sunday 11th February: Karlstad-Hagfors-Karlstad, 5 stages (98,01 km)

Starters - Finishers: 75 - 41

Conditions: Packed snow and ice.

TOP ENTRIES

1   Marcus Gronholm - Timo Rautiainen
Peugeot 206 WRC

2   Didier Auriol - Denis Giraudet
Peugeot 206 WRC

3   Carlos Sainz - Luis Moya
Ford Focus RS WRC

4   Colin McRae - Nicky Grist
Ford Focus RS WRC

5   Richard Burns - Robert Reid
Subaru Impreza WRC

6   Petter Solberg - Philip Mills
Subaru Impreza WRC

7   Tommi Makinen - Risto Mannisenmaki
Mitsubishi Lancer Evo 6

8   Freddy Loix - Sven Smeets
Mitsubishi Carisma GT

9   Kenneth Eriksson - Staffan Parmander
Hyundai Accent WRC

10   Alister McRae - David Senior
Hyundai Accent WRC

11   Armin Schwarz - Manfred Hiemer
Skoda Octavia WRC

12   Bruno Thiry - Stephane Prevot
Skoda Octavia WRC

16   Harri Rovanpera - Risto Pietilainen
Peugeot 206 WRC

17   Francois Delecour - Daniel Grataloup
Ford Focus RS WRC

18   Markko Martin - Michael Park
Subaru Impreza WRC

19   Thomas Radstrom - Tina Thorner
Mitsubishi Carisma GT

21   Tapio Laukkanen - Kaj Lindstrom
Toyota Corolla WRC

22   Pasi Hagstrom - Tero Gardemeister
Toyota Corolla WRC

23   Toni Gardemeister - Paavo Lukander
Peugeot 206 WRC

24   Janne Tuohino - Petri Vihavainen
Toyota Corolla WRC

25   Jani Paasonen - Arto Kapanen
Ford Focus RS WRC

26   Henrik Lundgaard - Jens Christian Anker
Toyota Corolla WRC

27   Kenneth Backlund - Tord Andersson
Mitsubishi Lancer Evo 6

28   Stig-Olov Walfridsson -
Lars Backman
Mitsubishi Lancer Evo 6

35   Abdullah Bakhashab - Bobby Willis
Toyota Corolla WRC

38   Hamed Al-Wahaibi - Tony Sircombe
Subaru Impreza WRC

39   Frederic Dor - Didier Breton
Subaru Impreza WRC

40   Stig Blomqvist - Ana Goni
Mitsubishi Lancer Evo 6

44   Daniel Carlsson - Benny Melander
Toyota Corolla WRC

64   Sebastien Loeb - Daniel Elena
Citroen Saxo Kit Car

Special Stage Times

SS1 Bjalverud 20,74 km
1.Gronholm 11'05"3; 2.Burns 11'09"2;
3.McRae 11'09"9; 4.Radstrom 11'10"9
5.Martin 11'11"1; 6.Rovanpera
11'11"2; Gr.N Walfridsson 11'44"2

SS2 Lonnhojden 18,82 km
1.Rovanpera 10'41"5; 2.McRae/Makinen
10'44"7; 4.Carlsson 10'47"3; 5.Eriksson
10'47"4; 6.Radstrom 10'47"6;
Gr.N Walfridsson 11'10"5

SS3 Bogen 12,78 km
1.Burns 7'31"7; 2.Sainz 7'35"2;
3.Radstrom 7'37"2; 4.Delecour 7'37"6;
5.Martin 7'38"5; 6.A. McRae 7'39"7;
Gr.N Walfridsson 7'58"4

SS4 Granberget 49,36 km
1.McRae 24'55"6; 2.Burns 25'05"5;
3.Sainz 25'15"0; 4.Radstrom 25'19"0;
5.Rovanpera 25'20"0; 6.Eriksson
25'21"2; Gr.N Walfridsson 26'39"4

SS5 Torntorp 20,38 km
1.McRae 10'30"0; 2.Burns 10'36"2;
3.Sainz 10'39"7; 4.Auriol/Delecour

10'40"5; 6.Rovanpera 10'44"4;
Gr.N Backlund 11'19"0

SS6 Sagfallet 26,48 km
1.McRae 13'22"3; 2.Burns 13'24"7;
3.Sainz 13'30"8; 4.Auriol 13'35"6;
5.Rovanpera 13'39"6; 6.Martin
13'40"0; Gr.N Backlund 14'22"6

SS7 Kullen 26,81 km
1.McRae 14'08"9; 2.Burns 14'16"2;
3.Makinen 14'20"7; 4.Sainz 14'23"5;
5.Delecour 14'25"0; 6.Rovanpera
14'25"1; Gr.N Walfridsson 15'11"5

SS8 Nyhammar 1 27,79 km
1.McRae 14'43"4; 2.Makinen 14'43"7;
3.Burns 14'44"7; 4.Radstrom 14'49"3;
5.Rovanpera 14'49"6; 6.Martin
14'55"1; Gr.N Walfridsson 15'40"6

SS9 Fredriksberg 34,07 km
1.McRae 19'21"7; 2.Burns 19'34"6;
3.Makinen 19'35"4; 4.Radstrom
19'37"5; 5.Rovanpera 19'39"4; 6.Martin
19'41"2; Gr.N Backlund 20'31"6

SS10 Silkesberg 15,30 km
1.McRae 7'52"6; 2.Burns 7'55"1;
3.Radstrom 7'58"8; 4.Rovanpera
7'59"3; 5.Makinen 8'01"4; 6.Carlsson
8'03"3; Gr.N Backlund 8'27"3

SS11 Nyhammar 2 27,79 km
1.Makinen 14'50"2; 2.Rovanpera
14'54"6; 3.Radstrom 14'56"5; 4.Burns
14'57"4; 5.Solberg 14'59"3;
6.Gardemeister 15'02"2;
Gr.N Backlund 15'41"7

SS12 Lugnet 2 km
1.Rovanpera 2'00"0; 2.Eriksson 2'00"6;
3.Sainz 2'00"8; 4.Makinen 2'01"5;
5.Auriol/Gardemeister 2'01"9;
Gr.N Blomqvist 2'06"7

SS13 Sagen 1 14,76 km
1.Burns 7'55"4; 2 Rovanpera 7'56"5;
3.Martin 7'57"4; 4.Sainz 7'59"9;
5.Makinen 8'01"6; 6.Rovanpera 8'04"0;
Gr.N Walfridsson 8'28"3

SS14 Rammen 1 23,41 km
1.Burns 12'11"8; 2.McRae 12'19"7;

3.Martin 12'20"4; 4.Rovanpera 12'20"9;
5.Sainz 12'21"4; 6. Gardemeister
12'24"9; Gr.N Walfridsson 12'56"9

SS15 Sagen 2 14,76 km
1.Burns 7'54"6; 2.Martin 7'58"7;
3.McRae 7'59"8; 4.Sainz 8'03"8;
5.Solberg 8'04"2; 6. Makinen / Loix /
Radstrom 8'07"5; Gr.N Walfridsson 8'27"7

SS16 Rammen 2 23,41 km
1.Burns 12'16"2; 2.Martin 12'26"4;
3.McRae 12'28"3; 4.Rovanpera
12'28"9; 5.Radstrom 12'30"0; 6.Sainz
12'32"1; Gr.N Walfridsson 12'59"9

SS17 Hagfors 21,21 km
1.Burns 12'26"8; 2.Eriksson 12'40"2;
3.Gardemeister 12'43"2; 4.Carlsson
12'47"6; 5.Rovanpera 12'55"3;
6.Martin 12'56"1; Gr.N Backlund
13'11"2

Results — WRC

	Driver/Navigator	Car	Gr.	Time
1	**Rovanpera - Pietilainen**	Peugeot 206 WRC	A	3h27'01"1
2	Radstrom - Thorner	Mitsubishi Carisma GT		+ 27"9
3	Sainz - Moya	Ford Focus RS WRC 01		+ 37"0
4	Gardemeister - Lukander	Peugeot 206 WRC		+ 2'05"3
5	Delecour - Grataloup	Ford Focus RS WRC 01		+ 2'25"2
6	Solberg - Mills	Subaru Impreza WRC 2001		+ 2' 48"5
7	Carlsson - Melander	Toyota Corolla WRC		+ 3'18"2
8	Eriksson - Parmander	Hyundai Accent WRC		+ 3'35"8
9	C. McRae - Grist	Ford Focus RS WRC 01		+ 4'28"0
10	Thiry - Prévot	Skoda Octavia WRC		+ 5'23"6
14	**Walfridsson - Backman**	Mitsubishi Lancer Evo 6	N	+ 10'37"2
15	**Lundgaard - Anker**	Toyota Corolla WRC Team's Cup		+ 10'44"0

Leading Retirements

SS.17	Makinen - Mannisenmaki	Mitsubishi Lancer Evo 6	Accident
SS.15	Auriol - Giraudet	Peugeot 206 WRC	Transmission
SS.7	Schwarz - Hiemer	Skoda Octavia WRC	Accident
SS.7	A. McRae - Senior	Hyundai Accent WRC	Engine
SS.6	Laukkanen - Lindström	Toyota Corolla WRC	Accident
SS.1	Gronholm - Rautiainen	Peugeot 206 WRC	Engine

Championship Classifications

Drivers
1. Tommi Makinen, Harri Rovanpera, Carlos Sainz 10; 4. Thomas Radstrom, François Delecour 6; 6.Toni Gardemeister 5; 7. Armin Schwarz 3; 8. Freddy Loix, Petter Solberg 1

Constructors
1. Mitsubishi 23; 2. Ford 14; 3. Skoda 6; 4. Hyundai 5; 5. Subaru 4

Group N
1. Olivier Gillet, Stig-Olov Walfridsson 10; 3. Manfred Stohl, Kenneth Backlund 6; 5. Gustavo Trelles, Stig Blomqvist 4...

Team's Cup
1. Toyota Castrol Team Denmark (Lundgaart) 10; 2. David Sutton Cars Ltd (Blomqvist) 6; 3. Marlboro Ford Mobil1 Team Poland (Kulig) 4; 4. Toyota Team Saudi Arabia (Bakashab) 3; 5. F. Dor Rally Team (Dor) 2; 6. World Rally Hire (Heath) 1

Performers

	1	2	3	4	5	6
C. McRae	7	2	3	-	-	-
Burns	6	7	1	1	-	-
Rovanpera	2	2	-	3	5	3
Makinen	1	2	2	1	2	1
Gronholm	1	-	-	-	-	-
Martin	-	2	2	-	2	4
Eriksson	-	2	-	-	1	1
Sainz	-	1	4	3	1	1
Radstrom	-	-	3	4	1	2
Gardemeister	-	-	1	-	1	2
Auriol	-	-	-	2	1	-
Delecour	-	-	-	2	1	-
Carlsson	-	-	-	2	-	1
Solberg	-	-	-	-	2	-
A. McRae	-	-	-	-	-	1

Event Leaders

SS.1	Gronholm
SS.2	Rovanpera
SS.3 > SS.4	Radstrom
SS.5 > SS.8	Sainz
SS.9 > SS.17	Rovanpera

Previous winners

1973	Blomqvist - Hertz Saab 96 V 4		1987	Salonen - Harjanne Mazda 323 Turbo
1975	Waldegaard - Thorszelius Lancia Stratos		1988	Alen - Kivimaki Lancia Delta HF 4WD
1976	Eklund - Cederberg Saab 96 V 4		1989	Carlsson - Carlsson Mazda 323 4WD
1977	Blomqvist - Sylvan Saab 99 ems		1991	Eriksson - Parmander Mitsubishii Galant VR-4
1978	Waldegaard - Thorszelius Ford Escort RS		1992	Jonsson - Backman Toyota Celica GT-Four
1979	Blomqvist - Cederberg Saab 99 Turbo		1993	Jonsson - Backman Toyota Celica Turbo 4WD
1980	Kullang - Berglund Opel Ascona 400		1994	Radstrom - Backman Toyota Celica Turbo 4WD
1981	Mikkola - Hertz Audi Quattro		1995	Eriksson - Parmander Mitsubishi Lancer Ev.2
1982	Blomqvist - Cederberg Audi Quattro		1996	Makinen - Harjanne Mitsubishi Lancer Ev.3
1983	Mikkola - Hertz Audi Quattro		1997	Eriksson - Parmander Subaru Impreza WRC
1984	Blomqvist - Cederberg Audi Quattro		1998	Makinen - Mannisenmaki Mitsubishi Lancer Ev.4
1985	Vatanen - Harryman Peugeot 205 T16		1999	Makinen - Mannisenmaki Mitsubishi Lancer Ev.6
1986	Kankkunen - Piironen Peugeot 205 T16		2000	Gronholm - Rautiainen Peugeot 206 WRC

Portugal

Run in infernal conditions, this 34th edition of the Portuguese event was without a doubt the toughest ever. Winning it would require an exceptional talent Makinen beat Sainz at the death

3

THE RALLY
MAKINEN MUD MASTER

One thing is certain about the 34th edition of this event. One day in the future, there will be drivers, mechanics, engineers, spectators and journalists, who will be able to say, "I was there!" It would be a motto on a badge of courage maybe, even if some people were not exactly there of their own free will. The whole event was run under a cloud, as a few days before the start, a coach full of passengers had crashed into the Douro river, at Castelo de Paiva, a village right in the middle of the rally route. The world championship crews turned up to find a country which had been ravaged by almost perpetual rain in that winter of 2001. Portugal seemed to have suffered more than most in what had been a terrible wet winter over almost all of Europe. The main image was one of a permanent fog which never seemed to clear throughout the rally, reducing visibility to nothing, in conditions where it was probably even more important than usual to be able to see what difficulties lay ahead. It was not much better for the spectators. As usual, at this event, they were wandering around in impressive numbers, except with the lack of visibility, this time they looked like ghosts stumbling around in the mist, having climbed the mud covered hills for mile to see the action. Heros on the ground, the Michelin and Pirelli men were working their fingers to the bone cutting and cutting again their tyres, in order to try and provide something resembling grip in the mud.

Did a rally really take place in all this? Yes, and even if the drivers did not have their hearts in it, the rally provided a thrilling climax. Before getting to the final leg which would decide the winner, the earlier stages served to eliminate the stars one at a time. Without doubt, the main victim on the opening leg was Colin McRae. Once again, Highlander paid a heavy price for the unreliability of his Ford engine. On top of that, he was the only one affected, as Sainz and Delecour managed to keep going to the end. Luck often sees to shine on Tommi Makinen and it did again, as he was first on the road. No two rallies are ever the same and just three weeks earlier, in Sweden, he was complaining about having to open the stages for the rest of the pack. But here in Portugal, there

Once again, Makinen showed off his skills and had the advantage of running first on the road.

Torrential rain in the Autumn of 2000 and the spring of 2001 had turned the Portuguese roads into bogs.

was no doubt that being the first away was a big advantage, as the more cars went through the stages, the bigger the ruts. Therefore, after an initial charge from Harri Rovanpera, the Mitsubishi driver quickly took the lead, making the most of some clever work on his Michelin tyres, suggested by his team. The other Michelin runners would only follow his example later on. On the evening of the first leg, Makinen had thus built a nice lead of 17 seconds over Sainz, 26 on Rovanpera and 1 minute 8 on Gronholm. Both Gronholm and fifth placed Burns had only one thing on their minds: to get out of the mud and hope for an illusory improvement in the conditions. It certainly was an illusion, because Portugal did not change overnight. The rally rapidly turned into a duel. Sainz yo-yoed behind a perfect Makinen, picking up the odd precious second here and there, just to lose them again, giving himself the odd scare in the process. In the end, the Spaniard only took four seconds from a hard day's work on Saturday,

leaving the four times world champion to win another leg. In the wake of these two men, Gronholm and Burns had a good tussle, in a repeat of their frequent battles the previous year.

Harri Rovanpera wasn't even there to referee the contest, as his Peugeot had succumbed to its favourite illness this season; a dead engine. He had already overheated the previous day. This time, the head-gasket let go in a cloud of smoke. It was a shame for the Swedish winner, who up until then, had looked capable of winning here. He was not the only one to throw in the towel that day, as Loix also retired with no clutch and Martin learned the pitfalls of driving with nil visibility. The Subaru team leader was chasing after third place on the podium for all he was worth. Halfway through, after setting two fastest times, he was only 3.7 seconds down on Gronholm. But he took the wrong fork and that cost him 54 seconds, leaving the Peugeot man with a comfortable advantage, before tackling the epilogue.

For three whole days, Auriol fought an uncooperative 206. It was only after the rally that the Peugeot engineers discovered they had made a mistake in installing the car's electronic mapping. A shame, given that Marcus Gronholm's third place proved the 206 WRC was on the pace.

Second win in three
rallies for Tommi
Makinen and Risto
Mannisenmaki,
deserved leaders of the
Drivers' classification.

Yet another
disappointment for
Colin McRae, who did
not even make it to the
end of the first leg,
after his engine broke.

And what a leg it was, with a thrilling fight between the two most crowned men in the field ; 6 titles, 44 wins and 242 world rally starts between them! Finally the rain had stopped and the rally was played out over just two stages, as the first of the three on the programme had to be cancelled. The course opening cars had to stop and help Gronholm's note crew extricate themselves from a canyon which had once been a road. The challenge for the Spanish Ford man was straightforward: in order to win, he had to make up 13 seconds on the leader over 34

kilometres. He did it in just one stage! At the end of its 23 kilometres, the two men were dead level. Sainz was quickest in 18'19"9 and Makinen was second, 13.3 seconds down. The order had changed and for the first time since the start, the Focus driver was in the lead by three measly tenths of a second! There were plenty of long faces in the Mitsubishi camp, who realised where the problem lay. The Michelins had been cut too much, as the opening crew had misjudged the level of mud on the road. More serious still, the driver would have

to tackle the final section on the same tyres. So, while the two men were level pegging on the clock, in reality the Finn was at a disadvantage. But Tommi Makinen is never stronger than when he is under pressure. At times of great tension, he has an incredible ability, not only to concentrate, but also to brush aside whatever has happened before. Splashing through the mud, he mounted a dazzling fight back, as can be seen from the time sheets. Ponte de Lima South, special stage 22, 11.51 km: 1. Makinen, 8'52"3; 2. Sainz, 8.9 seconds down. The

Mitsubishi, despite its unsuitable tyres, had made up almost a second per kilometre. When Sainz came to congratulate him, Makinen was in jovial mood: "Actually, I did it all in a straight line, even the corners. I never turned the steering wheel." Victory had once again tipped in his favour, simply because he was the best. Logically, Marcus Gronholm completed the podium, just ahead of Richard Burns. The main protagonists of the 2000 campaign had therefore both notched up their first points in a championship dominated by an on-form Makinen. ■

The condition of the roads in Portugal were particularly awful this year, as can be seen from this Subaru going through after the rain. It was enough to leave Alister McRae (bottom) daydream on the bonnet of his Hyundai Accent.

CONSISTENCY
FULL MARKS FOR FORD

On the eve of the new championship, Ford and Peugeot were the only two manufacturers who declared their intention of winning the Constructors' Championship. Even though it was comfortably in the lead after Portugal, Mitsubishi once again was putting all its irons in one fire, called Makinen. Subaru had opted for promising but inconsistent talent, in the shape of Solberg and Martin and could therefore kiss goodbye to this title. Hyundai did a remarkable job, as the only team to get both its cars into the points in Portugal, with its new evolution Accent, but at best, it could only hope to pick up the crumbs, as it had in fact been doing since the start of the year. Even so, at this stage they were lying a probing third. As for the valiant Czech Skoda team, its aim could only be to do as well as the Korean crews. Against this backdrop, Ford and its huge resources was going through an early part of the season that oscillated from the sublime to the ridiculous. Sublime had been the performance of Sainz and Delecour who, in the three rallies run so far, had finished in the points every time. The Spaniard definitely had the upper hand, as he picked up two second places and a third, fighting for victory to the bitter end in Portugal. Compared with the Frenchman, he had a better understanding of the Focus and no doubt, as was the case in Sweden, sometimes had access to the latest Pirellis, which gave him an edge. In this situation, Delecour had to pay the penalty of being the third driver. Nevertheless, his boss Malcolm Wilson was ceaseless in his praise for his latest recruit. "I am convinced Delecour is capable of winning the Drivers' title and we have not yet seen the best of him." It was a valid hope for this most consistent of drivers who had finished the last nine rallies in the points, without finishing in the top positions. He seemed to lack brio, something which could not be said about Colin McRae. It was luck the Scotsman seemed to lack. He had a catastrophic start to the 2001 season, never making it into the points. "At the moment, all the bad luck is going his way, but I think, and he agrees that he can still be world champion." The fact his team was second in the constructors' classification was down to the games fate had played on him. There was one big question mark over Ford's aspirations, namely that it had not won since Cyprus 2000, while all the other big teams had won since then. Was the Focus past its sell-by date? ■

34ᵗʰ PORTUGUESE RALLY

3ʳᵈ leg of the 2001 World Rally championship for constructors and drivers. **3ʳᵈ** leg of the Group N World Championship. **2ⁿᵈ** leg of the Team's cup.

Date 8ᵗʰ to 11ᵗʰ March 2001

Route
1794,47 km divided into 3 legs
22 special stages on dirt roads
(390,14 km) but 18 ran
(300,88 km)

Prologue
Thursday 8ᵗʰ March: Santa Maria da Feira, 1 stages (3,20 km)

1ˢᵗ leg
Friday 9ᵗʰ March: Santa Maria da Feira-Celorico de Basto-Santa Maria da Feira, 9 stages and 7 ran (110,84 km)

2ⁿᵈ leg
Saturday 10ᵗʰ March: Santa Maria da Feira-Tabua-Santa Maria da Feira, 9 stages but 8 ran (153,43 km)

3ʳᵈ leg
Sunday 11ᵗʰ March: Santa Maria da Feira-Ponte de Lima-Santa Maria da Feira, 3 stages but 2 ran (34,41 km)

Starters - Finishers: 94 - 26

Conditions: constant rain and mud.

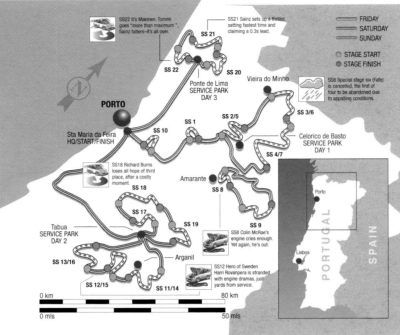

Map legend:
FRIDAY
SATURDAY
SUNDAY
○ STAGE START
● STAGE FINISH

SS22 It's Makinen. Tommi goes "more than maximum". Sainz falters–it's all over.

SS21 Sainz sets up a thriller, setting fastest time and claiming a 0.3s lead.

SS6 Special stage six (Fafe) is cancelled, the first of four to be abandoned due to appalling conditions.

SS21
SS22
SS20
Ponte de Lima SERVICE PARK DAY 3
Vieira do Minho
PORTO
Sta Maria da Feira HQ/START/FINISH
SS 10
SS 1
SS 2/5
SS 3/6
Celorico de Basto SERVICE PARK DAY 1
SS 4/7
SS18 Richard Burns loses all hope of third place, after a costly moment.
Amarante
SS 8
SS 18
SS 17
SS 19
SS 9
SS8 Colin McRae's engine cries enough. Yet again, he's out.
Tabua SERVICE PARK DAY 2
Arganil
SS 13/16
SS12 Hero of Sweden Harri Rovanpera is stranded with engine dramas, just yards from service.
SS 12/15
SS 11/14

PORTO
Porto
Lisboa
PORTUGAL SPAIN

0 km 80 km
0 mls 50 mls

TOP ENTRIES

1 Marcus Gronholm - Timo Rautiainen
Peugeot 206 WRC

2 Didier Auriol - Denis Giraudet
Peugeot 206 WRC

3 Carlos Sainz - Luis Moya
Ford Focus RS WRC

4 Colin McRae - Nicky Grist
Ford Focus RS WRC

5 Richard Burns - Robert Reid
Subaru Impreza WRC

6 Petter Solberg - Philip Mills
Subaru Impreza WRC

7 Tommi Makinen - Risto Mannisenmaki
Mitsubishi Lancer Evo 6

8 Freddy Loix - Sven Smeets
Mitsubishi Carisma GT

9 Kenneth Eriksson - Staffan Parmander
Hyundai Accent WRC

10 Alister McRae - David Senior
Hyundai Accent WRC

11 Armin Schwarz - Manfred Hiemer
Skoda Octavia WRC

12 Bruno Thiry - Stephane Prevot
Skoda Octavia WRC

16 Harri Rovanpera - Risto Pietilainen
Peugeot 206 WRC

17 Francois Delecour - Daniel Grataloup
Ford Focus RS WRC

18 Markko Martin - Michael Park
Subaru Impreza WRC

19 Toshihiro Arai - Glenn Mac Neall
Subaru Impreza WRC

20 Gilles Panizzi - Herve Panizzi
Peugeot 206 WRC

21 Henrik Lundgaard - Jens Christian Anker Toyota Corolla WRC

22 Pedro Matos Chaves - Sergio Paiva
Toyota Corolla WRC

23 Adruzilo Lopes - Luis Lisboa
Peugeot 206 WRC

24 Rui Madeira - Fernando Prata
Ford Focus RS WRC

27 Pasi Hagstrom - Tero Gardemeister
Toyota Corolla WRC

29 Abdullah Bakhashab - Bobby Willis
Toyota Corolla WRC

39 Manfred Stohl - Peter Muller
Mitsubishi Lancer Evo 6

41 Gustavo Trelles - Jorge Del Buono
Mitsubishi Lancer Evo 6

42 Gabriel Pozzo - Daniel Luis Stillo
Mitsubishi Lancer Evo 6

43 Stig Blomqvist - Ana Goni
Mitsubishi Lancer Evo 6

47 Marcos Ligato - Ruben Garcia
Mitsubishi Lancer Evo 6

54 Philippe Bugalski - Jean-Paul Chiaroni
Citroen Saxo Kit Car

55 Thomas Radstrom - Tina Thorner
Citroen Saxo Kit Car

Special Stage Times

SS1 Baltar 3,20 km
1.Makinen 3'46"9; 2.Gronholm 3'47"9; 3.Rovanpera 3'51"0; 4.Sainz 3'52"9; 5.Loix/Martin 3'54"7; Gr.N Trelles 4'09"0

SS2 Viso 1 11,84 km
1.Rovanpera 7'57"6; 2.Sainz 7'56"1; 3.Makinen 8'05"5; 4.Gronholm 8'07"4 5 McRae 8'13"3; 6.Burns 8'14"2; Gr.N Pozzo 8'57"8

SS3 Fafe - Lameirinha 1 15,16 km
1.Makinen 10'51"8; 2.Rovanpera 10'53"7; 3.Sainz 10'59"2; 4.Burns 11'01"5; 5.Delecour 11'12"4; 6.Loix 11'12"5; Gr.N Stohl 12'29"2

SS4 Vieira - Cabeceiras 1 26,68 km
1.Makinen 20'36"2; 2.Rovanpera 21'01"7; 3.Sainz 21'15"2; 4.Gronholm 21'31"9; 5.Loix 21'46"1; 6.Burns 22'09"0; Gr.N Pozzo 24'20"9

SS5 Viso 2 11,84 km
1.Sainz 8'17"0; 2.Gronholm 8'21"2; 3.Burns 8'21"7; 4.Rovanpera 8'22"4; 5.Makinen 8'23"7; 6.McRae 8'28"4; Gr.N Stohl 9'20"8

SS6 Fafe - Lameirinha 2 15,16 km
Cancelled - during the first run, several competitors got stuck in the mud.

SS7 Vieira - Cabeceiras 2 26,68 km
Cancelled - after the delay, spectators leave the stage in the fog and the drivers refuse to start.

SS8 Amarante 18,44 km
1.Rovanpera 14'19"9; 2.Gronholm 14'26"6; 3.Sainz 14'28"4; 4.Makinen 14'37"1; 5.Burns 14'40"2; 6.Delecour 14'44"5; Gr.N Stohl 16'28"5

SS9 Mondim de Basto 22,08 km
1.Sainz 17'41"9; 2.Makinen 17'48"3; 3.Gronholm 17'56"2; 4.Burns 18'01"1; 5.Rovanpera 18'04"0; 6.Loix 18'17"4; Gr.N Stohl 20'08"2

SS10 Lousada 3,69 km
1.Sainz 3'19"5; 2.Rovanpera 3'20"8; 3.Martin 3'21"1; 4.Delecour 3'21"3; 5.Burns 3'23"1; 6.Loix 3'25"0; Gr.N Stohl 3'47"3

SS11 Oliveira do Hospital 1 24,78 km
1.Makinen 18'14"3; 2.Sainz 18'15"8; 3.Rovanpera 18'21"0; 4.Burns 18'25"1; 5.Loix 18'42"9; 6.Gronholm 18'51"2; Gr.N Ligato 21'30"1

SS12 Arganil 1 14,27 km
1.Makinen 11'13"2; 2.Sainz 11'21"5; 3.Burns 11'21"7; 4.Gronholm 11'25"8; 5.Delecour 11'31"0; 6.Loix 11'33"8; Gr.N Ligato 13'25"7

SS13 Gois 1 19,62 km
1.Burns 12'26"1; 2.Sainz 12'32"8; 3.Makinen 12'33"7; 4.Gronholm 12'40"5; 5.Loix 12'45"0; 6.Delecour 12'55"6; Gr.N Stohl 14'41"0

SS14 Oliveira do Hospital 2 24,78 km
1.Burns 18'42"0; 2.Sainz 18'43"5; 3.Loix 18'44"1; 4.Gronholm 18'44"9; 5.Makinen 18'45"9; 6.Auriol 19'13"1; Gr.N Ligato 21'15"8

SS15 Arganil 2 14,27 km
1.Sainz 11'15"0; 2.Makinen 11'22"2; 3.Burns 11'27"0; 4.Gronholm 11'29"5; 5.Delecour 11'40"3; 6.Eriksson 11'48"7; Gr.N Ligato 13'54"4

SS16 Gois 2 19,62 km
1.Makinen 12'33"0; 2.Gronholm 12'37"0;3.Burns 12'39"1; 4.Sainz 12'45"0; 5.Delecour 12'52"7; 6.Auriol 12'53"1; Gr.N Ligato 14'37"9

SS17 Tabua 14,71 km
1.Makinen 11'13"3; 2.Sainz 11'14"4; 3.Gronholm 11'15"0; 4.Burns 11'30"2; 5.Carlsson 11'30"2; 6.A. McRae 11'36"4 Gr.N Stohl 12'11"9

SS18 Mortagua 21,38 km
1.Sainz 15'30"1; 2.Gronholm 15'31"6; 3.Makinen 15'46"9; 4.A. McRae 15'54"7; 5.Burns 16'05"6; 6.Eriksson 16'22"9; Gr.N Stohl 17'15"2

SS19 Aguieira 23,93 km
Cancelled - impassable, too muddy.

SS20 Ponte de Lima Este 23,49 km
Cancelled - impassable, road washed away.

SS21 Ponte de Lima Oeste 23,26 km
1.Sainz 18'19"2; 2.Makinen 18'32"5; 3.Gronholm 18'34"1; 4.Burns 18'34"4; 5.A. McRae 19'00"2; 6.Auriol 19'04"9; Gr.N Stohl 19'55"9

SS22 Ponte de Lima Sul 11,15 km
1.Makinen 8'52"3; 2.Sainz 9'01"2; 3.Burns 9'08"0; 4.Delecour 9'26"3; 5.A. McRae 9'34"1; 6.Gronholm 9'34"2; Gr.N Stohl 10'07"5

Results · WRC

	Driver/Navigator	Car	Gr.	Time
1	Makinen - Mannisenmaki	Mitsubishi Lancer Evo 6	A	3h46'42"2
2	Sainz - Moya	Ford Focus RS WRC		+ 8"6
3	Gronholm - Rautiainen	Peugeot 206 WRC		+ 2'55"6
4	Bruns - Reid	Subaru Impreza WRC		+ 3'24"3
5	Delecour - Grataloup	Ford Focus RS WRC		+ 3'24"3
6	A. McRea - Senior	Hyundai Accent WRC		+ 12'08"4
7	Eriksson - Parmander	Hyundai Accent WRC		+ 13'32"5
8	Auriol - Giraudet	Peugeot 206 WRC		+ 16'08"6
9	Laukkanen - Lindström	Toyota Corolla WRC		+ 16'35"9
10	Hagstrom - gardemeister	Toyota Corolla WRC	Team's Cup	+ 19'32"5
14	Ligato - Garcia	Mitsubishi Lancer Evo 6	N	+ 38'53"7

Leading Retirements

SS.15	Martin - Park	Subaru Impreza WRC 2001	Off
SS.15	Loix - Smeets	Mitsubishi Carisma GT	Clutch
SS.13	Rovanpera - Pietilainen	Peugeot 206 WRC	Engine
SS.10	P. Solberg - Mills	Subaru Impreza WRC 2001	Suspension
SS.8	C. McRea - Grist	Ford Focus RS WRC	Engine
SS.4	Arai - Mac Neall	Subaru Impreza WRC 2001	Off
SS.2	Schwarz - Hiemer	Skoda Octavia WRC	Clutch
SS.1	Thiry - Prevot	Skoda Octavia WRC	Electronics

Championship Classifications

Drivers
1. Makinen 20; 2. Sainz 16; 3. Rovanpera 10; 4. Delecour 8; 5. Radstrom 6; 6. Gardemeister 5; 7. Gronholm 4; 8. Burns, Schwarz 3; 10. Loix, Solberg, A. McRae 1

Constructors
1. Mitsubishi 33; 2. Ford 20; 3. Hyundai 8; 4. Subaru 7; Skoda 6; 5. Peugeot 4

Group N
1. Stohl, Ligato 12; 3. Gillet, Walfridsson 10; 4. Backlund 6; 6. Trelles, Blomqvist, Dias da Silva 4...

Team's Cup
1. Toyota Castrol Team Denmark (Lundgaart), Toyota Castrol Finland (Hagstrom) 10; 3. David Sutton Cars Ltd (Blomqvist), Oman Arab World Rally Team (Al Wahaibi) 6; 5. Marlboro Ford Mobil1 Team Poland (Kulig) 4...

Performers

	1	2	3	4	5	6
Makinen	8	3	3	1	2	-
Sainz	6	7	3	2	-	-
Rovanpera	2	3	1	1	1	-
Burns	2	-	5	5	3	2
Gronholm	-	5	3	5	-	2
Loix	-	-	1	-	4	4
Martin	-	-	1	-	1	-
Delecour	-	-	-	2	4	2
A. McRae	-	-	-	1	2	1
C. McRae	-	-	-	-	1	1
Carlsson	-	-	-	-	1	-
Auriol	-	-	-	-	-	3
Erikson	-	-	-	-	-	2

Event Leaders

SS.1	Makinen
SS.2 & 3	Rovanpera
SS.4 > SS.18	Makinen
SS.19 & 20	*annulées*
SS.21	Sainz
SS.22	Makinen

Previous winners

1973	Thérier - Jaubert Alpine Renault A 110	1987	Alen - Kivimäki Lancia Delta HF 4WD
1974	Pinto - Bernacchini Fiat 124 Abarth	1988	Biasion - Cassina Lancia Delta Integrale
1975	Alen - Kivimäki Fiat 124 Abarth	1989	Biasion - Siviero Lancia Delta Integrale
1976	Munari - Maiga Lancia Stratos	1990	Biasion - Siviero Lancia Delta Integrale
1977	Alen - Kivimäki Fiat 131 Abarth	1991	Sainz - Moya Toyota Celica GT-Four
1978	Alen - Kivimäki Fiat 131 Abarth	1992	Kankkunen - Piironen Lancia HF Integrale
1979	Mikkola - Hertz Ford Escort RS	1993	Delecour - Grataloup Ford Escort RS Cosworth
1980	Röhrl - Geistdörfer Fiat 131 Abarth	1994	Kankkunen - Grist Toyota Celica Turbo 4WD
1981	Alen - Kivimäki Fiat 131 Abarth	1995	Sainz - Moya Subaru Impreza
1982	Mouton - Pons Audi Quattro	1996	Madeira - Da Silva Toyota Celica GT-Four
1983	Mikkola - Hertz Audi Quattro	1997	Makinen - Harjanne Mitsubishi Lancer Ev.4
1984	Mikkola - Hertz Audi Quattro	1998	McRae - Grist Subaru Impreza WRC
1985	Salonen - Harjanne Peugeot 205 T16	1999	McRae - Grist Ford Focus WRC
1986	Moutinho - Fortes Renault 5 Turbo	2000	Burns - Reid Subaru Impreza WRC 2000

Spain

Catalunya

The extraordinary demonstration by the Xsaras, on their first world championship outing did not go the distance. It fell to Auriol, one of the few not to have thrown down his arms, to take the victory.

THE RALLY
AURIOL DESPITE THE CITROENS

To say that everyone had been eagerly awaiting the Citroens' Catalan debut would be a masterpiece of understatement. Everyone was staring and smiling inquisitively, watching every step the cars took and every spanner that was laid on them. On the day the Red Army made its first appearance in action, it was obvious it would be the "bête noire" of the WRC class. The chevron-clad Puras and Bugalski tried to be cunning during the shakedown, but they were not cunning enough. The times of the shakedown are not supposed to mean anything but both men lifted off the loud pedal as they approached the timing beam, so as not to give away any clues to the opposition, but the signs were plain to see.

Change of scene two days later on the Catalunya asphalt, with its wide roads and flowing corners in the gentle hills which roll down to the base of the Pyrenees and the bucolic Mediterranean. The Xsara put on a very convincing performance for its first steps on the world championship stage. Not only did it take the lead, just like the 206 in the 1999 Tour of Corsica, but better still, it led the first leg from start to finish, thanks to a very stylish performance from Puras. Just like the Toyota Corolla in 1997 in Finland, it won the first leg of its

world championship career and to top it all, it was fastest on four of the six stages. There was even some icing on the cake, in that Bugalski in the other red devil was second. Stop the clocks! No new car had ever done as well. However, unlike the other examples of debut brilliance, the Xsara was not exactly a virgin as it had first turned a wheel back in May '99 and had a triumphant season in the French Championship in 2000. Nevertheless, there could not have been a prouder man on earth that day than team boss Guy Frequelin, the man who runs Citroen Sport. "I am reassured and happy. Really. Despite all our preparation, we did not know how competitive we would be. I just hoped

we would be on the pace!" He probably hadn't dared expect anything like this. Puras was delighted and took fastest time on the first stage, before running consistently for the rest of the day, to be the "de facto" winner of the leg. Only Bugalski drove better, but he had to deal with brake problems. "I took a lot of risks," explained the Spanish Champion. "Because, as I started a long way down the order, I was driving on a track which had been made dirty by the early runners. When the first cars clip the kerbs, they throw a lot of gravel, mud and stones onto the road. So that meant, my aim was to start the second leg as near to the front as possible."

Behind the two impeccable Citroens, the order had a strange look about it. Gronholm had been very strong at the start of the leg, but then made mistakes. "I got caught out by some gravel. It was my fault because I did not listen properly to the pace notes. The car got away from me and I hit something and the right rear wheel was pulled off."

For his part, Burns was slowed by a gearbox gremlins, before a slight knock meant he had to run on a damaged rim. Fifteenth, around two minutes down, the number one Subaru driver was down in the dumps. "It's too much, it's over!" As for McRae, he almost incited pity, such had been his bad luck. While all three Fords were hit with fuel injection problems, his was the only one not to get past stage five.

That left the effective trio of Makinen, Auriol and Panizzi to try and put up some resistence. In aggressive mood at the start of the rally, the Finn was finally slowed with brake bothers. "The cooling system was damaged and I found myself with a long pedal several times." So, he had to give best to the Peugeots, with Auriol finishing just ahead of Panizzi, as the first non-Citroen runner. The gap between the top five was less than 25 seconds. There was to be no god for Citroen's Jesus, as his Xsara ground to a halt, just when he thought his home event was his for the taking. It was a fuel problem. "Whether it's the fuel pump or a possible knock under the car

As usual, the Catalunya Rally drew a very big crowd, keen to cheer on the tarmac artists like Gilles Panizzi.

With Puras out, his team-mate Philippe Bugalski picked up the baton to run at the head of the field in the Xsara WRC's debut on the world stage.

With each passing rally, Marcus Gronholm improved his mastery of tarmac driving.

on this tarmac surface and the proverbial reliability of his Citroen had never been brought into question, about from Puras' misfortune. "It's the aspect we had the least doubts about which finally let us down," regretted Guy Frequelin, "the reliability of our car." At the exit to stage 14, Osor 1, the clutch master cylinder broke. In order to keep going, the crew had to change the part and take great care on the next stage. It was not a problem while the car was moving, but it was the moment it had

to stop for any reason. Bugalski was aware of it. He left the next section, Collsesplanes 1, late and took a two minute penalty. The mechanics might have done a great job to change the gearbox and clutch in just 20 minutes, but the penalty robbed him of any hopes. It was all falling into place for Auriol and the Peugeot driver picked up the winner's trophy. He had gone looking for the win, never easing up throughout the rally. Even though he must have thought he had no hope as he approached the final leg, he still

which did something to the circuit, it really doesn't matter," lamented Frequelin. "We've lost one car, but the important thing is that Bug is still leading!" The grizzled general still kept his head as high as his hopes. Because despite this faux pas, the Citroen once again proved it had something in reserve. The rest of the field were doing all they could to push the leader hard, in the hope that the second Citroen would fail. "I am pushing very hard," confided Didier Auriol. "Really hard. The car is great; without a doubt the best I have driven on tarmac and that's saying something." Meanwhile, Panizzi was playing with his central diff settings. Winner of the second leg, Bugalski led Auriol by 27.7 seconds and was about a week ahead (1'10"4) of Panizzi, as they prepared to tackle the final leg. It seemed as though the final 118 timed kilometres would go off smoothly. There were three concrete reasons to believe that to be the case: the speed of the Xsara WRC, which had been obvious from the start; the surefootedness of the driver

Always dangerous on tarmac, Makinen finished third and first non-French car.

Like his team-mates, sixth-placed Francois Delecour had to make do with Pirellis which were not on the pace on tarmac.

attacked it with more vigour than usual. Two kilometres into the first stage, his rally almost came to an end. "We were deep in the apex of a right-hander, two wheels in the dirt, two on the road," explained co-driver Denis Giraudet. "The car went sideways and was about to hit the mountain with the back end. But Didier suddenly put on full opposite lock and the car shot off in the other direction. So, now we were facing the mountain! More opposite lock and we nearly ended up in the ditch. Basically, for a hundred metres we went down the road in every

direction. If we had gone off, it would have been worse for the 206 than for us." Four rallies with Peugeot and the driver was now all smiles, having been down in the dumps two weeks earlier in Portugal.

Third behind Auriol and Panizzi, Makinen tightened his grip on the championship. "Maybe the Peugeot men will be the toughest this year," laughed the Finn with a malicious grin. "We won't talk about the title yet. But it's got off to a good start with this third place, after two wins." ∎

Citroen did not win, but its Xsara WRCs put on a remarkable show. They were not the most reliable, but they were the quickest.

THE WINNER
AURIOL JOINS THE CLUB

Of all the key players in the world championship, Didier Auriol was the one who had gone the longest without a win. His victory in China was now eighteen months old. Sure, the 2000 season was not the sort of adventure which would allow a driver to add any lustre or wins to his record book, but to a champion of his calibre, this

hiatus must have seemed like the eternity that accompanies waiting for a bus in the rain. But in Catalunya, there must be some sort of Auriol winning manual. Get him well wound up and the man gets up on his high horse, grabs the road by the scruff of the neck, dominates the opposition and wins. In the 1998 edition, Toyota never stopped expressing its lack of confidence in the driver and he crushed the opposition with a steel boot. This season, two weeks before the Spanish event, he went home

Tommi Makinen seems to appreciate his sponsor's promo girls, who make the Mitsubishi service areas a nice place to be!

Bruno Thiry can still do the business on tarmac, even in an underpowered Skoda.

destroyed and bemoaning his fate, after a desperate Portuguese Rally. He didn't know where he was and began to question his abilities, while others pointed to his age and his motivation or lack of it. Once the technical error in Portugal was discovered and put behind him, Didier Auriol returned to form. He dominated the non-Citroen class, even beating his team-mate Gilles Panizzi, who is reckoned to be the fastest man on tarmac these days.

This return to the top step of the podium was welcomed by one and all. It also allowed him to join the "20 Club," for drivers who had won at least twenty rounds of the world championship. It is a select band, including Sainz, Kankkunen, Makinen and McRae. It is a symbolic number and he reached it at the wheel of a French car; something he had never done before and had always wanted. More than ever, the dream could go on. ■

37th SPANISH RALLY

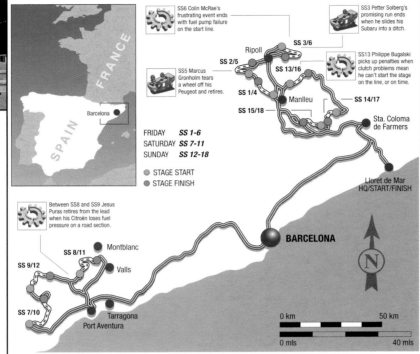

SS6 Colin McRae's frustrating event ends with fuel pump failure on the start line.

SS3 Petter Solberg's promising run ends when he slides his Subaru into a ditch.

Ripoll

SS 3/6

SS 2/5

SS13 Philippe Bugalski picks up penalties when clutch problems mean he can't start the stage on the line, or on time.

SS5 Marcus Gronholm tears a wheel off his Peugeot and retires.

SS 13/16

SS 1/4

Manlleu

SS 15/18

SS 14/17

Sta. Coloma de Farmers

FRIDAY **SS 1-6**
SATURDAY **SS 7-11**
SUNDAY **SS 12-18**

● STAGE START
● STAGE FINISH

Barcelona

SPAIN

FRANCE

Lloret de Mar HQ/START/FINISH

Between SS8 and SS9 Jesus Puras retires from the lead when his Citroën loses fuel pressure on a road section.

BARCELONA

SS 8/11   Montblanc

SS 9/12   Valls

SS 7/10   Tarragona
Port Aventura

N

0 km		50 km
0 mls		40 mls

4th leg of the 2001 World Rally Championship for constructors and drivers. **4th** leg of the Group N World Championship. **1st** leg FIA Super 1600 Championship. **1st** leg of the Team's cup.

Date 23th - 25th March 2001

Route
1815.02 km divided into 3 legs
18 special stages on tarmac roads (383,18 km) but 17 ran (347,29 km)

1st leg
Friday 23th March: Lioret de Mar - Manlleu - Lioret de Mar, 6 stages (101 km)

2nd leg
Saturday 24th March: Lioret de Mar-Salou- Lioret de Mar, 6 stages and 5 ran (127,89 km)

3rd leg
Sunday 25th March: Lioret de Mard - Manlleu - Lioret de Mar, 6 stages (118,40 km)

Starters - Finishers: 74 - 36

Conditions: nice and dry.

TOP ENTRIES

1 Marcus Gronholm - Timo Rautiainen
   Peugeot 206 WRC

2 Didier Auriol - Denis Giraudet
   Peugeot 206 WRC

3 Carlos Sainz - Luis Moya
   Ford Focus RS WRC

4 Colin McRae - Nicky Grist
   Ford Focus RS WRC

5 Richard Burns - Robert Reid
   Subaru Impreza WRC

6 Petter Solberg - Philip Mills
   Subaru Impreza WRC

7 Tommi Makinen - Risto Mannisenmaki
   Mitsubishi Lancer Evo 6

8 Freddy Loix - Sven Smeets
   Mitsubishi Carisma GT

9 Piero Liatti - Carlo Cassina
   Hyundai Accent WRC

10 Alister McRae - David Senior
    Hyundai Accent WRC

11 Armin Schwarz - Manfred Hiemer
    Skoda Octavia WRC

12 Bruno Thiry - Stephane Prevot
    Skoda Octavia WRC

14 Philippe Bugalski - Jean-Paul
    Chiaroni Citroen Xsara WRC

15 Jesus Puras - Marc Marti
    Citroen Xsara WRC

16 Gilles Panizzi - Herve Panizzi
    Peugeot 206 WRC

17 Francois Delecour - Daniel Grataloup
    Ford Focus RS WRC

18 Markko Martin - Michael Park
    Subaru Impreza WRC

19 Simon Jean-Joseph - Jacques
    Boyere Peugeot 206 WRC

22 Adruzilo Lopes - Luis Lisboa
    Peugeot 206 WRC

26 Gustavo Trelles - Jorge Del Buono
    Mitsubishi Lancer Evo 6

27 Gabriel Pozzo - Daniel Luis Stillo
    Mitsubishi Lancer Evo 6

28 Stig Blomqvist - Ana Goni
    Mitsubishi Lancer Evo 6

29 Marcos Ligato - Ruben Garcia
    Mitsubishi Lancer Evo 6

50 Manfred Stohl - Ilka Petrasko
    Fiat Punto

51 Patrick Magaud - Guylene Brun
    Ford Puma

52 Andrea Dallavilla - Danilo Fappani
    Fiat Punto

53 Sebastien Loeb - Daniel Elena
    Citroen Saxo

54 Larry Cols - Yasmine Gerard
    Peugeot 206

55 Niall McShea - Michael Orr
    Ford Puma

57 Cedric Robert - Marie-Pierre Billoux
    Peugeot 206

Special Stage Times

SS1 La Trona 1 12,90 km
1.Puras 8'24"8; 2.Auriol 8'25"8;
3.Gronholm 8'26"0; 4.Panizzi 8'26"6;
5.Burns 8'27"2; 6.Solberg 8'29"5; Gr.N
Trelles 9'05"6; S16 Robert 9'06"1

SS2 Alpens - Les Lloses 1 21,80km
1.Makinen 13'30"3 2.Puras 13'34"0
3.Gronholm 13'34"7 4.Auriol 13'35"1
5.Loix 13'36"7 6.Delecour 13'37"9 Gr.N
Ligato 14'46"1; S16 Loeb 14'37"6

SSS3 Vallfogona 1 15,80 km
1.Bugalski 9'21"2; 2.Puras 9'22"7;
3.Panizzi 9'26"2; 4.Auriol 9'26"3;
5.Gronholm 9'26"5; 6.Makinen
9'26"9;Gr.N Ligato 10'15"0;
S16 Loeb 10'01"1

SS4 La Trona 2 12,90 km
1.Auriol 8'26"2; 2.Gronholm/Bugalski
8'26"5; 4.Panizzi 8'28"5; 5.Puras
8'29"2; 6.Burns 8'30"8; Gr.N Trelles
9'07"9; S16 Duval 9'05"2

SS5 Alpens - Les Lloses 2 21,80 km
1.Bugalski 13'32"7; 2.Puras 13'34"0;
3.Panizzi 13'38"1; 4.Auriol 13'38"7;
5.Makinen 13'43"5; 6.Loix 13'45"2;

Gr.N Ligato 13'45"3; S16 Loeb 14'34"3

SS6 Vallfogona 2 15,80 km
1.Bugalski 9'19"3; 2.Puras 9'20"2;
3.Auriol 9'24"0; 4.Panizzi 9'25"0;
5.Makinen 9'26"8; 6.Martin 9'32"8;
Gr.N Ligato 10'12"6; S16 Loeb 10'07"0

SS7 Pratdip 1 31,57 km
1.Puras 19'12"0; 2.Bugalski 19'21"3;
3.Burns 19'24"3; 4.Auriol 19'26"5;
5.Panizzi 19'31"5; 6.Makinen 19'38"3;
Gr.N Pozzo 21'01"2; S16 Stohl 21'01"2

SS8 Escaladei 1 14,43 km
1.Bugalski 10'26"6; 2.Auriol 10'31"2;
3.Panizzi 10'32"7; 4.Makinen 10'35"3;
5.Puras/Delecour 10'37"7; Gr.N Ligato
11'20"1; S16 Loeb 11'10"5

SS9 La Riba 1 35,89 km
1.Bugalski 21'56"6; 2.Auriol 22'05"0;
3.Puras 22'06"0; 4.Delecour 22'12"1;
5.Makinen 22'16"6; 6.Burns 22'16"9;
Gr.N Trelles 24'10"4; S16 Loeb 23'38"6

SS10 Pratdip 2 31,57 km
1.Bugalski 19'17"8; 2.Puras 19'19"8;
3.Auriol 19'26"7; 4.Burns 19'28"2;

5.Makinen 19'33"8; 6.Sainz&Panizzi
19'39"7; Gr.N Pozzo 20'56"1;
S16 Loeb 20'48"5

SS11 Escaladei 2 14,43 km
1.Auriol 10'44"5; 2.Bugalski 10'46"4;
3.Panizzi 10'47"0; 4.Puras 10'48"0;
5.Delecour 10'51"6; 6.Makinen
10'52"1; Gr.N Trelles 11'36"5;
S16 Loeb 11'32"3

SS12 La Riba 2 35,89 km
Cancelled - too many spectators.

SS13 Coll de Bracons 1 19,66 km
1.Panizzi 12'51"3; 2.Bugalski 12'55"7;
3.Loix 12'58"0; 4.Burns 12'59"7;
5.Delecour 13'00"8; 6.Delecour
13'00"8; Gr.N Trelles 14'18"3;
S16 Loeb 14'01"0

SS14 Osor 1 13,26 km
1.Auriol 8'12"4; 2.Panizzi 8'13"1;
3.Makinen 8'17"4; 4.Burns 8'18"8;
5.Sainz 8'19"0; 6.Bugalski 8'21"3; Gr.N
Pozzo 9'07"6; S16 Loeb 8'57"3

SS15 Collsesplanes 1 26,28 km
1.Bugalski 16'28"0; 2.Panizzi 16'30"1;

3.Makinen 16'32"9; 4.Auriol 16'33"1;
5.Loix 16'37"9; 6.Delecour 16'43"2; Gr.N
Feghali 18'17"6; S16 Loeb 18'02"0

SS16 Coll de Bracons 2 19,66 km
1.Auriol 12'56"5; 2.Panizzi 12'56"8;
3.Panizzi 12'59"5; 4.Loix 13'00"5;
5.Makinen 13'01"7; 6.Burns 13'04"2;
Gr.N Pozzo 14'12"1; S16 Robert
14'08"9

SS17 Osor 2 13,26 km
1.Panizzi 8'10"9; 2.Bugalski 8'13"0;
3.Loix 8'14"3; 4.Makinen 8'14"5;
5.Delecour 8'16"2; 6.Auriol 8'16"5;
Gr.N/S16 ES neutralisée

SS18 Collsesplanes 2 26,28 km
1.Bugalski 16'33"3; 2.Panizzi 16'40"3;
3.Makinen 16'44"7; 4.Auriol 16'44"8;
5.Delecour 16'49"2; 6.Loix 16'49"4;
Gr.N Pozzo 18'24"7; S16 Robert
18'21"4

Results WRC

	Driver/Navigator	Car	Gr.	Time
1	**Auriol - Giraudet**	**Peugeot 206 WRC**	A	3h40'54"7
2	Panizzi - Panizzi	Peugeot 206 WRC		+ 23"2
3	Makinen - Mannisenmaki	Mitsubishi Lancer Evo 6		+ 1'01"4
4	Loix - Smeets	Mitsubishi Carisma GT		+ 2'16"7
5	Sainz - Moya	Ford Focus RS WRC 01		+ 2'35"7
6	Delecour - Grataloup	Ford Focus RS WRC 01		+ 2'43"7
7	Burns - Reid	Subaru Impreza WRC 2001		+ 3'02"8
8	Bugalski - Chiaroni	Citroën Xsara WRC		+ 3'25"7
9	Jean-Joseph - Boyere	Peugeot 206 WRC		+ 4'59"3
10	Thiry - Prévot	Skoda Octavia WRC		+ 6'03"9
15	**Loeb - Eléna**	**Citroen Saxo**	**Super 1600**	**+ 19'23"9**
18	**Pozzo - Stillo**	**Mitsubishi lancer Ev 6**	**N**	**+ 23'41"4**

Leading Retirements
SS.16	Martin - Park	Subaru Impreza WRC 2001	Gearbox
SS.14	Liatti - Cassina	Hyundai Accent WRC	Brakes
SS.11	Ligato - Garcia	Mitsubishi Lancer Evo 6	Accident
SS.11	Puras - Marti	Citroen Xsara WRC	Fuel pressure
SS.7	Schwarz - Hiemer	Skoda Octavia WRC	Steering
SS.6	C. McRae - Grist	Ford Focus RS WRC	Fuel pump
SS.5	Gronholm - Rautiainen	Peugeot 206 WRC	Wheel torn off
SS.3	Solberg - Mills	Subaru Impreza WRC 2001	Accident

Performers

	1	2	3	4	5	6
Bugalski	8	6	-	-	-	1
Auriol	4	3	2	6	-	1
Puras	2	6	1	6	-	1
Panizzi	2	3	5	3	-	1
Makinen	1	-	3	2	6	3
Gronholm	-	1	2	-	1	-
Loix	-	-	2	1	2	2
Burns	-	-	1	3	1	3
Delecour	-	-	-	1	3	4
Sainz	-	-	-	-	1	1
Solberg	-	-	-	-	-	1
Martin	-	-	-	-	-	1

Event Leaders

SS.1 > SS. 8	Puras
SS.9 > SS. 14	Bulgalski
SS.15 > SS.18	Auriol

Championship Classifications

Drivers
1. Makinen 24; 2. Sainz 18; 3. Rovanpera, Auriol 10; 5. Delecour 9;
6. Radstrom, Panizzi 6; 8. Gardemeister 5; 9. Gronholm, Loix 4;
11. Burns, Schwarz 3; 13. Solberg, A. McRea 1

Constructors
1. Mitsubishi 40; 2. Ford 22; 3. Peugeot 20; 4. Hyundai, Subaru 8;
6. Skoda 6

Group N
1. Pozzo 13; 2. Gillet, Walfridsson, Dias da Silva 5...

Team's Cup
1. Toyota Castrol Team Denmark (Lundgaard), Team Toyota Castrol
Finland (Hagstrom) 10; 3. David Sutton Cars Ltd (Blomqvist), Oman
Arab World Rally Team (Al Wahaibi) 6...

FIA Super 1600
1. Loeb 10; 2. Basso 6; 3. Fontana 4; 4. Stenshorne 3; 5. Dallavilla 2...

Previous winners

1991	Schwarz - Hertz Toyota Celica GT-Four		1996	McRae - Ringer Subaru Impreza
1992	Sainz - Moya Toyota Celica Turbo 4WD		1997	Makinen - Harjanne Mitsubishi Lancer Ev.4
1993	Delecour - Grataloup Ford Escort RS Cosworth		1998	Auriol - Giraudet Toyota Corolla WRC
1994	Bertone - Chiapponi Toyota Celica Turbo 4WD		1999	Bugalski - Chiaroni Citroen Xsara Kit Car
1995	Sainz - Moya Subaru Impreza		2000	C. McRea - Grist Ford Focus WRC

Argentina

Argentina

Another faultless performance saw McRae make the most of a course that had never favoured him before. He dominated his car, the opposition and other fears with panache, on an event which was marked by a incredible catastrophe for Skoda

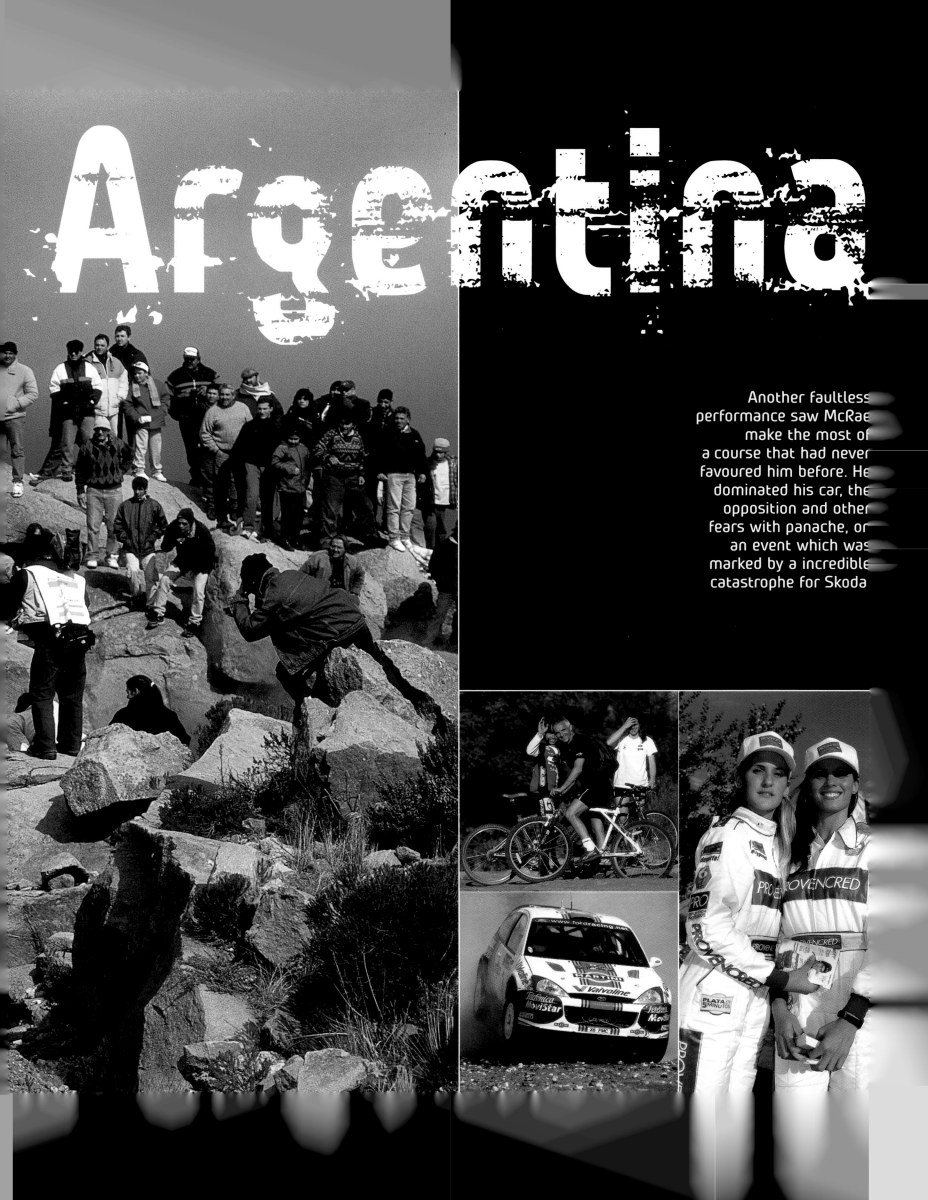

THE RALLY
McRAE IN THE LAND OF GIANTS

There are some who reckon that the Argentinian event separates the men from the boys. It's shorter now of course, but it still requires a superhuman effort mixed with courage and a degree of impetuousness. The 2001 event stuck to the script.

The first leg, which meandered around the heights of Sierra Chica, beat a path back to the great grassy plain of Cumbre, a delicate town with an English look to it and it was certainly a tough overture. When Colin McRae is on a charge, it is usually only his own folly or mechanical failure which can stop him. At the start of the rally, he never encountered either of these two misfortunes and he swallowed up the first five special stages. "I never held back, never. Halfway through the leg is not the time to play it safe. I was pushing all the way to the end. I just want a big enough lead to be able to ease up for the rest of it. In this rally, everything can change so quickly." Even though a poor tyre choice - too hard - towards the end of the leg, slowed him a tad, his lead over second placed Burns was a considerable 41.4 seconds.

In very determined mood, the Subaru driver had lived through a few heart stopping moments: a spin cost him almost 23 seconds, the power steering lost power and his rear brakes were inconsistent.

What with the Fords (McRae first, Sainz, in trouble with back pains, a brave third) and the Subaru leading the way, it seemed the Pirelli tyres were doing well in these cold and slightly damp climes, while the tracks dried a bit at the end of the day. This did not suit Makinen one bit. "As it gets drier and drier, a layer of dust appears making the surface very slippery. Starting further down the order, and a long way down the order in Colin's case, is definitely a big advantage compared with my position, opening the stage."

The Mitusbishi man finished this leg in fourth place, giving away over a minute to the leader. These were the sort of gaps we had not seen for some time on the world championship trail. The others, all of them, were finding it hard to keep up. Best of the three Peugeots, Auriol was 1'35 down. Not only was this poor unfortunate dragged down by the 19.6 seconds he had picked up the previous night because a bank of fog floated across the super stage just as he was tackling it, but he also had to lift off mid-stage, having heard a loud crack come from the left rear corner of his car.

Gronholm had even more serious problems. Right from the morning's

The Argentinian Rally can prove very treacherous: here, Freddy Loix and his Mitsubishi prove the point. Despite getting out of shape, the Belgian finished sixth.

Sainz was third, adding to Ford's points collected by McRae the winner.

Petter Solberg is very much at his ease on the Argentinian tracks.

Jorge Recalde was the darling of the locals and he was in their thoughts, having died a few days before the Argentinian event.

first special stage, the wastegate on his turbo seemed to have caught a cold, preventing the engine from using all its power. He had to put up with it for 41 kilometres before the faulty part was replaced.
As for Rovanpera, he drowned his engine in a ford at the end of the day,

before retiring with a broken suspension. It was inevitable that the second leg should kick off with a fascinating Anglo-Scottish duel for the lead.
Richard Burns was tackling the assault on the Sierra Morena with every intention on making up all or

most of his gap to Colin McRae. At the same time, the Ford driver had no intention of giving anything away, not even a tenth of a second! So, between them they swopped fastest times throughout the day. The British version of the tango was a thriller, with both men totally committed. By the end of the leg, the Sauber managed to eat up a few seconds deficit on the Ford, sniffing round its exhaust pipes.
However, when it came to them having to explain quite how their different driving styles had been so effective, they were unable to find the words to match their brio at the wheel.
Colin McRae: "Everything's going well. I'm pushing, but I don't think I'm taking too big a risk. I have to be careful all the same."
Richard Burns: "I am doing all I can. I am going as fast as I can. Of course I am going to fight for the win. But what else would I say?"
In their wake, the day turned sour, what with the Skoda drama (see below) and a storm of problems which wiped out Peugeot, as Auriol's

turbo failed and so did Gronholm's power steering. "I don't know what's happened to the Lion," whinged the world champion, who was still capable of getting to the podium. Then, for the first time since he joined Peugeot, this nice young man gave vent to a few probing remarks regarding his team. "I have never complained. But this time, we have to admit our lack of reliability has been catastrophic."
Along with the Peugeot drivers, Makinen was not in the best of moods. A recalcitrant transmission had slowed him early in the leg and the Finn was spiralling down the order, but still fifth and first of the Michelin runners. In fact, since 1999, the Italian tyres always seemed to have the edge in Argentina.
This was certainly one of the elements of McRae's and Burns' superiority, separated by 37.1 seconds at the start of the final day, the one which held all the dangers, in Giulio Cesare and El Condor, the terrible sections which snake through the Sierra de Gigantes. With its hellish roads and slippery

While leaping forward, Gustavo Trelles was still unable to contain the local man Pozzo, in the Group N category.

Denis Giraudet casts a bitter eye over the wreck of the 206 he shared with Didier Auriol. The accident in the penultimate stage was fatal for their car.

tracks, which would even give a donkey a few headaches, the drivers have to pick a path through blocks of rock which would serve to build the Arc de Triomphe. No wonder the spectacular mountain is called the land of giants. Colin McRae had never tasted success here in the past. He had never been able to tame his aggression to come out of it in one piece. Two years earlier, just before tackling Giulio Cesare, his faithful co-driver Nicky Grist explained: "it is not important to lead going into this stage. You have to lead coming out of it." Back then, the British crew destroyed their suspension on the Ford. Two years later, they set the fastest time,

beating Makinen's old record to win the rally. Better still, they went on to wrap up the final stage, El Condor, as well, despite its dangerous reputation.

Richard Burns had shot off like a British bulldog, determined to bite his rival. After only managing to nibble a few fractions here and there, he admitted "I don't want to take any unnecessary risks. I'll continue at a good pace. Second is better than nothing, but not as good as winning. Things could have been different if I had not spun on the first day. These days, the slightest mistake is very hard to make up." McRae made no mistakes, despite running flat out for three days. A

rare event which paid off. For the two Brits, this result came at just the right time. It meant they were still in with a chance of the Drivers' title. "I've scored my first ten points of the year on this rally, which I've wanted to win one day," rejoiced the winner. "Finally I've done it. I've never felt so relieved in my life. I hope this is the start of a new race for the title. The next two events (Cyprus and the Acropolis) will be crucial. I will have to score big on both of them!"

The gauntlet had been thrown down. The crew's happiness was mirrored by the team, which had finally won a rally for the first time this season. Thanks to the fourteen points picked up by McRae and Sainz, it also went some way to reduce the gap to Mitsubishi, the imperturbable leader of the Constructors' series in the way of Makinen in the Drivers' classification. It was about time the Blue Oval proved that its avowed intention of finally taking the constructors' title was more than just a lot of hot air. Not all the constructors could say the same. ■

THE DRAMA
SKODA IN TORMENT

Saturday 5th May 2001 will forever be a black day for the Czech team. It threw up a series of terrible events which were all linked by a series of awful

coincidences. It proved the theory that, "when a butterfly's wings beat in China, it can cause a tidal wave in America." The dramatic accident occurred halfway through the second leg. The Argentinian spectators love having an "asados"; a sort of impromptu barbecue, where they cook steaks as big as houses, alongside delicious sausages. At the finish of the Amboy-Santa Rosa de Calamuchita stage, a helicopter landed in a parking area full with well over a hundred cars. Wind generated by its rotor blades sparked a fire which spread to around fifteen cars. The firemen were soon on the scene. Unfortunately, a water truck came barrelling into the holding area for the rally cars, at far too great a speed. It flew into the entrance to the Santa Rosa de Calamuchita service area, which seemed an odd route to chose. As it tried to negotiate a tight right hand bend with negative camber, the truck hit Jens Polhmann, the German second in command at Skoda, in charge of engineering and the boss of the company's motorsport department. At the time he was talking to Armin Schwarz. Then, the out of control truck went off the road to the left and both its water tanks landed on the Octavia WRC of Bruno Thiry and Stephane Prevot. "I only just had time to jump out of the way," explained the driver in a state of shock. "It's lucky we had a roll-over cage, or we would have been

On its first run in Argentina, the Skoda team saw its efforts come to nothing when a water tank fell of a fire engine, crushing both Octavia WRCs and badly injuring one of the team personnel.

crushed." Not only was the Belgian's Skoda destroyed, but the runaway truck also hit the Schwarz-Hiemer car at full pelt. Luckily, it was parked and the crew were not in the car. More worrying than the loss of these two cars, the Czech team faced the worry of waiting for news of their boss, who had immediately been helicoptered to the Cordoba hospital. He had cranial bruising, internal bleeding and four left ribs broken. Luckily, after a thorough examination the next day, there were no neurological problems to report. Polhmann spent several days in Argentina before being repatriated to Europe, where he slowly recovered from his injuries. Skoda will not forget its first Argentinian Rally in a hurry. ∎

21th RALLY OF ARGENTINA

5th leg of the 2001 World Rally championship for constructors and drivers. 5th leg of the Group N World Championship.

Date 3rd to 6th May 2001

Route
1345,07 km divided into 3 legs
21 special stages on dirt roads (389,58 km)

Prologue
Thursday 3rd May: Pro Racing Complex Villa Carlos Paz - Villa Carlos Paz, 2 stages (6,88 km)

1st leg
Friday 4th May: Villa Carlos Paz - La Cumbre - Villa Carlo Paz, 6 stages (150,59 km)

2nd leg
Saturday 5th May: Villa Carlo Paz - Santa Rosa de Calamuchita - Villa Carlo Paz, 7 stages (120,43 km)

3rd leg
Sunday 6th May: Villa Carlo Paz - Mina Clavero - Cordoba, 6 stages (118,56 km)

Starters - Finishers: 65 - 32

Conditions: fog and damp loose surface road (1st leg.) The surface got progressively drier.

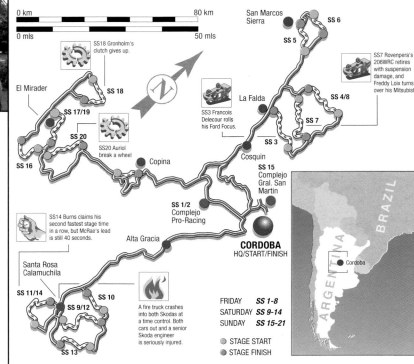

SS18 Gronholm's clutch gives up.

SS20 Auriol break a wheel

SS3 Francois Delecour rolls his Ford Focus.

SS7 Rovenpera's 206WRC retires with suspension damage, and Freddy Loix turns over his Mitsubishi.

SS14 Burns claims his second fastest stage time in a row, but McRae's lead is still 40 seconds.

A fire truck crashes into both Skodas at a time control. Both cars out and a senior Skoda engineer is seriously injured.

FRIDAY   SS 1-8
SATURDAY   SS 9-14
SUNDAY   SS 15-21

● STAGE START
● STAGE FINISH

CORDOBA
HQ/START/FINISH

Special Stage Times

SS1 Complejo PRO-RACING 1 3,44 km
1.McRae 2'27"9; 2.Sainz 2'30"6;
3.Solberg 2'30"6; 4.Delecour 2'31"9;
5.Burns 2'32"2; 6.Blazquez 2'32"9; Gr.N
Ligato 2'37"1

SS2 Complejo PRO-RACING 2 3,44 km
1.McRae 2'25"1; 2.Sainz 2'27"7;
3.Solberg 2'28"9; 4.Burns 2'29"8;
5.A. McRae 2'30"5; 6.Makinen/Blazquez
2'30"7; Gr.N Ligato 2'34"6

SS3 La Falda – Rio Ceballos 29,96 km
1.McRae 22'34"1; 2.Makinen 22'51"3;
3.Burns 22'56"9; 4.Auriol 23'00"3;
5.Sainz 23'04"1; 6.A. McRae 23'05"7;
Gr.N Pozzo 24'16"6

SS4 Ascochinga – La Cumbre 1 28,83 km
1.McRae 18'39"9; 2.Auriol 18'43"5;
3.Sainz 18'43"9; 4.Makinen 18'49"8;
5.Burns 18'50"0; 6.Rovanpera 18'52"2;
Gr.N Pozzo 19'38"6

SS5 Capilla del Monte – San Marcos Sierra 23,02 km
1.McRae 17'09"1; 2.Burns 17'14"7;
3.Gronholm 17'18"0; 4.Rovanpera
17'20"5; 5.Makinen 17'28"9; 6.Auriol
17'29"3; Gr.N Pozzo 18'24"6

SS6 San Marcos Sierra – Charbonier 9,61 km
1.Burns 6'33"6; 2.McRae 6'34"7;
3.Rovanpera 6'36"5; 4.Makinen 6'37"0;

5.Gronholm 6'37"1; 6.Sainz 6'37"3; Gr.N
Pozzo 7'07"9

SS7 La Cumbre – Agua de Oro 23,46 km
1.Sainz 19'45"8; 2.Makinen 19'52"5;
3.Delecour 19'53"3; 4.Burns 19'56"5;
5.Auriol 20'00"7; 6.McRae 20'03"0;
Gr.N Pozzo 21'39"7

SS8 Ascochinga – La Cumbre 2 28,83 km
1.McRae 18'24"2; 2.Burns 18'25"7;
3.Sainz 18'31"5; 4.Makinen 18'34"2;
5.Gronholm 18'34"9; 6.Delecour
18'37"4; Gr.N Pozzo 19'31"6

SS9 Santa Rosa de Calamuchita – San Agustin 1 26,10 km
1.Burns 15'22"6; 2.McRae 15'22"8;
3.Gronholm 15'24"8; 4.Auriol 15'25"1;
5.Sainz 15'25"5; 6.Delecour 15'27"1;
Gr.N Pozzo 16'20"6

SS10 San Agustin – Villa General Belgrano 12,65 km
1.McRae 9'19"2; 2.Burns 9'20"4;
3.Sainz 9'22"6; 4.Delecour 9'23"7;
5.Gronholm 9'26"7; 6.Solberg 9'28"5;
Gr.N Pozzo 10'04"1

SS11 Amboy – Santa Rosa de Calamuchita 1 17,48 km
1.Burns 9'13"6; 2.McRae 9'16"3;
3.Makinen 9'20"3; 4.Gronholm 9'21"2;
5.Delecour 9'22"9; 6.Solberg 9'24"6;
Gr.N Pozzo 10'01"2

SS12 Santa Rosa de Calamuchita – San Agustin 2 26,10 km
1.McRae 15'10"4; 2.Gronholm 15'10"5;
3.Burns 15'14"2; 4.Sainz 15'17"2;
5.Auriol 15'17"8; 6.Solberg 15'20"0;
Gr.N Pozzo 16'16"0

SS13 Las Bajadas – Villa del Dique 16,42 km
1.Burns 8'48"3; 2.McRae 8'48"9;
3.Sainz 8'52"8; 4.Auriol 8'53"2;
5.Delecour 8'53"5; 6.Makinen 8'55"6;
Gr.N Pozzo 9'32"3

SS14 Amboy – Santa Rosa de Calamuchita 2 17,48 km
1.Burns 9'09"2; 2.McRae 9'14"6;
3.Makinen 9'16"8; 4.Sainz 9'17"6;
5.Delecour 9'17"7; 6.Loix 9'19"4;
Gr.N Pozzo 10'03"7

SS15 Camping General San Martin 4,20 km
1.Makinen 3'04"1; 2.Solberg 3'04"3;
3.A. McRae 3'04"8; 4.Burns 3'05"7;
5.McRae 3'06"1; 6.Loix 3'06"6;
Gr.N Ligato 3'15"1

SS16 Cura Brochero – Cienaga de Allende 13,63 km
1.Makinen 6'43"1; 2.Burns 6'45"8;
3.Sainz 6'47"6; 4.Solberg 6'48"0;
5.Auriol 6'48"2; 6.Eriksson 6'51"0;
Gr.N Ligato 7'14"8

SS17 El Mirador – San Lorenzo 1 20,65 km
1.Gronholm 11'29"5; 2.McRae 11'35"3;
3.Burns 11'35"5; 4.Sainz 11'36"4;
5.Auriol 11'36"8; 6.A. McRae 11'38"7;
Gr.N Ligato 12'16"4

SS18 Chamico – Ambul 24,60 km
1.Burns 17'50"4; 2.Makinen 17'55"2;
3.McRae 17'56"8; 4.Sainz 18'00"1;
5.Auriol 18'06"6; 6.Loix 18'11"0;
Gr.N Ligato 19'13"2

SS19 El Mirador – San Lorenzo 2 20,65 km
1.McRae 11'25"3; 2.Auriol 11'27"1;
3.McRae 11'28"9; 4.Solberg 11'31"7;
5.Makinen 11'32"1; 6.Delecour
11'32"3; Gr.N Ligato 12'15"5

SS20 Mina Clavero – Giulio Cesare 22,26 km
1.McRae 18'06"4; 2.Burns 18'08"9;
3.Sainz 18'17"3; 4.Makinen 18'17"4;
5.Delecour 18'25"2; 6.Loix 18'28"4;
Gr.N Ligato 19'21"7

SS21 El Condor – Copina 16,77 km
1.McRae 13'50"3; 2.Makinen 13'50"4;
3.Burns/Delecour 13'52"8; 5.Sainz
13'53"5; 6.Solberg 13'59"1; Gr.N Trelles
14'35"6

Results WRC

	Driver/Navigator	Car	Gr.	Time
1	C. McRae – Grist	Ford Focus RS WRC 01	A	4h18'25"3
2	Burns – Reid	Subaru Impreza WRC 2001		+ 26"9
3	Sainz – Moya	Ford Focus RS WRC 01		+ 1'46"4
4	Makinen – Mannisenmaki	Mitsubishi Lancer Ev.6		+ 3'12"6
5	Solberg – Mills	Subaru Impreza WRC 2001		+ 3'47"0
6	Loix – Smeets	Mitsubishi Carisma GT		+5'40"1
7	Delecour – Grataloup	Ford Focus RS WRC 01		+ 6'10"9
8	Arai – McNeall	Subaru Impreza WRC 2001		+ 10'55"7
9	A. McRae – Senior	Hyundai Accent WRC 2		+ 13'58"9
10	Pozzo – Stillo	Mitsubishi Lancer Ev.6	N	+ 20'15"1

Leading Retirements

SS.21	Ligato – Garcia	Mitsubishi Lancer Ev.6	Gearbox
SS.20	Eriksson – Parmander	Hyundai Accent WRC 2	Lost a wheel
SS.20	Auriol – Giraudet	Peugeot 206 WRC	Wheel torn off
SS.18	Gronholm – Rautianen	Peugeot 206 WRC	Clutch
SS.11	Thiry – Prévot	Skoda Octavia WRC	Accident
SS.11	Schwarz – Hiemer	Skoda Octavia WRC	Accident
SS.7	Rovanpera – Pietilainen	Peugeot 206 WRC	Suspension
SS.6	Blazquez – Mercader	Seat Cordoba WRC	Engine

Championship Classifications

Drivers
1. Makinen 27; 2. Sainz 22; 3. Rovanpera, Auriol, C. McRae 10;
6. Delecour, Burns 9; 8. Radstrom, Panizzi 6; 10. Gardenmeister, Loix 5;
12. Gronholm 4; 13. Schwarz, Solberg 3; 14. A. McRae 1

Constructors
1. Mitsubishi 44; 2. Ford 36; 3. Peugeot 20; 4. Subaru 16;
5. Hyundai 8; Skoda 6

Group N
1. Pozzo 23; 2. Gillet, Walfridsson, Dias da Silva, Trelles 10...

Team's Cup
1. Toyota Castrol Team Denmark (Lundgaard), Team Toyota Castrol
Finland (Hagström) 10; 3. David Sutton Cars Ltd (Blomqvist), Oman
Arab World Rally Team (Al Wahaibi) 6...

FIA Super 1600
1. Loeb 10; 2. Basso 6; 3. Fontana 4; 4. Stenshorne 3; 5. Dallavilla 2...

Performers

	1	2	3	4	5	6
C. McRae	10	7	2		1	1
Burns	7	5	4	3	2	–
Makinen	2	4	2	4	2	2
Sainz	1	2	6	4	3	1
Gronholm	1	1	2	1	3	–
Auriol	–	2	–	3	5	1
Solberg	–	1	2	2	–	4
Delecour	–	–	2	2	4	3
Rovanpera	–	–	1	1	–	1
A. McRae	–	–	1	–	1	2
Loix	–	–	–	–	–	4
Blazquez	–	–	–	–	–	2
Eriksson	–	–	–	–	–	1

Event Leaders

SS.1 > SS.21   C. McRae

Previous winners

1980	Rohrl – Geistdorfer Fiat 131 Abarth		1993	Kankkunen – Grist Toyota Celica Turbo 4WD
1981	Fréquelin – Todt Talbot Sunbeam Lotus		1994	Auriol – Occelli Toyota Celica Turbo 4WD
1983	Mikkola – Hertz Audi Quattro		1995	Recalde – Christie Lancia Delta HF Integrale
1984	Blomqvist – Cederberg Audi Quattro		1996	Makinen – Harjanne Mitsubishi Lancer Ev.3
1985	Salonen – Harjanne Peugeot 205 T16		1997	Makinen – Harjanne Mitsubishi Lancer Ev.4
1986	Biasion – Siviero Lancia Delta S4		1998	Makinen – Mannisenmaki Mitsubishi Lancer Ev.5
1987	Biasion – Siviero Lancia Delta HF Turbo		1999	Kankkunen – Repo Subaru Impreza WRC
1988	Recalde – Del Buono Lancia Delta Integrale		2000	Burns – Reid Subaru Impreza WRC 2000
1989	Ericsson – Billstam Lancia Delta Integrale			
1990	Biasion – Siviero Lancia Delta Integrale 16v			
1991	Sainz – Moya Toyota Celica GT4			
1992	Auriol – Occelli Lancia Delta HF Integrale			

MICHELIN

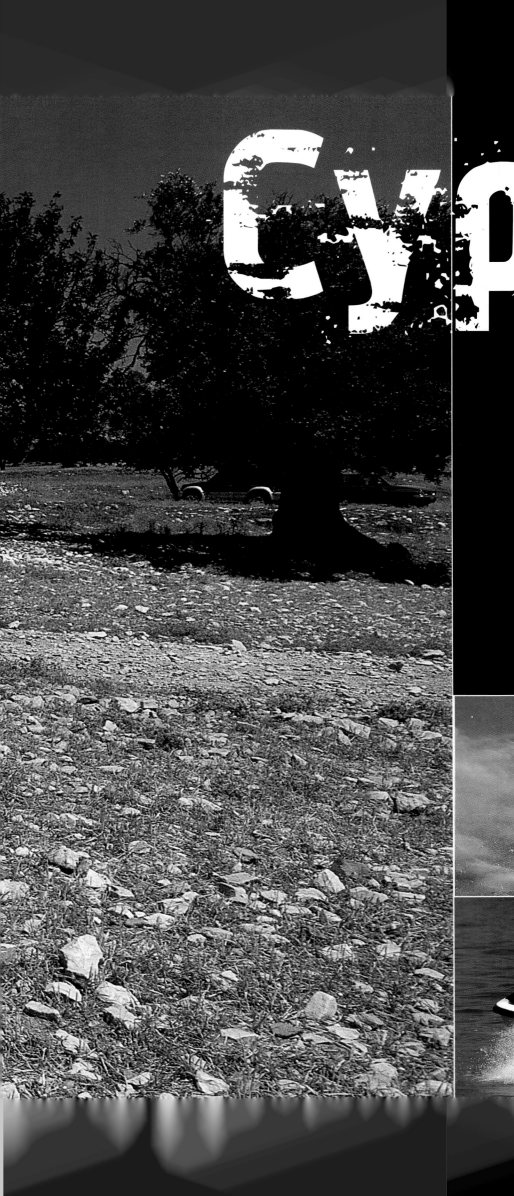

Cyprus

Rally savvy and a bit of brio brought Colin McRae victory in what is reckoned to be the toughest event on the calendar. It came at just the right time to revive his and the team's hopes in the title chase.

Both Skodas (here we see Thiry) made it to the finish of this testing event.

THE RALLY
McRAE, A MAN OF
FEW WORDS

What is amazing about Colin McRae is that it is impossible to misunderstand his declarations. "I am going to win here, to get back in contention for the championship," he had announced before the start, fully aware that wanting was not enough on a rally as probing as this one, both for man and machine. Since Ancient times, Cyprus has been blessed with roads to challenge the best. Just like McRae, Hippomene

was also a winner and he won the love of Atlanta. Unfortunately, the two lovers forgot to offer a sacrifice to the Goddess of Beauty, Aphrodite, who was the mistress of the island. She was not best pleased and turned them both into lions. As he had not joined the Peugeot ranks, despite coming pretty close over the winter, Highlander managed to escape the punishment: he drives a Ford, not a lion and in Cyprus this year, that was definitely the better option. This simple fact, coupled of course with his talent, meant he was able to wring the neck of the rally in the final leg, dealing with the opposition

one at a time. In Cyprus, McRae was quite simply the strongest and maybe the maddest. Because a deal of courage was certainly needed, allied to a whim of lunacy, in order to spend days at a time in an overheated cockpit. It was more than 35 degrees in the shade and around 60 inside the car, where the drivers were having to work harder than usual. Was heatstroke the cause of the first day's two most spectacular retirements? Maybe. On the road to Koilineia, a little village tucked away with its church of Agios Nikolaos disappearing in a heat haze, Harri Rovanpera was the first to get it wrong. He failed to

Fighting for the Team's Cup, the Saudi Bakashab was again driving his private Toyota.

In terms of potential, the 206 was keeping its promises, but Gronholm retired with a fuel feed problem.

spot a rock and the result was a broken suspension on his Peugeot, which put paid to his efforts. A few hours later, Tommi Makinen went one better, throwing his Mitsubishi down a ravine. Both he and his co-driver escaped unharmed. Risto Mannisenmaki still managed to radio through to the team, but it was not good news. "You're going to need some very special equipment to get it out from where it's landed!"
In terms of competition, the first leg was significant for a Solberg hurricane, as he set two remarkable fastest times, before being slowed by a failing power steering. He then

stopped for good, when a jolly engine fire added to the heat. It was Gronholm who then thundered onto centre stage, dazzling on his way to fastest times in the two final stages, to win the leg, ahead of an ever present Burns and Delecour, who was a revelation, making the most of his start number, coming through the stages well behind the leaders. Once again, it was the usual discussion about the relative merits of sweeping the stages for the pursuing pack. "I won the leg, but the rest is going to be very difficult," was Gronholm's analysis. "I think Delecour and McRae will be best placed for what comes next as they start 3rd and 4th."
The four front runners were all within 15 seconds of one another, as they set off on the second leg. Delecour was the first to crack, or rather his engine did. "It stopped suddenly on a link section," recounted the Ford driver. "A little bit of smoke coming out of the bonnet was the only sign something was

Gronholm and indeed all the crews were feeling the heat, with cockpit temperatures being particularly unbearable.

wrong. It fired up again, but only on three cylinders and it was impossible to continue." It was a terrible disappointment. "Of course, I wasn't guaranteed to win, but I was fighting and everything was going really well."
This meant that the team leaders now had to take over the fight. McRae and Sainz finished the leg in second and fourth places, with top honours going to Richard Burns and Marcus Gronholm taking the third slot.
With the same equipment, the Scotsman and the Spaniard had endured different fortunes. Colin McRae was on a charge and took the lead for a while, before cleverly slowing the pace, well aware that the Cyprus roads did not do any favours to those who had the honour of being first through the stages. Gronholm learnt this by bitter experience on this beautiful Saturday in June.
This tactical game was best played by Ford and Peugeot, so that the role of road sweeper fell to Burns. With a 3 second lead over McRae, 18.6 over

McRae was charging to his second consecutive win and was able to rely on the strength of his Ford.

A flamboyant Delecour was sadly let down by his engine. He could have won.

With Makinen having crashed out, Loix brought home three points for Mitsubishi.

Gronholm and 24.6 on Sainz, the final leg was going to be very close and intense.

Marcus Gronholm tackled this final day, hungry for victory, as could be seen from the fastest time the Finn posted on the opening stage. But it did not help make up much time on the man who was only just in the lead, Burns. The world champion, who had not won since Australia in 2000, was really hoping to make it stick this time, but the fuel feed on his 206 was to let him down.
This left the door open to a very confident McRae. He had put down a marker in the form of a fastest time on the Saturday afternoon and that showed him that an attacking pace would be enough to take the win. The next day, he evidently set about adopting this strategy, going quickest on four of the five stages, some of the performances being totally stupefying. "I thought Marcus and Carlos would be quicker, given they had a better start position than mine," was his analysis half way

through the day. With that, he set off again, really attacking the stages, robbing Burns of any slight hopes he might have been harbouring. The others were out of the running. McRae, Burns, Sainz; the Cyprus podium smacked of "déjà vu", as this had been the final order in the previous round in Argentina! After the Makinen period, tempered by the Peugeot wins - Rovanpera in Sweden and Auriol in Catalunya - a new cycle looked as though it was establishing itself this season. Was it the McRae push? "I've won what I reckon is the hardest rally of the season," was his straightforward comment, although he was obviously delighted. "You cannot imagine how happy that makes me!" ∎

THE NOVELTY "206 EVO. III"

For Peugeot, a 206 WRC is always a 206 WRC. There are no curlicues added when a new version appears. There is no such

thing as an Evo X, or some other Pythagorian nomenclature which results in a name longer than a day without rallying. Nevertheless, in Cyprus, a new version of the French pocket rocket appeared. Evolution 1 made its debut in Corsica in 1999 and the 2 followed in Catalunya the next year. Now we had the third version. This meant that, apart from Skoda, Peugeot was the only one of the six full-time listed constructors not to have already brought out its 2001 car. "There's nothing revolutionary about it," said its "father" Michel Nandan, by way of introduction. It had just been given a few new touches, more technical than aesthetic, which it was hoped, would give it a bit more go.
"I don't know if we had got the new car earlier, if we would have had a better start to the season," continued the technical director. "What I do know is that, in January, we had only just started work on the programme and that by April, we were not ready."

Hence this new homologation in early June. The engineer tasked with taking control of the project, Julien Loisy, had started work in October 2000, just a few months after the engine people at Pipo Moteurs.
Point by point, here are the new areas, as outlined by Nandan.
- Cooling. The water radiator and the air/air exchanger are new. Globally, the modifications to the front of the car optimise the diffusion inside and the new vents on the bonnet improve extraction. All of this was tested in the wind tunnel.
- Engine. It has had a general makeover in order to improve its driveability, as it is not possible to extract more power. Therefore the idea is to have an engine that works well at both low and high revs, which should make it easier to tackle tight corners. The inlet, exhaust, turbo, fresh-air and wastegate are the main new components. The new engine has also necessitated new mapping.
- Running gear. We have worked on

Although 8th, Thiry picked up a point for Skoda as Arai and Hagstrom, who finished ahead of him were not eligible for constructors' points.

The new evolution of the 206 had a lot of problems on its first outing. Auriol retired with a blown engine after a radiator failed and Gronholm also went out.

strengthening the suspension to improve reliability with quite a few new pieces, like the wishbones and pull rods.
-Weight. We have slightly optimised the body to lose weight in certain areas and some parts, in order to be able to use ballast in others. Overall, the car is still at the minimum weight (1,230 kilos), with a bit more bias towards the rear.
- Gearbox. Apart from the annual homologation, we are allowed to homologate one additional gearbox per year. Since the end of 2000, we have a five-speed box (Harri Rovanpera already used it in Sweden). Its layout is different and, in some cases, it will better suit the new engine characteristics."
At the end of February, this third evolution ran for the first time, covering about 2,500 kilometres of testing prior to the Cyprus rally.
The French team was really taking a gamble, as the first three events for the 206 WRC 2001, Cyprus, Acropolis and Safari, are the most car-breaking as well as being the ones run in the hottest conditions.
As far as the rally itself was concerned, Rovanpera retired through youthful exuberance, while Auriol went out because of the youth of his car. Slowed on the first day by a faulty rear differential, he was forced

to retire the next day when a broken radiator caused the engine to die. This new part had evidently lacked testing miles. "I can take some consolation from the fact we did good times, including one fastest," said the driver. "I am reassured. The new 206 is alright." Gronholm's performance, almost always fighting for the lead, was further proof, even though he too had to retire with reliability problems. So, despite the fact that all three works cars failed to see the finish, there was a light at the end of the tunnel for the Lion team.
Out of eight 206 WRCs at the start, not one made it to the end. Apart from the three factory cars, Gilles Panizzi retired with four punctures on Friday and the Englishman, Wearden went out on Saturday with a broken sump. Simon Jean-Joseph suffered exactly the same fate. Driving for the Belgian Kronos team, Kris Princen put his Peugeot off the road right at the start of the event. Finally, Greece's Papadimitriou rolled, before his car caught fire. Cyprus might well be a land of legend, but Peugeot would not be adding to it this year. ∎

A steady drive brought Arai home fourth.

29th CYPRUS RALLY

6th leg of the 2001 World Rally championship for constructors and drivers. 6th leg of the Group N World Championship. 3th leg of the Team's cup.

Date 1st to 3rd June 2001

Route
1252,53 km divided into 3 legs
22 special stages on dirt road
(341,40 km)

1st leg
Friday 1st June: Limassol - Paphos - Limassol, 6 stages (137,98 km)
2nd leg
Saturday 2nd June: Limassol - Limassol, 8 stages (105,96 km)
3rd leg
Sunday 3rd June: Limassol - Limassol, 8 stages (97,46 km)

Starters - Finishers: 76 - 30

Conditions: good weather and hot, dusty gravel dirt road.

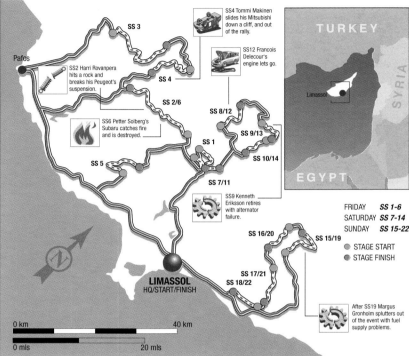

SS4 Tommi Makinen slides his Mitsubishi down a cliff, and out of the rally.

SS12 Francois Delecour's engine lets go.

SS2 Harri Rovanpera hits a rock and breaks his Peugeot's suspension.

SS6 Petter Solberg's Subaru catches fire and is destroyed.

SS9 Kenneth Eriksson retires with alternator failure.

After SS19 Margus Gronholm splutters out of the event with fuel supply problems.

TURKEY
SYRIA
EGYPT
Limassol

Pafos
LIMASSOL
HQ/START/FINISH

FRIDAY *SS 1-6*
SATURDAY *SS 7-14*
SUNDAY *SS 15-22*

● STAGE START
● STAGE FINISH

0 km — 40 km
0 mls — 20 mls

TOP ENTRIES

1. Marcus Gronholm - Timo Rautiainen
   Peugeot 206 WRC
2. Didier Auriol - Denis Giraudet
   Peugeot 206 WRC
3. Carlos Sainz - Luis Moya
   Ford Focus RS WRC
4. Colin McRae - Nicky Grist
   Ford Focus RS WRC
5. Richard Burns - Robert Reid
   Subaru Impreza WRC
6. Petter Solberg - Philip Mills
   Subaru Impreza WRC
7. Tommi Makinen - Risto Mannisenmaki
   Mitsubishi Lancer Evo 6
8. Freddy Loix - Sven Smeets
   Mitsubishi Carisma GT
9. Kenneth Eriksson - Staffan Parmander
   Hyundai Accent WRC
10. Alister McRae - David Senior
    Hyundai Accent WRC
11. Armin Schwarz - Manfred Hiemer
    Skoda Octavia WRC
12. Bruno Thiry - Stephane Prevot
    Skoda Octavia WRC
16. Harri Rovanpera - Risto Pietilainen
    Peugeot 206 WRC
17. Francois Delecour - Daniel Grataloup
    Ford Focus RS WRC
18. Toshihiro Arai - Glenn Mac Neall
    Subaru Impreza WRC
19. Katsuhiko Taguchi - Derek Ringer
    Mitsubishi Lancer Evo 6
20. Piero Liatti - Carlo Cassina
    Hyundai Accent WRC
21. Gilles Panizzi - Herve Panizzi
    Peugeot 206 WRC
22. Frederic Dor - Didier Breton
    Subaru Impreza WRC
24. Simon Jean-Joseph - Jack Boyere
    Peugeot 206 WRC
25. Henrik Lundgaard - J.-C. Anker
    Toyota Corolla WRC
26. Pasi Hagstrom - Tero Gardemeister
    Toyota Corolla WRC
27. Hamed Al-Wahaibi - Tony Sircombe
    Subaru Impreza WRC
28. Abdullah Bakhashab - Bobby Willis
    Toyota Corolla WRC
29. Gustavo Trelles - Jorge Del Buono
    Mitsubishi Lancer Evo 6
30. Manfred Stohl - Peter Muller
    Mitsubishi Lancer Evo 6
31. Stig Blomqvist - Ana Goni
    Mitsubishi Lancer Evo 6
33. Gabriel Pozzo - Daniel Luis Stillo
    Mitsubishi Lancer Evo 6
35. Marcos Ligato - Ruben Garcia
    Mitsubishi Lancer Evo 6
39. Kris Princen - Dany Colebunders
    Peugeot 206 WRC

Special Stage Times

SS1 Platres - Saittas 11,48 km
1.Solberg 9'31"4; 2.Eriksson 9'36"7; 3.Burns 9'37"1; 4.Gronholm/Panizzi 9'39"0; 6.Arai 9'39"4; Gr.N Ligato 10'13"8

SS2 Foini - Koilinia 1 30,29 km
1.Gronholm 27'51"0; 2.Eriksson 28'02"0; 3.McRae 28'06"2; 4.Burns 28'08"5; 5.Delecour 28'11"0; 6.Panizzi 28'25"4; Gr.N Stohl 29'59"3

SS3 Simou - Stravos 35,57 km
1.Gronholm 31'13"0; 2.Burns 31'15"1; 3.Eriksson 31'19"0; 4.McRae 31'19"5; 5.Jean-Joseph 31'21"4; 6.Loix 31'23"0; Gr.N Ligato 32'50"8

SS4 Selladi - Panagia 19,29 km
1.Solberg 16'37"6; 2.Delecour 16'58"6; 3.Sainz 16'59"8; 4.Burns 17'00"0; 5.McRae 17'00"8; 6.Gronholm 17'09"5; Gr.N Trelles 18'04"4

SS5 Prastio - Pachna 11,06 km
1.Delecour 6'40"2; 2.Burns 6'41"8; 3.McRae 6'44"8; 4.Loix 6'46"8; 5.Auriol 6'48"2; 6.Sainz 6'49"0; Gr.N Pozzo 7'16"4

SS6 Foini - Koilinia 2 30,29 km
1.Delecour 27'36"8; 2.Gronholm 27'41"1; 3.McRae 27'44"4; 4.Burns

27'46"4; 5.Loix 28'00"2; 6.Sainz 28'12"2; Gr.N Stohl 29'42"7

SS7 Platres - K.Amiantos 1 11,99 km
1.Sainz 9'45"0; 2.McRae 9'51"6; 3.Burns 9'52"3; 4.Arai 9'53"6; 5.Auriol 9'53"8; 6.Delecour 9'55"4; Gr.N Stohl 10'25"5

SS8 Stravroulia - Orkontas 15,73 km
1.Sainz 16'53"3; 2.Auriol 16'56"0; 3.Burns 16'59"8; 4.McRae 16'59"9; 5.Gronholm 17'01"8; 6.A.McRae 17'05"3; Gr.N Stohl 17'40"2

SS9 Agios Theodoros - Assinou 9,61 km
1.Auriol 9'29"8; 2.Sainz 9'30"4; 3.Delecour 9'34"0; 4.Burns 9'35"2; 5.McRae 9'36"0; 6.Gronholm 9'38"2; Gr.N Pozzo 10'06"7

SS10 Assinou - Spilia 1 15,65 km
1.Sainz 14'51"9; 2.McRae 14'58"5; 3.Delecour 15'04"0; 4.Arai 15'05"1; 5.Burns 15'05"6; 6.Gronholm 15'07"3; Gr.N Stohl 15'37"7

SS11 Platres - K.Amiantos 11,89 km
1.Sainz 9'47"6; 2.Burns 9'52"7; 3.Delecour/Arai 9'53"4; 5.Loix 9'53"9; 6.McRae 9'54"3; Gr.N Stohl 10'31"2

SS12 Stravroulia - Orkontas 15,73 km
1.McRae 16'44"3; 2.Sainz 16'46"0; 3.Burns 16'51"8; 4.Gronholm 16'52"3;

5.Arai 16'58"5; 6.A. McRae 17'01"8; Gr.N Stohl 17'28"1

SS13 Agios Theodoros - Assinou 9,61 km
1.Sainz 9'30"7; 2.Burns 9'32"5; 3.Gronholm 9'34"4; 4.McRae 9'35"1; 5.Loix 9'40"7; 6.A. McRae 9'42"2; Gr.N Stohl 9'51"2

SS14 Assinou - Spilia 2 15,65 km
1.Sainz 14'48"2; 2.Arai 14'52"5; 3.Gronholm 14'52"6; 4.Loix 14'57"3; 5.Burns 15'05"6; 6.McRae 15'02"7; Gr.N Stohl 15'38"8

SS15 Vavatsinia - Mandra Kambiou 19,02 km
1.Gronholm 17'17"0; 2.Sainz 17'18"1; 3.McRae 17'20"1; 4.Burns 17'21"1; 5.A.McRae 17'25"9; 6.Loix 17'34"3; Gr.N Trelles 18'22"2

SS16 Macheras - Agioi Vavatsinias 1 13,09 km
1.McRae 11'41"2; 2.Sainz 11'45"2; 3.Gronholm 11'45"3; 4.Loix 11'47"1; 5.Burns 11'49"0; 6.Arai 11'54"7; Gr.N Pozzo 12'47"0

SS17 Lageia - Kalavasos 1 9,53 km
1.McRae 8'37"3; 2.Sainz 8'37"5; 3.Loix 8'43"1; 4.Gronholm 8'43"5; 5.Burns 8'46"4; 6.Arai 8'50"2; Gr.N Stohl 9'04"8

SS18 Mari - Monagrouli 1 7,07 km
1.Burns 4'36"1; 2.Sainz 4'38"2; 3.Gronholm 4'38"7; 4.McRae 4'40"4; 5.Loix 4'43"6; 6.Schwarz 4'48"8; Gr.N Stohl 5'24"6

SS19 Vavatsinia - Mandra Kambiou 2 19,02 km
1.McRae 16'59"8; 2.Sainz 17'05"7; 3.Burns 17'07"2; 4.Loix 17'15"3; 5.Arai 17'16"8; 6.Hagstrom 17'24"5; Gr.N Stohl 18'15"7

SS20 Macheras - Agioi Vavatsinias 2 13,09 km
1.Sainz 11'36"0; 2.McRae 11'36"8; 3.Burns 11'37"6; 4.Loix 11'46"9; 5.Hagstrom 12'01"4; 6.A. McRae 12'04"7; Gr.N Stohl 12'56"1

SS21 Lageia - Kalavasos 2 9,53 km
1.McRae 8'37"5; 2.Sainz 8'37"7; 3.Burns 8'38"9; 4.Loix 8'41"4; 5.Arai 8'48"1; 6.A. McRae 8'48"6; Gr.N Stohl 8'52"8

SS22 Mari - Monagrouli 2 7,07 km
1.Burns 4'35"5; 2.Sainz 4'38"2; 3.McRae 4'39"3; 4.A. McRae 4'45"6; 5.Loix 4'46"0; 6.Arai 4'48"0; Gr.N Pozzo 5'18"3

Results WRC

	Driver/Navigator	Car	Gr.	Time
1	McRae - Grist	Ford Focus RS WRC 01	A	5h07'32"7
2	Burns - Reid	Subaru Impreza WRC 2001		+ 16"4
3	Sainz - Moya	Ford Focus RS WRC 01		+ 26"5
4	Arai - McNeall	Subaru Impreza WRC 2001		+ 5'38"3
5	Loix - Smeets	Mitsubishi Carisma GT		+ 6'10"2
6	Hagstrom - Gardemeister	Toyota Corolla WRC Teams' Cup		+ 9'32"5
7	A. McRae - Senior	Hyundai Accent WRC 2		+ 10'35"6
8	Thiry - Prevot	Skoda Octavia WRC		+ 11'38"0
9	Schwarz - Hiemer	Skoda Octavia WRC		+ 12'48"1
10	Bakashab - Willis	Toyota Corolla WRC		+ 22'12"1
11	Trelles - Del Buono	Mitsubishi Lancer Evo 6	N	+ 27'11"3

Leading Retirements

SS.18	Gronholm - Rautianen	Peugeot 206 WRC	Fuel feed
SS.11	Delecour - Grataloup	Ford Focus RS WRC 01	Engine
SS.10	Auriol - Giraudet	Peugeot 206 WRC	Water radiator leak
SS.9	Eriksson - Parmander	Hyundai Accent WRC 2	Alternator
SS.6	Solberg - Mills	Subaru Impreza WRC 2001	Fire
SS.4	Lundgaard - Anker	Toyota Corolla WRC	Puncture, accident
SS.4	Panizzi - Panizzi	Peugeot 206 WRC	Puncture, accident
SS.4	Makinen - Mannisenmaki	Mitsubishi Lancer Evo 6	Accident
SS.2	Rovanpera - Pietilainen	Peugeot 206 WRC	Suspension

Performers

	1	2	3	4	5	6
Sainz	7	9	1	-	-	2
C. McRae	5	3	5	4	2	2
Gronholm	3	1	4	3	1	3
Burns	2	4	7	5	4	-
Delecour	2	1	3	-	1	1
Solberg	2	-	-	-	-	-
Auriol	1	1	-	-	2	-
Eriksson	-	2	1	-	-	-
Arai	-	1	1	3	3	4
Loix	-	-	1	5	5	2
A. McRae	-	-	-	1	1	5
Panizzi	-	-	1	-	1	-
Hagstrom	-	-	-	-	1	1
Jean-Joseph	-	-	1	-	-	-
Schwarz	-	-	-	-	-	1

Event Leaders

SS.1	Solberg
SS.2 > SS.6	Gronholm
SS.7 > SS.11	Burns
SS.12 > SS.13	C. McRae
SS.14 > SS.15	Burns
SS.16 > SS.22	C. McRae

Championship Classifications

Drivers
1. Makinen 27; 2. Sainz 26; 3. C. McRae 20; 4. Burns 15;
5. Rovanpera 10, Auriol 10; 7. Delecour 9; 8. Loix 7; 9. Radstrom 6;
10. Panizzi 6; 11. Gardemeister 5; 12. Gronholm 4; 13. Schwarz 3, Solberg 3, Arai 3; 16. A. McRae 1, Hagstrom 1

Constructors
1. Ford 50; 2. Mitsubishi 47; 3. Subaru 22; 4. Peugeot 20;
5. Hyundai 10; 6. Skoda 7

Group N
1. Pozzo 27; 2. Trelles 20; 3. Stohl 12; 4. Gillet, Walfridsson, Dias da Silva 10...

Team's Cup
1. Team Toyota Castrol Finland (Hagstrom) 20; 2. Toyota Castrol Team Denmark (Lundgaard) 10; 3. Toyota Team Saudi Arabia (Bakashab) 9...

FIA Super 1600
1. Loeb 10; 2. Basso 6; 3. Fontana 4; 4. Stenshorme 3; 5. Dallavilla 2...

Greece

Acropolis

Impeccable from start
to finish, McRae went
and took another win,
built not just on
straightforward talent,
but also thanks to the
misfortune of others.

7

Sainz retired on the last stage, when lying second. His engine had failed at the end of a remarkable drive.

THE RALLY
McRAE'S PANTHEON

A lanky silhouette walked mournfully through the Parnassos service area, throwing up a slim shadow and small puffs of dust behind it, kicked up by his feet. His cap on back to front, with a blank look and no sign of a smile, Marcus Gronholm strolls away from the rally. His Greek journey had lasted less than three stages, not even half a day, not even fifty kilometres. It's not a lot when you carry the Number 1 on your doors. "There was a big stone in the middle of the track," explains the world champion, in a dull monotone. "I tried to pass over it, but it went through the sump and caused an oil leak. It's just bad luck and not the team's fault. The car was perfect and I was attacking." And how, given that Gronholm was lying second at the time.

He only just finishes his explanation, when the sound of another 206 can be heard behind him. It is Didier Auriol at the wheel of his car. He is still running, but the car had needed repairs, because earlier it had refused to cover more than 3,000 metres. "After one kilometre in the first stage, I felt the clutch wasn't working properly," related the fatalist Frenchman. "Two more klix and it was over, with black smoke coming out from the bonnet. What else can I say?" That he is downhearted and sick? That much is obvious, just as it is with Gronholm, who felt the first symptoms on the road section from Itea to the service area, located before the stages. After the control, the Peugeot mechanics had let the 206 leave, without having found any problem. Usually, they would have changed the offending item, which is no more than a five minute job. But this time, they did not bother; a question of saving new clutches, as they did not have that many spares. It was a big mistake and the wolf had run riot in the mechanical sheep run.

After just three stages of this seventh round of the world championship, the French team's score was a perfect zero, the third in three events. Yes, its last remaining official WRC car was still running, with Rovanpera lying eighth, after the management had told him to be very careful. But this Finn was not the one eligible to score Constructors' points, as this role fell to Auriol and Gronholm.

Peugeot took little consolation from the fact that its sworn enemies in the Citroen camp where having a more than impressive debut on the loose. For their first championship event on this surface, the Xsaras look perfectly at ease, thanks mainly to remarkably good road handling. Bugalski, considered a tarmac man, was putting in some encouraging times, as was Radstrom his team-mate, a workman-like performer, but no McRae, Gronholm or Makinen. To look at, it seemed that this WRC car was capable of doing the business. Before retiring with electrical problems, the Swede had actually been confident enough to predict that, "we can think in terms of getting on the podium."

That was all well and good, except for the fact that, on the first leg, neither his determination, nor that of

Thanks to a flood of retirements in the closing stages, Solberg found himself promoted to second for the first time in his career.

For all the teams, be they Michelin or Pirelli runners, tyres are of primordial importance.

Sainz, McRae, Makinen et al, was not enough to stop the Subarus. Burns was the first to lead, before handing over to the two young mad dogs, Solberg and Martin.

They made the most of the fact that they did not come on stage until, respectively, 11 and 17 cars had gone on before them. In this, their exploits were imitated by Panizzi, 6th and Bugalski. On the other hand, Makinen was first to perform and admitted he couldn't stop haemorrhaging seconds because of the rigours of sweeping the tracks. Right at the end of the first leg, strategy took over from speed. All three Subarus did terrible times on the last timed section, although

Solberg was genuinely slowed with gearbox worries, thus leaving the lead to the Ford duo of McRae and Sainz.

The Mediterranean event continued to cull the field on the second leg, with Markko Martin's remarkable performance coming to an end. A broken suspension, following a puncture, prevented him from finishing the first timed section on Saturday. Gilles Panizzi had been a strong 5th at the end of the previous day with his private 206 WRC, but it all came to nothing with continual damper problems and then a faulty fuel feed. In the Mitsubishi camp, Makinen and Loix were still going,

but they had been delayed so much that they really had no chance of troubling the leaders. This team even had to change both gearboxes; the Finn's being reduced to a three-speed and the Belgian's being stuck in 5th. This, added to a severe lack of grip and a nasty knock for Loix, contributed to a further slide down the order.

More seriously, Francois Delecour had a physical injury. He had broken his right wrist before the event, falling off his bicycle. Nevertheless, the Ford man was enjoying a good run, even setting three fastest stage times. Alas, the power steering on his Focus gave up halfway through the rally, which left him in a lot of

(top)
Bugalski brought the surviving Xsara home to a good sixth place.

(bottom)
The world champion was still missing the mark. This time a big stone punctured the sump on the first leg.

Steady yes, but not really quick: Schwarz finished seventh, just outside the points.

On the Greek roads, signs are often indispensable and here a Subaru crew tells Martin where to go.

pain, as he battled to get the car to service, before continuing. "I really fed up, because if it wasn't for this injury, this rally was mine for the taking," he cursed.

His troubles were all the more regrettable, given that his fellow Ford co-workers, McRae and Sainz were whizzing along at the front. Indeed, together I am really with the Subarus of Burns and Solberg, they were the only ones to be spared any major bothers. Having cunningly lost the lead on the evening of the first leg, the Subaru boys had every intention of making up all or most of the deficit. It was not to be.

"I have to admit I can't do anything about catching McRae," confessed Burns. "He's very strong."

But he still managed a day of damage limitation.

That meant that as dawn rose on the final day, there were really only three men in the running for victory: McRae, Sainz and Burns. Fourth-placed Solberg was already too far back. Firing first, Burns was giving it plenty, really plenty and actually too much. In the second stage, the Englishman made a mistake in a right-hand hairpin, after he was distracted by a sign board hung out by members of his team.

By the time the Impreza was back on track again, with help from the spectators, he had lost three minutes. "I'm disappointed, but it's not a disaster," he explained shortly afterwards. "I can't complain, as it

was entirely my own fault." The chance of a good win had gone, as had the small collection of points he could have expected to take with him, when his transmission let go at the end of the leg.

This left the two Ford men out in front on their own. Preferring not to

Along with its drivers, Panizzi on left and Rovanpera, Peugeot was struggling at the mid-point of the season. The new 206 (here with Rovanpera at the wheel) was promising but lacked reliability. The Lion was now 4th in the championship, 40 points adrift of Ford!

up in the final kilometre of the last stage. Sainz thus recorded his first retirement of the season, leaving yet another win to McRae, his third in a row. Behind him came Solberg, getting on to the podium for the first time in a world championship event and Rovanpera, who was delighted to end a pretty anonymous event with a third place. ∎

THE THIRD MAN
THE ROVANPERA PARADOX

Argentina, Cyprus, Acropolis: three rallies and no points for Peugeot. By the mid-point of the season, the reigning world champions were frittering away their chances. Its driver Harri Rovanpera, very much the third driver in the team, was not eligible to score points for Peugeot in the Constructors' championship, as this role fell to the unfortunate Auriol and Gronholm, who had gone out very early. This meant that the Lion limped home from Greece with the same measly 20 points with which it had arrived. While, over in the Ford camp, its boys would head home to Cockermouth with a handy total of 60. Three times more than their French opponents no less! "The end result is hard to take. There is no need to comment," sighed a dispirited Corrado Provera, the

Peugeot boss. "We can only take consolation from the fact that, once again, our 2001 car has proved it is quick." That was not enough to increase its lamentable points total. It was a strange paradox, when the comparison was made with the Drivers' classification, which often seemed of little interest to the French squad, because Harri Rovanpera was the best placed of their drivers. Sure, he only had fourteen points at the time, which was sixteen less than the leaders, Makinen and McRae. But the previous year, at the same point in the season, a certain Marcus Gronholm was fourteen points down on the then leader, Richard Burns.
Seven rallies later, the Espoo giant was crowned world champion. It was a worrying coincidence. "It's much too early to talk about that," insisted the Finn. "Let's just take the rallies one at a time." This one for certainly going well for him, if not his team-mates. "I was not very happy with the handling on Friday. We changed so many things on the car, that I am not sure which bit actually changed its behaviour. But from Saturday, it was back to normal." He was entitled to a few regrets all the same, as his team had asked him to take it easy, right from the start of the rally. But for that, his score might have been better; even better than Gronholm's a year earlier. How does one say "ifs and buts" in Finnish? ∎

hand out any team orders, team boss Malcolm Wilson, left his two big predators to devour themselves. No doubt he could remember the awful psycho-drama which unfolded here a year ago, when he ordered his men to hold station, to the benefit of the Scotsman. He certainly didn't want

to live through a situation which had caused waves in his team for months after. This meant that, as they prepared to tackle the final stage, McRae led Sainz by just 5.7 seconds! But worse still than in 2000, it was destined that Greece would not be kind to the Spaniard, his engine giving

48ᵗʰ ACROPOLIS RALLY

7ᵗʰ leg of the 2001 World Rally Championship for constructors and drivers. 7ᵗʰ leg of the Group N World Championship. 4ᵗʰ leg of the Team's cup. 2ⁿᵈ leg FIA Super 1600 Championship.

Date 14ᵗʰ - 17ᵗʰ June 2001

Route
1645.38 km divided into 3 legs
20 special stages on dirt roads
(398.91 km)

1ˢᵗ leg
Friday 15 June: Itea-Parnassos-Itea, 6 stages (143,54 km)
2ⁿᵈ leg
Saturday 16 June: Itea-Parnassos-Itea, 7 stages (123,36 km)
3ʳᵈ leg
Sunday 17 June: Itea-Parnassos-Itea, 7 stages (132,01 km)

Starters - Finishers: 110 - 47

Conditions: good weather and very hot, dusty dirt roads.

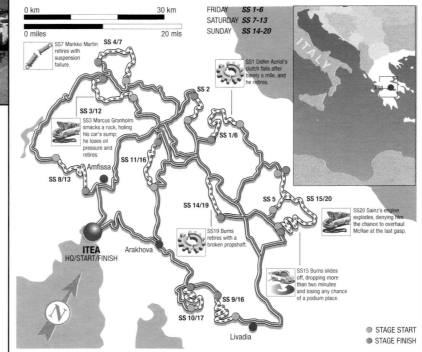

0 km   30 km
0 miles   20 mls

FRIDAY *SS 1-6*
SATURDAY *SS 7-13*
SUNDAY *SS 14-20*

SS7 Markko Martin retires with suspension failure.

SS1 Didier Auriol's clutch fails after barely a mile, and he retires.

SS3 Marcus Gronholm smacks a rock, holing his car's sump; he loses oil pressure and retires.

SS20 Sainz's engine explodes, denying him the chance to overhaul McRae at the last gasp.

SS19 Burns retires with a broken propshaft.

SS15 Burns slides off, dropping more than two minutes and losing any chance of a podium place.

SS 4/7
SS 2
SS 1/6
SS 11/16
SS 8/13
Amfissa
SS 3/12
SS 14/19
SS 5
SS 15/20
ITEA HQ/START/FINISH
Arakhova
SS 9/16
SS 10/17
Livadia

● STAGE START
● STAGE FINISH

ITALY
Itea

Special Stage Times

SS1 Mendenitsa 1 26,92 km
1.Burns 19'14"0; 2.Solberg 19'14"1; 3.Gronholm 19'14"2; 4.McRae 19'16"7 5.Martin 19'20"6; 6.Sainz 19'21"3; Gr.N Blomqvist 21'08"1; S16 Galanti 22'49"2

SS2 Paleohori 10,85 km
1.Solberg 8'07"8; 2.Martin 8'08"2 3 Gronholm 8'08"5; 4.Panizzi 8'09"6 5.Sainz 8'09"8; 6.Burns 8'10"4; Gr.N Pozzo 8'50"5; S1600 Magaud 9'32"8

SS3 Inohori 23,00 km
1.Martin 18'27"1; 2.Panizzi 18'31"3 3.Solberg 18'31"5; 4.Radstrom 18'31"9; 5.McRae 18'36"1; 6.Burns 18'37"4; Gr.N Pozzo 19'43"6; S16 Loeb 20'04"0

SS4 Pavliani 1 24,45 km
1.McRae 20'17"2; 2.Delecour 20'17"3 3.Panizzi 20'17"7; 4.Solberg 20'18"4; 5.Martin 20'21"3; 6.Radstrom 20'24"6 Gr.N Pozzo 21'22"6; S16 Dallavilla 22'22"6

SS5 Etalia 31,40 km
Annulée - trop de spectateurs.

ES6 Mendenitsa 2 26,92 km
1.McRae 19'14"2; 2.Sainz 19'24"0; 3.Rovanpera 19'27"8; 4.Makinen 19'29"4; 5.Loix 19'34"0; 6.Burns

19'44"8; Gr.N Trelles 21'58"0; S16 Duval 23'53"0

SS7 Pavliani 2 24,45 km
1.Delecour 19'46"0; 2.Rovanpera 19'54"7; 3.Solberg 19'55"2; 4.McRae 19'56"7; 5.Burns 19'57"2; 6.Sainz 20'03"1; Gr.N Pozzo 21'22"9; S16 Loeb 22'51"3

SS8 Karoutes 1 18,89 km
1.Delecour 12'12"8; 2.Burns 12'19"5; 3.Makinen/Rovanpera 12'21"5; 5.Sainz 12'23"0; 6.Solberg 12'23"2; Gr.N Hatzitsopanis 13'28"4; S16 Loeb 13'37"6

SS9 Livadia 1 11,66 km
1.Sainz 9'26"2; 2.Delecour 9'27"2; 3.Rovanpera 9'27"8; 4.Burns 9'28"9; 5.Solberg 9'31"2; 6.Solberg 9'33"7; Gr.N Pozzo 10'05"8; S16 Dallavilla 10'35"9

SS10 Stiri 1 3,59 km
1.Delecour 1'57"3; 2.Sainz 1'57"4; 3.Makinen 1'57"5; 4.McRae 1'57"9; 5.Burns 1'58"3; 6.Thiry 1'58"8; Gr.N Pozzo 2'06"5; S16 Dallavilla 2'16"3

SS11 Gravia 1 17,13 km
1.Sainz 13'17"3; 2.Burns 13'20"3; 3.McRae 13'22"4; 4.Rovanpera 13'24"8; 5.Makinen 13'24"9; 6.Bugalski 13'26"4; Gr.N Pozzo

14'08"8; S16 Dallavilla 14'40"2

SS12 Inohori 2 23,00 km
1.Delecour 18'13"2; 2.Sainz 18'13"5; 3. Solberg 18'15"4; 4.Burns 18'16"2; 5.Rovanpera 18'17"5; 6.McRae 18'18"0; Gr.N Pozzo 19'35"2; S16 Dallavilla 20'29"1

SS13 Karoutes 2 18,89 km
1.Burns 12'03"4; 2.Delcour 12'04"5; 3.Solberg 12'08"8; 4.McRae 12'09"5; 5.Sainz 12'10"2; 6.Rovanpera 12'12"8; Gr.N Pozzo 13'17"0; S16 Loeb 13'38"4

SS14 Amfiklia 1 8,25 km
1.Burns 4'49"6; 2.McRae 4'51"6; 3.Sainz 4'52"4; 4.Solberg 4'53"0; 5.Rovanpera 4'4'53"1; 6.Makinen 4'54"4; Gr.N Trelles 5'17"9; S16 Loeb 5'44"2

SS15 Elatia - Rengini 1 38,69 km
1.Solberg 25'37"5; 2.McRae 24'42"4; 3.Delecour 24'44"6; 4.Sainz 25'46"6; 5.Rovanpera 25'55"5; 6.Loix 25'55"7; Gr.N Trelles 27'36"0; S16 Loeb 29'20"

SS16 Livadia 1 11,66km
1.Burns 9'19"2; 2.Sainz 9'19"4; 3.Rovanpera 9'20"2; 4.Delecour 9'20"8; 5.Solberg 9'21"4; 6.McRae 9'23"8; Gr.N Trelles 9'56"9; S16 Robert 10'52"4

SS17 Stiri 2 3,59 km
1.Sainz 1'55"6; 2.Burns 1'55"9; 3.McRae 1'56"0; 4.Solberg 1'57"2; 5.Makinen 1'57"5; 6.Delecour 1'57"8; Gr.N Trelles 2'08"6; S16 Loeb 2'19"2

SS18 Gravia 2 17,13 km
1.Sainz 13'03"2; 2.Delecour 13'05"5; 3.McRae 13'05"7; 4.Rovanpera 13'06"8; 5.Burns 13'07"7; 6.Solberg 13'08"7; Gr.N Pozzo 14'00"9; S16 Loeb 14'52"9

SS19 Amfiklia 2 8,25 km
1.Sainz 4'49"2; 2.Makinen 4'49"5; 3.McRae 4'50"8; 4.Solberg 4'52"7; 5.Delecour 4'54"0; 6.Rovanpera 4'55"5; Gr.N Trelles 5'17"0; S16 Magaud 5'47"7

SS20 Elatia - Rengini 2 38,69 km
1.Makinen 25'32"5; 2.Delecour 25'35"9; 3.Solberg 25'36"9; 4.Loix 25'48"8; 5.McRae 25'49"4; 6.Rovanpera 25'52"1; Gr.N Pozzo 27'33"0; S16 Ceccato 30'05"8

Results — WRC

	Driver/Navigator	Car	Gr.	Time
1	C. McRae - Grist	Ford Focus RS WRC 01	A	4h19'01"9
2	Solberg - Mills	Subaru Impreza WRC 2001		+ 49"0
3	Rovanpera - Pietilainen	Peugeot 206 WRC		+ 1'35"7
4	Makinen - Mannisenmaki	Mitsubishi Lancer Evo 6		+ 2'15"3
5	Delecour - Grataloup	Ford Focus RS WRC 01		+ 2'35"4
6	Bugalski - Chiaroni	Citroen Xsara WRC		+ 4'00"2
7	Schwarz-Hiemer	Skoda Octavia WRC		+ 5'56"7
8	Jean-Joseph - Boyere	Peugeot 206 WRC		+ 7'27"1
9	Loix - Smeets	Mitsubishi Carisma GT		+ 8'00"9
10	Thiry - Prevot	Skoda Octavia WRC		+ 8'35"7
11	Lundgaard - Haker	Toyota Corolla WRC	Team's Cup	+ 15'26"4
13	Pozzo - Stillo	Mitsubishi Lancer Evo 6	N	+ 21'16"0
19	Loeb - Elena	Citroen Saxo	Super 1600	+ 41'50"0

Leading Retirements

SS.20	Sainz - Moya	Ford Focus RS WRC 01	Oil pressure
SS.19	Burns - Reid	Subaru Impreza WRC 2001	Propshaft
SS.7	Martin - Park	Subaru Impreza WRC 2001	Suspension
SS.7	Eriksson - Parmander	Hyundai Accent WRC 2	Turbo
SS.6	Radstrom - Thorner	Citroen Xsara WRC	Electrics
SS.6	Richelmi -Barjou	Peugeot 206 WRC	Wheel torn off
SS.4	Arai - McNeall	Subaru Impreza WRC 2001	Fire
SS.3	Gronholm - Rautiainen	Peugeot 206 WRC	Sump
SS.1	Auriol - Giraudet	Peugeot 206 WRC	Clutch

Performers

	1	2	3	4	5	6
Sainz	5	4	1	1	3	2
Delecour	4	5	1	1	1	1
Burns	4	3	-	2	3	3
C. McRae	2	2	4	4	3	2
Solberg	2	1	5	4	1	3
Makinen	1	1	2	1	2	1
Martin	1	1	-	-	2	-
Rovanpera	-	1	3	-	3	3
Panizzi	-	1	1	1	-	-
Gronholm	-	2	-	-	-	-
Loix	-	-	-	1	1	1
Radstrom	-	-	-	1	-	1
Bulgalski	-	-	-	-	1	1
Thiry	-	-	-	-	-	1
Eriksson	-	-	-	-	-	1

Event Leaders

SS.1	Burns
SS.2 > SS.4	Solberg
SS.5	*cancelled*
SS.6 > SS.20	C. McRae

Previous winners

1973	Thérier - Delferrier Alpine Renault A110		1988	Biasion - Siviero Lancia Delta Integrale
1975	Rohrl - Berger Opel Ascona		1989	Biasion - Siviero Lancia Delta Integrale
1976	Kallstrom - Andersson Datsun 160J		1990	Sainz - Moya Toyota Celica GT4
1977	Waldegaard - Thorszelius Ford Escort RS		1991	Kankkunen - Piironen Lancia Delta Integrale 16v
1978	Rohrl - Geistdorfer Fiat 131 Abarth		1992	Auriol - Occelli Lancia Delta Integrale
1979	Waldegaard - Thorszelius Ford escort RS		1993	Biasion - Siviero Ford Escort RS Cosworth
1980	Vatanen - Richards Ford Escort RS		1994	Sainz - Moya Subaru Impreza
1981	Vatanen - Richards Ford Escort RS		1995	Vovos - Stefanis Lancia Delta Integrale
1982	Mouton - Pons Audi Quattro		1996	McRae - Ringer Subaru Impreza
1983	Rohrl - Geistdorfer Lancia Rally 037		1997	Sainz - Moya Ford Escort WRC
1984	Blomqvist - Cederberg Audi Quattro		1998	McRae - Grist Subaru Impreza WRC
1985	Salonen - Harjanne Peugeot 205 T16		1999	Burns - Reid Subaru Impreza WRC
1986	Kankkunen - Piironen Peugeot 205 T16		2000	C. McRae - Grist Ford Focus WRC
1987	Alen - Kivimaki Lancia Delta HF Turbo			

Championship Classifications

Drivers
1. McRae, Makinen 30; 3. Sainz 26; 4. Burns 15; 5. Rovanpera 14; 6. Delecour 11; 7. Auriol 10; 8. Solberg 9; 9. Loix 7; 10. Radstrom, Panizzi 6; 12. Gardemeinster 5; 13.Gronholm 4; 14. Schwarz, Arai 3; 16. A McRae, Hagstrom, Bugalski 1

Constructors
1. Ford 60; 2. Mitsubishi 53; 3. Subaru 28; 4. Peugeot 20; 5. Skoda 11; 6. Hyundai 10

Group N
1. Pozzo 37; 2. Trelles 26; 3. Stohl 12...

Team's Cup
1. Team Toyota Castrol Finland (Hagstrom), Toyota Castrol Team Denmark (Lundgaard) 20; 3. Toyota Team Saudi Arabia (Bakashab) 15...

FIA Super 1600
1. Loeb 20; 2. Dallavilla 8; 3. Stenshorne 7; 4. Basso 6; 5. Fontana 4...

Kenya

Safari

Making the most of a fantastic job by Michelin, Tommi Makinen flew to victory on the Safari, helped by the early retirements of Burns, McRae, Auriol, Gronholm and Sainz. As far as the championship was concerned, the Finn had really taken a firm grip on things.

WRC
WORLD RALLY
CHAMPIONSHIP

8

Masai or not – there are so many different races in Kenya that some people see Masai everywhere. There are always more spectators lining the Kenyan roads.

THE RALLY
MAKINEN'S STROLL

There was once a team of beautiful horses, which decided to take a gallop through the savannah, confident they had the legs of the zebras, antelopes, lions and leopards which lived there. The confidence came from the fact they had already beaten the Argentinian jaguars and the beasts of myth and legend in Cyprus and Greece.

So, on this grey July morning, an unusual time of year for the annual African reunion, not one saddle or stirrup was empty, no jockeys were absent and all the tyres were on hand for this meeting in the Rift Valley. But the cavalcade was not to last and neither was the dream. After just 200 competitive kilometres, the proudest horseman of all, a Scot going by the name of Colin McRae, was already out of the running as his mount had gone lame. In so doing, he was imitating the previous year's winner, Richard Burns, who had kicked off the round of retirements after just sixty kilometres, when a knock to his Subaru had broken the front left shock absorber. The British crown had thus lost two jewels in the space of one leg; two drivers who had shared the Kenyan trophies between them, every year since 1997. The Union Jack would not

Last hope for Subaru, Solberg went out of the rally when he lost a wheel, while lying third.

be flying over Nairobi.
With no Ford or Subaru at the head of the field, the job of leading the event fell to a Skoda! Armin Schwarz created an enormous surprise, setting fastest time on the first section, taking four seconds less to cover the distance in his Skoda than Makinen did in a Lancer! The bubbly German had therefore hoisted a Czech car to the top of the leaderboard on a world championship event for the very first time, much to the great delight of his team boss. While all his opposite numbers had urged their drivers to exercise caution, Pavel Janeba had given his driver the order to go for it. It might have been daylight robbery,

but the crook was quickly apprehended, as he tried to make good his getaway. From the very next stage, Tommi Makinen was in the lead. The Finn was delighted and it was enough for him to forget his sad encounter with a bird, a now late bird, which had flapped across his path, smashing the upper left corner of the Mitsubishi's windscreen, sending a shower of glass dust into Tommi's eyes. But that didn't matter now. "The car was perfect, and the tyres were really fantastic!" In the week prior to the event, his team had completed a massive test session, racking up 450 kilometres a day. That, coupled with its experience of the terrain, the talent of its driver and a

Michelin was the best option for this year's Safari. Ford (here we see McRae) did not and failed to score a single point.

Nairobi, where the leg was based. Between Mali Tisia and Olorian, from one lost hamlet to a forgotten one, the black mud, heavy, sticky and very slippery once wet, was about to toll the bell for the over-ambitious. Subaru lost a second Impreza, when Arai went off and Peugeot left two of their 206s there!

The first unfortunate was Auriol. The car had been misting up, so he and Giraudet were running with the window open. The extra noise this generated meant that the driver misheard his co-drivers advice about the imminent approach of a huge hole, to be taken in second gear and no faster. The driver apparently heard,

"flat in fifth." Tackling the obstacle at 170 km/h, the Peugeot barrel-rolled twice, landing very heavily on its left side. The wreck immediately caught fire and the co-driver only just had enough time to haul his partner out through the right-hand door, the two men escaping unharmed.

Much less dramatic, but producing the same end result was Marcus Gronholm's retirement a few minutes later, this one caused by broken steering. This meant that, as the second leg got under way, the last of the Lions, driven with extreme caution by Rovanpera, was now third, 5 minutes 16 seconds down on the

solid job from the French tyre men had done the rest.
The previous year, the Pirelli runners had suffered all sorts of torture and turmoil with punctures forcing cars to run on their rims and the drivers were left with nothing to do but complain about their fate.

Along with Mitsubishi and Skoda, Peugeot were making the most of the fact their 206s were running on Mr. Bibendum's product. Auriol however, was slowed from the start with a transmission problem, which triggered a power steering glitch, which culminated in a small fire. Gronholm and Rovanpera were being careful and paying attention. "I think I have found the right rhythm," explained the reigning world champion. "I am running at 75% of my capability and that of the car and I am being especially careful in the really rough bits. It's more like a rally-raid than a rally and I'm not enjoying it at all!" The final kilometres of this first day were not much fun for Didier Auriol either. A violent storm hit the plains of Athi and Kapiti, to the south of

Peugeot took the strange decision of nominating Rovanpera to score points, which he did, coming second, rather than Auriol.

leader Makinen, who was 1'32" up on Sainz. The Spanish inquisition would not last long. Thirty-five kilometres after Marigat, not far from Lake Bogoria, where hosts of flaming red flowers decorated the landscape, the Spaniard just lifted off the throttle for a moment, simply to avoid yet another unknown beast wandering across his path. "In that instant, the engine cut to just three cylinders and then died," reported the dispirited man from Madrid. "I don't think it had anything to do with the difficult terrain. It's all the more disappointing, as I really thought we could beat Tommi and win."

In the Ford camp, they were trying to console themselves with humour after this second retirement in two days. "It must be written in the rules that it is forbidden to win four rallies in a row," joked the Blue Oval's chief designer, Gunther Steiner. "It's really a shame for Carlos that he has had another broken engine, after the Acropolis." The Spaniard's power failure was the main event of this interminable day, even though it was the equivalent of driving from London to Edinburgh and back, over mountains and down dale! In fact this year's Safari covered a total distance which equalled the drive from Helsinki to Madrid and not a single decent road in sight.

The gaps rapidly became so big, not just between Makinen and his immediate pursuers, but also the tail-end Charlies, that all these guys were interested in was getting through the treacherous terrain.

The Finn was certainly flying out in front. Keeping his driving well under control, he arrived in Nairobi with a lead of 6 minutes 14 seconds over Rovanpera and 10'24" over Solberg. The final leg had to be cut short as some stages were reduced in length with the helicopters unable to take off because of fog, a hundred kilometres away from the action. It messed up the order a bit, but a very relaxed Makinen wasn't complaining about having less miles to drive. The rest of the day, over the three stages still on the programme, were a comfortable Sunday afternoon drive for the Finn, who cruised home to yet another trouble-free win. However, for two of his competitors, this day proved a day too far. Solberg had been lying a solid third behind Makinen and Rovanpera, but he fell victim to the vagaries of the terrain, unsure whether or not it had been his fault. Thiry went off in the final kilometres. Both he and his co-driver had to be heli-lifted to hospital in Nairobi, but they escaped without too serious injury. The driver was simply exhausted, while Stephane Prevot was found to have a cracked lumber vertebra.

As for Francois Delecour, despite a final charge, he was unable to overtake Armin Schwarz. Tommi Makinen therefore left the Safari with a nice trophy to add to the one he picked up here in 1996. "I can't say this was an easy win," was his analysis of events, "but I stayed in control throughout the event."

His car had performed faultlessly, with only a turbo problem on Saturday night to cause him concern. But it was changed the following morning and from then on, the Finn was untouchable. He had driven a remarkably intelligent rally. He had attacked cleverly in the early stages, wearing out Burns, McRae and Auriol. Once Sainz went out on Saturday morning, he was able to back off. "When he's feeling confident, his driving and his handling of the car are absolutely the best," reckoned Timo Joukhi, his manager, who had made a special trip to attend this event. Strange then, that some people had doubted Tommi's ability, given he had now won 23 world championship rallies, making him joint record-holder with Messrs. Kankkunen, McRae and Sainz no less! ∎

Makinen was the winner and Loix (here in action) came fifth, bringing Mitsubishi enough points to take the lead in the Constructors' Championship.

Rovanpera was unfamiliar with the Safari, but he managed to avoid the pitfalls and got to the finish.

After three wins on the trot, McRae was unable to make it four.

THE TRAGI-COMEDY
AURIOL-PEUGEOT: NO GO

A few weeks before the start of the Safari, Peugeot dropped a bombshell. It had "nominated" Gronholm and Rovanpera to score points in its name, counting towards the Constructors' World Championship, preferring the younger Finn to Didier Auriol.
The French team bosses took this surprising decision (*) even though Harri had neither Auriol's "savoir-faire" on this event, nor his impressive Kenyan track record: three podium finishes from four starts for the French driver against a fifth and

sixth place from two starts for the boy from Finland. Strange, given that experience counts for so much on this event. Of course, Auriol was free to run his own rally and to score as many points as possible in the Drivers' classification. But the man himself saw the decision as a slight. It was the same situation when Loix was preferred to Auriol by Toyota in Catalunya in 1998. On that occasion, the "outcast" scored one of his finest wins!
It might have been wiser to leave Gronholm off the nominated list. He might be the reigning world champion, but Big Marcus was and, the least experienced of the three, but on top of that, he hated the African event.

With that in mind, most people reckoned he would not have taken umbrage at being left out of the Constructors' squad. The reasons put forward by Peugeot concerned the quality of Auriol's mechanics, apparently inferior to those working on Rovanpera's car. Another theory was that they did not want to put Auriol under too much pressure at this point in the season. "If anyone's under pressure in the Peugeot camp, it's not me," cursed a seriously hurt driver. "I still don't get the message," he added, totally confused at the end of a surreal press conference held in Nairobi by the French team, who proved pretty hopeless at defending their decision.

In the race, Auriol retired, as did Gronholm. Rovanpera finished second with his 206, struggling after breaking two drive-shafts, which at least provided some justification for the decision to nominate him. But this fortuitous result could not hide a serious problem. Auriol had now lost all faith in Peugeot. ■

*: In the next rally, in Finland, Auriol was not nominated yet again, but this logical decision had been accepted by the Frenchman, when he signed his contract at the end of 2000. At the time, there was no indication that this would also apply to Kenya.

49ᵗʰ SAFARI RALLY - KENYA

8ᵗʰ leg of the 2001 World Rally championship for constructors and drivers. **8ᵗʰ** leg of the Group N World Championship.

Date 20ᵗʰ to 22ⁿᵈ July 2001

Route
2958,47 km divided into 3 legs
13 timed sections (1129,76 km) but
12 ran (1079,81 km)

1ˢᵗ leg
Friday 20ᵗʰ July: Nairobi – Whistling Thorns – Nairobi, 4 SC (351,76 km)
2ⁿᵈ leg
Saturday 21ˢᵗ July: Nairobi – Equator Park – Nairobi, 5 SC (426,24 km)
3ʳᵈ leg
Sunday 22ⁿᵈ July: Nairobi – Whistling Thorns – Nairobi, 4 timed sections but 3 ran (301,81 km)

Starters – Finishers: 41 – 15

Conditions: dry tracks with some muddy sections, storm at the end of the first leg and fog at the start of the last one.

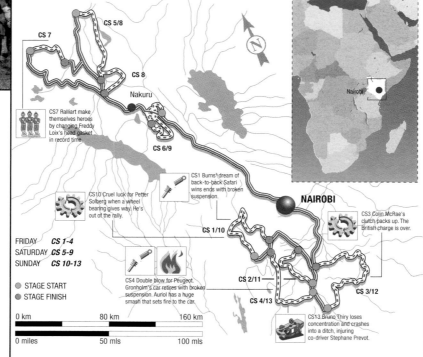

FRIDAY CS 1-4
SATURDAY CS 5-9
SUNDAY CS 10-13

● STAGE START
● STAGE FINISH

CS7 Ralliart make themselves heroes by changing Freddy Loix's head gasket in record time.

CS10 Cruel luck for Petter Solberg when a wheel bearing gives way. He's out of the rally.

CS1 Burns's dream of back-to-back Safari wins ends with broken suspension.

CS4 Double blow for Peugeot. Gronholm's car retires with broken suspension. Auriol has a huge smash that sets fire to the car.

CS3 Colin McRae's clutch packs up. The British charge is over.

CS13 Bruno Thiry loses concentration and crashes into a ditch, injuring co-driver Stephane Prevot.

TOP ENTRIES

1 Marcus Gronholm – Timo Rautiainen
   Peugeot 206 WRC
2 Didier Auriol – Denis Giraudet
   Peugeot 206 WRC
3 Carlos Sainz – Luis Moya
   Ford Focus RS WRC
4 Colin McRae – Nicky Grist
   Ford Focus RS WRC
5 Richard Burns – Robert Reid
   Subaru Impreza WRC
6 Petter Solberg – Philip Mills
   Subaru Impreza WRC
7 Tommi Makinen – Risto Mannisenmaki
   Mitsubishi Lancer Evo 6
8 Freddy Loix – Sven Smeets
   Mitsubishi Carisma GT
11 Armin Schwarz – Manfred Hiemer
   Skoda Octavia WRC
12 Bruno Thiry – Stephane Prevot
   Skoda Octavia WRC
16 Harri Rovanpera – Risto Pietilainen
   Peugeot 206 WRC
17 Francois Delecour – Daniel Grataloup
   Ford Focus RS WRC
19 Toshihiro Arai – Glenn Mac Neall
   Subaru Impreza WRC
20 Frederic Dor – Didier Breton
   Subaru Impreza WRC
21 Roman Kresta – Jan Tomanek
   Skoda Octavia WRC
22 Gabriel Pozzo – Daniel Luis Stillo
   Mitsubishi Lancer Evo 6
23 Stig Blomqvist – Ana Goni
   Mitsubishi Lancer Evo 6
24 Marcos Ligato – Ruben Garcia
   Mitsubishi Lancer Evo 6
27 Paul Bailey – Raju Sehmi
   Toyota Celica GT-Four
50 Rudi Stohl – Peter Muller
   Mitsubishi Lancer Evo 6

Special Stage Times

SC1 Oltepesi 1 117,46 km
1.Schwarz 55'05"; 2.Makinen 55'09";
3.McRae 55'33"; 4.Solberg 55'38";
5.Sainz 56'54"; 6.Gronholm 57'12";
Gr.N Pozzo 1h06'25"

1h03'03"; 6.Delecour 1h06'43"; Gr.N
Ligato 1h10'14"

SC6 Mbaruk 1 84,58 km
1.Makinen 46'23"; 2.Rovanpera
46'52"; 3.Schwarz 46'56"; 4.Delecour
47'43"; 5.Solberg 48'58"; 6.Thiry
50'19"; Gr.N Pozzo 54'36"

SC2 Kajiado 1 49,95 km
1.Makinen/Loix 24'06"; 3.McRae 24'15";
4.Solberg 24'24"; 5.Auriol 24'32";
6.Schwarz 24'36"; Gr.N Ligato 30'03"

SC7 Nyaru 72,37 km
1.Solberg 41'16"; 2.Rovanpera 41'21";
3.Delecour 41'55"; 4.Makinen 42'04";
5.Schwarz 42'34"; 6.Loix 43'34";
Gr.N Ligato 47'58"

SC3 Orien 1 112,52 km
1.Sainz 48'40"; 2.Makinen 48'57";
3.Auriol 48'58"; 4.Delecour 49'18";
5.Rovanpera 49'37"; 6.Gronholm
51'00"; Gr.N Pozzo 57'20"

SC8 Marigat 60,23 km
1.Solberg 27'27"; 2.Delecour 27'29";
3.Makinen 27'38"; 4.Rovanpera
27'43"; 5.Schwarz 27'45"; 6.Thiry
29'20"; Gr.N Ligato 32'11"

SC4 Maili Tisa 1 71,83 km
1.Sainz 35'42"; 2.Makinen 36'22";
3.Solberg 36'39"; 4.Rovanpera 37'02";
5.Delecour 37'46"; 6.Loix 44'01";
Gr.N Pozzo 54'44"

SC9 Mbaruk 2 84,58 km
1.Makinen 45'40"; 2.Rovanpera 46'53";
3.Schwarz 47'10"; 4.Loix 47'42";
5.Solberg 47'45"; 6.Thiry 49'18";
Gr.N Ligato 55'54"

SC5 Marigat 1 24,48 km
1.Solberg 1h00'05"; 2.Rovanpera
1h00'31"; 3.Makinen 1h00'37";
4.Schwarz 1h00'55"; 5.Thiry

SC10 Oltepesi 1 17,46 km
1.Makinen 1h01'02"; 2.Rovanpera
1h01'27"; 3.Delecour 1h01'41";
4.Schwarz 1h02'09"; 5.Thiry
1h08'14"; 6/Gr.N Ligato 1h12'46"

SC11 Kajiado 2 49,95 km
Cancelled - too big a delay

SC12 Orien 2 112,52 km
1.Delecour 50'09"; 2.Makinen 51'36";
3.Schwarz 51'46"; 4.Rovanpera
53'02"; 5.Loix 54'08"; 6.Thiry
1h00'54"; Gr.N Pozzo 1h01'41"

SC13 Maili Tisa 2 71,83 km
1.Delecour 38'08"; 2.Schwarz 38'33";
3.Makinen 38'53"; 4.Loix 39'38";
5.Rovanpera 43'25"; 6/Gr.N Ligato
50'41"

Results ᴡᴚᴄ

	Driver/Navigator	Car	Gr.	Time
1	Makinen - Mannisenmaki	Mitsubishi Lancer Evo.	A	8h57'37"
2	Rovanpera - Pietilainen	Peugeot 206 WRC		+ 12'37"
3	Schwarz - Hiemer	Skoda Octavia WRC		+ 17'35"
4	Delecour - Grataloup	Ford Focus RS WRC		+ 20'36"
5	Loix - Smeets	Mitsubishi Carisma GT		+ 1h44'02"
6	**Pozzo - Stillo**	**Mitsubishi Lancer Evo.**	**N**	**+ 2h06'46"**
7	Lifato - Garcia	Mitsubishi Lancer Evolution		+ 2h07'50"
8	Green - Taylor	Subaru Impreza		+ 2h55'56"
9	Anwar - Muriuki	Mitsubishi Lancer Evolution		+ 3h13'03"
10	Stohl - R. Muller	Mitsubishi Lancer Evolution		+ 4h41'03"

Leading Retirements

SC.13	Thiry - Prevot	Skoda Octavia WRC	Accident
SC.10	Solberg - Mills	Subaru Impreza 2001	Wheel bearing
SC.6	Sainz - Moya	Ford Focus WRC	Engine
SC.4	Arai - McNeall	Subaru Impreza WRC	Suspension
SC.4	Gronholm - Rautiainen	Peugeot 206 WRC	Accident
SC.4	Auriol - Giraudet	Peugeot 206 WRC	Accident
SC.3	Kresta - Tomanek	Skoda Octavia WRC	Suspension
SC.3	C. McRae - Grist	Ford Focus WRC	Clutch
SC.1	Burns - Reid	Subaru Impreza WRC	Suspension

Championship Classifications

Drivers
1. Makinen 40; 2. C. McRae 30; 3. Sainz 26; 4. Rovanpera 20;
5. Burns 15; 6. Delecour 14; 7. Auriol 10; 8. Solberg, Loix 9;
10. Schwarz 7; 11. Radstrom, Panizzi 6; 13. Gardemeister 5;
14. Gronholm 4; 15. Arai 3; 16. A. McRae, Hagstrom, Bugalski, Pozzo 1

Constructors
1. Mitsubishi 66; 2. Ford 60; 3. Subaru 28; 4. Peugeot 26;
5. Skoda 15; 6. Hyundai 10

Group N
1. Pozzo 47; 2. Trelles 26; 3. Stohl, Ligato 12; 5. Gillet, Walfridsson,
Da Silva 10; 8.Blomqvist 8; 9. Backlund, Pascoal, Feghali, Baldacci 6...

Team's Cup
1. Toyota Castrol Team Finland (Hagstrom), Toyota Castrol Team
Denmark (Lundgaard) 20; 3. Toyota Team Saudi Arabia (Bakashab) 15...

FIA Super 1600
1. Loeb 20; 2. Dallavilla 8; 3. Stenshorne 7; 4. Basso 6; 5. Fontana 4...

Performers

	1	2	3	4	5	6
Makinen	4	4	3	1	-	-
Solberg	3	-	1	2	2	-
Delecour	2	1	2	2	1	1
Sainz	2	-	-	-	1	-
Schwarz	1	1	3	2	2	1
Loix	1	-	-	2	1	2
Rovanpera	-	5	-	3	2	-
C. McRae	-	-	2	-	-	-
Auriol	-	-	1	-	1	-
Thiry	-	-	-	-	2	4
Gronholm	-	-	-	-	-	2
Ligato	-	-	-	-	-	2

Event Leaders

SC.1	Schwarz
SC.2 > SC.13	Makinen

Previous winners

1973	Mehta - Drews Datsun 240 Z		1987	Mikkola - Hertz Audi 200 Quattro
1974	Singh - Doig Mitsubishi Colt Lancer		1988	Biasion - Siviero Lancia Delta Intégrale
1975	Andersson - Hertz Peugeot 504		1989	Biasion - Siviero Lancia Delta Integrale
1976	Singh - Doig Mitsubishi Colt Lancer		1990	Waldegaard - Gallagher Toyota Celica GT-Four
1977	Waldegaard - Thorszelius Ford Escort RS		1991	Kankkunen - Piironen Lancia Delta Integrale
1978	Nicolas - Lefebvre Peugeot 504 v6 Coupé		1992	Sainz - Moya Toyota Celica Turbo 4WD
1979	Metha - Doughty Datsun 160 J		1993	Kankkunen - Piironen Toyota Celica Turbo 4WD
1980	Metha - Doughty Datsun 160 J		1994	Duncan - Williamson Toyota Celica Turbo 4WD
1981	Metha - Doughty Datsun Violet GT		1995	Fujimoto - Hertz Toyota Celica Turbo 4WD
1982	Metha - Doughty Datsun Violet GT		1996	Makinen - Harjanne Mitsubishi Lancer EV.3
1983	Vatanen - Harryman Opel Ascona 400		1997	McRae - Grist Subaru Impreza WRC
1984	Waldegaard - Thorzelius Toyota Celica Turbo		1998	Burns - Reid Mitsubishi Carisma GT
1985	Kankkunen - Gallagher Toyota Celica Turbo		1999	Colin Mc Rae - Nicky Grist Ford Focus WRC
1986	Waldegaard - Gallagher Toyota Celica Turbo		2000	Burns - Reid Subaru Impreza WRC

Finland

The world champion finally returned to his winning ways with victory at the end of an event, where he had to fight off the advances of team-mate Rovanpera, as well as those of Burns and McRae. It was a very welcome win for Peugeot.

9

Always higher in Finland as proved here by Solberg.

THE RALLY
"MADE FOR MAGIC MARCUS"

Okay, it might be a bad joke that the journalists have relied on to keep themselves amused when they need someone to poke fun at. Ever since the 2000 Corsica Rally, they came up with the very official Freddy Loix Trophy, named after the likeable Belgian, because of his unfortunate habit of throwing his car off the road with monotonous regularity. Of course, he did it in Corsica. So, the trophy goes to the driver who puts up the

earliest retirement on a rally. It can go to the very best and in Finland it went to Tommi Makinen. He was so confident on this event, which he has won no less than five times, that on this occasion, it was all over after just four kilometres! The Finn quite simply destroyed his Mitusubishi's front left suspension on a tree stump. "It's my fault", he admitted with alacrity. "I didn't have this obstacle in my notes." This really amazed his fellow competitors, given how well the lad knows the roads on his home event. "Every year, this track gets wider and wider, through being resurfaced

With the return of Kankkunen (in action on right), it meant that the four holders of the record for number of wins (23) were all present. The other three are McRae, Sainz and Makinen.

Marcus Gronholm proved untouchable with a 206 WRC that was on the pace and finally reliable.

McRae did some damage limitation for Ford, coming home third behind the Peugeots.

over the winter," he explained. "I did not cut the corner too much, but the stump was just below the level of the road and, as we were sliding, it was the most fragile part of the car which hit it." One little detail omitted by Makinen was the fact this stump was a good 80 centimetres from the edge of the road...

Rather despondent and without his usual smile, he came back to apologise to the team, before the smile finally came back again: "Well, at least it makes the championship more interesting!" Delighted with this mistake, actually quite similar to the one he made on the Swedish Rally, when

he planted the Mitsu in a snowdrift, as he was heading for second place, his opponents were quick to praise Tommi's act of generosity. But before looking at what this meant in terms of the championship, which Makinen still led, there was the small matter of a rally to run. Rovanpera kicked off by setting the first fastest time to take the lead. It only lasted two stages, or the time needed for Gronholm to get his eye in and put the hammer down in Laukaa, the stage which runs through Juha Kankkunen country, with a phenomenal quickest time. It was a masterful display. Rovanpera had no excuses. "Basically, Marcus is quicker than me today, simply

because he is driving better."
So the world champion was back on form, and as the English contingent are fond of saying, the Nordic event was "made for Magic Marcus." And "Magic Marcus did not need to be asked twice. He conscientiously pressed the pedal to the metal, putting his 206 through paces it probably never knew it had, at incredible speeds. All the records tumbled one after the other, with average speeds over an hour well in excess of 120 km/h at times. He really screwed home the advantage. This first leg belonged exclusively to the two Peugeots, chased by two Subarus, while, surprisingly, the Fords could not match the pace of

the leaders. Burns and Martin had really been going well. "I am really happy," reckoned the big blue redhead. "I'm driving at the pace I want and I don't feel as though I'm pushing too hard."

Nevertheless, it seemed as though the final day would come down, in part, to strategy, drivers yet again manoeuvring not to run first on the road. Gronholm's punctures right at the end of the leg, could not have come at a more opportune moment, as they meant the Englishman would be first off. Was it a stunt, or a bit of luck? No matter, the Finn timed it well, only giving away 3.5 seconds.

Retaking the lead, in the first stage on the final day, was just child's play for the world champion, especially as it was Burns' turn to be slowed by a faulty tyre.

Not that big Marcus needed any help. He continued giving his 206 socks, so that the Englishman slipped further back. In fact, the Finn almost gave it a bit too much, halfway through the leg. "It was nearly over," he explained. "In Ehikki, I went too wide in a corner and the right rear hit something. It damaged the suspension, so I eased off a bit." But this time, he did not have to pay the bill, as others had already picked up the tab.

In the Peugeot camp, there was Auriol, who had driven faultlessly up until then, but half-way through the day, a suspension arm broke, even though he had never hit anything. The old reliability demons were waking up in the French quarter.

Over at Subaru, there was Martin. He was doing a remarkable job of mastering the terrain at speed, but the young Estonian was a bit too enthusiastic over a bump and had a minor off. The 18 seconds lost as he grabbed himself some air,

Makinen's faux pas (centre) just after the start meant that McRae closed on the Finn in the championship.

relegated him to fifth place.
On this rally, just the slightest error or whiff of bad luck costs dear. The Finnish Rally makes cruel demands for perfection.
And perfect is just what Rovanpera was. Fifth at the start of this leg, he ran off a stunning series of fastest times, moving up one place at a time, to end up second, 14.2 seconds behind Gronholm. "My aim was not to be left behind before the final leg," he said, delighted with himself. "Now, everything is fine. But it's funny, I think taking the lead might be a bit more difficult."
In the wake of the two Peugeots, the order was sorting itself out and the gaps were getting bigger. Burns, along with Sainz and Solberg were gradually losing ground, with McRae, the only one capable of closing on the leaders. Compared with the previous leg, Ford was looking in good shape. A few adjustments to the Focus, wider roads which suited it better and a more favourable running

order: these were the key factors according to the Scotsman, who was finally challenging Burns for third place.
At the same time, the two 206s were far enough ahead for the French team to decide on team orders for the final leg, giving Gronholm the win. It was not a case of slowing dramatically, more a desire to avoid a case of fratricide, leading to the cars knocking one another out of the running. Peugeot absolutely needed the sixteen points for a one-two finish and they did not want their drivers at each other's throats. Strategy had therefore dictated what would happen next. But the fall from grace was played out in three acts over the last leg. On Sunday's first stage, a torn valve released the anti-puncture foam in one of Rovanpera's tyres, upsetting the handling of his car. Sensibly, he backed off, but that allowed Burns to threaten his second place. So, in the very next stage, the Finn pushed very hard.

However, the left front shock absorber cracked under the pressure. "It's happened often in rallies on his car and never on the others," explained a disappointed Jean-Charles Odon, his engineer. "No doubt, it is down to his driving style, as he tends to have heavier landings over the bumps than Marcus or Didier." Poor Rovanpera was now facing the 25.20 kilometres of the toughest stage of the rally, Ouninpohja. The 206 tackled them bravely but slowly, too slowly, so slowly that first Burns, then McRae made up the gap and passed ahead of the unlucky Finn in the overall classification. "That's rallying," was all poor Rovanpera could find to say about it, as he went on to finish an eventual fourth, while Gronholm won as he pleased to take his fifth victory.
Those 13 points, which should have been 16, that Peugeot brought home, in front of the big PSA boss, Jean-Martin Folz, on his first rally visit, had a bigger effect

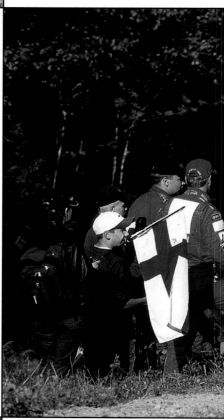

Burns is always on the case in Finland and finished second.

on the Constructors' table, while the Drivers' classification closed up at the front. The reigning World Championship team closed the gap even more, given that Mitsubishi still led, but came away from Finland with a blank score sheet. It was time for the Lion to show it still knew how to roar! ∎

SUPER 1600
LOEB'S HAT-TRICK

The Finnish Rally was also the scene of the third round of the Super 1600 Championship. At the start, there were two novelties

Paasonen never stopped beating his Ford
Focus to death and of course his rally
ended with a roll!

worthy of note: the sad departure of
the talented Swiss, Cyril Henny,
apparently short of a budget and
the Brit McShea's switch from Ford
to Citroen, preferring the
conservative choice of the category,
the Saxo, to the quick but often
unreliable Puma. Sebastien Loeb,
the winner in Catalunya and Greece,
had a difficult job in the early
stages, fighting off the advances of
Andrea Dallavilla and Manfred Stohl,
who were on fine form. The Austrian
was the first to give up the chase,
going off on stage 5 and wrecking
his Fiat. At the end of the first leg,
the Italian was slowed by a broken
drive-shaft on his Punto. This left
the Citroen man in the lead as the

crews returned to Jyvaskyla, ahead
of Belgium's Francois Duval, who
was doing a remarkable job at the
wheel of his Puma. And it was only
his third ever appearance on a loose
surface rally!
The Peugeot runners had a
particularly disappointing start,
plagued with radiator worries, as
earth was getting into the air
intakes doing irreparable damage.
This caused the retirements of
Robert and Bernardi, while Finland's
Valimaki had to cope with a
capricious and failing gearbox.
On the second leg, while well in
control of the Super 1600 class,
Loeb came under attack from a
determined Duval. The Belgian even

led briefly, making the most of the
one minute penalty imposed on the
man from Alsace, after he clocked
into a control early, before stage 13.
Forced to attack like a mad thing, he
finally made up the gap, securing a
17.2 second lead over his
opponent's Puma. But yet again, the

Ford would prove to be as fragile as
glass. Right from the first stage on
the final leg, the engine broke,
leaving Loeb to claim victory,
heading calmly for his third win on
the trot. "It was the hardest of the
three," said the delighted
Frenchman. "I had to fight almost
right to the end. Anyway, I love this
event, especially driving so quickly
on these tracks!" Loeb had made a
clean sweep of it so far, but the title
was not yet in the bag. A few days
later, he learned he would be driving
a Xsara WRC in the Sanremo and
would therefore be unable to take
part in the fourth round of the
Super 1600, to be run at the same
event. But he was not about to turn
down the chance of being part of
the world championship and he
would have to wait until Corsica and
Great Britain to get back together
with his little two-wheel driver car.
It would be a shame not to take the
offer. ■

50th RALLY OF FINLAND

9th leg of the 2001 World Rally championship for constructors and drivers. 9th leg of the Group N World Championship. 3rd leg FIA Super 1600 Championship

Date 24th to 26th August 2001

Route
1678,26 km divided into 3 legs
21 special stages on dirt roads
(407,70 km)

1st leg
Friday 24th August: Jyvaskyla -
Paviljonki - Jyvaskyla, 9 stages
(130,15 km)
2nd leg
Saturday 25th August: Jyvaskyla - Halli
- Jyvaskyla, 9 stages (181,21 km)
3rd leg
Sunday 26th August: Jyvaskyla - Halli
- Jyvaskyla, 7 stages (96,34 km)

Starters - Finishers: 160 - 79

Conditions: dry weather and roads, which cleaned up as the cars passed through.

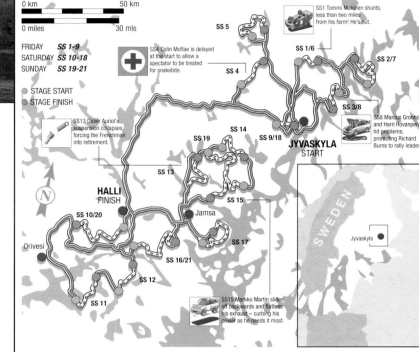

0 km   50 km
0 miles   30 mls

FRIDAY   *SS 1-9*
SATURDAY   *SS 10-18*
SUNDAY   *SS 19-21*

● STAGE START
● STAGE FINISH

SS1 Tommi Makinen shunts, less than two miles from his farm! He's out.

SS4 Colin McRae is delayed at the start to allow a spectator to be treated for snakebite.

SS13 Didier Auriol's suspension collapses, forcing the Frenchman into retirement.

SS8 Marcus Gronholm and Harri Rovanpera hit problems, promoting Richard Burns to rally leader.

SS15 Markko Martin slides off backwards and flattens his exhaust - curbing his power as he needs it most.

HALLI FINISH
JYVASKYLA START
Orivesi
Jamsa
SWEDEN
Jyvaskyla

TOP ENTRIES

1   Marcus Gronholm - Timo Rautiainen
    Peugeot 206 WRC

2   Didier Auriol - Denis Giraudet
    Peugeot 206 WRC

3   Carlos Sainz - Luis Moya
    Ford Focus RS WRC

4   Colin McRae - Nicky Grist
    Ford Focus RS WRC

5   Richard Burns - Robert Reid
    Subaru Impreza WRC

6   Petter Solberg - Philip Mills
    Subaru Impreza WRC

7   Tommi Makinen - Risto Mannisenmaki
    Mitsubishi Lancer Evo 6

8   Freddy Loix - Sven Smeets
    Mitsubishi Carisma GT

9   Kenneth Eriksson - Staffan Parmander
    Hyundai Accent WRC

10   Alister McRae - David Senior
    Hyundai Accent WRC

11   Armin Schwarz - Manfred Hiemer
    Skoda Octavia WRC

12   Bruno Thiry - Georges Biar
    Skoda Octavia WRC

16   Harri Rovanpera - Risto Pietilainen
    Peugeot 206 WRC

17   Francois Delecour - Daniel Grataloup
    Ford Focus RS WRC

18   Markko Martin - Michael Park
    Subaru Impreza WRC

19   Toni Gardemeister - Paavo Lukander
    Mitsubishi Carisma GT

20   Juha Kankkunen - Juha Repo
    Hyundai Accent WRC

21   Stig Blomqvist - Ana Goni
    Skoda Octavia WRC

22   Pasi Hagstrom - Tero Gardemeister
    Toyota Corolla WRC

23   Sebastian Lindholm - Timo Hantunen
    Peugeot 206 WRC

24   Jani Paasonen - Arto Kapanen
    Ford Focus WRC

25   Gilles Panizzi - Herve Panizzi
    Peugeot 206 WRC

26   Janne Tuohino - Petri Vihavainen
    Toyota Corolla WRC

29   Markku Alen - Ilkka Riipinen
    Ford Focus WRC

38   Jouko Puhakka - Keijo Eerola
    Mitsubishi Carisma GT

40   Gabriel Pozzo - Daniel Luis Stillo
    Mitsubishi Lancer Evo 6

47   Marcos Ligato - Ruben Garcia
    Mitsubishi Lancer Evo 6

50   Manfred Stohl - Peter Muller
    Fiat Punto

52   Andrea Dallavilla - Giovanni Bernacchini
    Fiat Punto

53   Sebastien Loeb - Daniel Elena
    Citroen Saxo

Special Stage Times

SS1 Valkola 1 8,42 km
1.Rovanpera 4'27"2; 2.Gronholm 4'28"0; 3.Burns 4'29"1; 4.Auriol 4'29"3; 5.Martin 4'29"6; 6.Paasonen 4'30"9; Gr.N Puhakka 4'46"6; S16 Loeb 5'05"6

SS2 Lankamaa 1 23,47 km
1.Gronholm 11'33"5; 2.Rovanpera 11'33"8; 3.Paasonen 11'36"2; 4.Burns 11'36"5; 5.Martin 11'41"7; 6.Sainz 11'44"7; Gr.N Puhakka 12'17"4; S16 Dallavilla 13'01"2

SS3 Laukaa 1 12,40 km
1.Gronholm 6'06"6; 2.Rovanpera 6'10"2; 3.Martin 6'10"4; 4.Paasonen 6'11"9; 5.Pykalisto 6'12"7; 6.Lindholm 6'13"4; Gr.N Salo 6'32"8; S16 Loeb 6'48"7

SS4 Mokkipera 13,38 km
1.Burns 6'26"8; 2.Gronholm 6'27"1; 3.Martin 6'28"0; 4.Rovanpera 6'28"5; 5.Auriol 6'30"8; 6.Solberg 6'30"9; Gr.N Puhakka 6'55"6; S16 Stohl 7'14"9

SS5 Palsankyla 25,47 km
1.Gronholm 13'48"7; 2.Burns 13'49"2; 3.Martin 13'50"7; 4.Rovanpera 13'52"9; 5.Auriol 13'56"7; 6.Paasonen 14'01"2; Gr.N Puhakka 14'47"0; S16 Dallavilla 15'32"0

SS6 Valkola 2 8,42 km
1.Gronholm 4'27"4; 2.Auriol 4'27"5; 3.Sainz 4'27"9; 4.Solberg 4'28"0; 5.Rovanpera 4'28"1; 6.C. McRae 4'28"4; Gr.N Ipatti 4'53"2; S16 Duval 5'14"1

SS7 Lankamaa 2 23,47 km
1.Burns 11'35"4; 2.Solberg 11'36"8; 3.McRae 11'37"3; 4.Sainz 11'37"7; 5.Rovanpera 11'42"0; 6.Rovanpera 11'42"1; Gr.N Ipatti 12'37"3; S16 Loeb 13'18"7

SS8 Laukaa 2 12,40 km
1.Martin 6'06"0; 2.Solberg 6'06"5; 3.Auriol 6'09"6; 4.Burns 6'10"1; 5.Lindholm 6'11"1; 6.Kankkunen 6'12"1; Gr.N Salo 6'32"2; S16 Loeb 6'49"3

SS9 Killeri 1 2,06 km
1.Sainz/Solberg 1'21"2; 3.McRae 1'21"6; 4.Auriol/Martin 1'21"8; 6.Burns 1'22"0; Gr.N Pozzo/Ipatti 1'25"8; S16 Loeb 1'31"1

SS10 Talvianen 1 30,30 km
1.Gronholm 15'06"2; 2.Rovanpera 15'09"6; 3.C. McRae 15'10"1; 4.Delecour 15'12"3; 5.Sainz 15'15"6; 6.Martin 15'18"2; Gr.N Sohlberg 16'04"1; S16 Duval 16'40"1

SS11 Vastila 17,40 km
1.Rovanpera 8'22"4; 2.Delecour 8'23"1; 3.Martin 8'23"6; 4.Gronholm/McRae 8'23"7; 6.Lindholm 8'25"8; Gr.N Sohlberg 8'52"9; S16 Dallavilla 9'06"9

SS12 Paijala 12,81 km
1.Sainz 6'01"9; 2.Rovanpera 6'02"1; 3.Lindholm 6'02"2; 4.Gronholm 6'02"4; 5.Martin 6'03"2; 6.Burns 6'03"9; Gr.N Sohlberg 6'18"1; S16 Loeb 6'36"6

SS13 Ehikki 19,07 km
1.Rovanpera 9'18"5; 2.McRae 9'20"7; 3.Gronholm 9'25"3; 4.Paasonen 9'26"7; 5.Burns 9'27"2; 6.Martin 9'27"9; Gr.N Puhakka 9'59"9; S16 Loeb 10'35"9

SS14 Parkkola 15,80 km
1.McRae 8'03"6; 2.Rovanpera 8'04"2; 3.Burns 8'05"7; 4.Sainz 8'06"0; 5.Gronholm 8'07"1; 6.Delecour 8'08"8; Gr.N Puhakka 8'34"0; S16 Loeb 8'59"5

SS15 Leustu 23,58 km
1.Rovanpera 11'38"3; 2.Gronholm 11'43"5; 3.McRae 11'44"4; 4.Burns 11'46"7; 5.Delecour 11'48"1; 6.Sainz 11'49"8; Gr.N Puhakka 12'36"5; S16 Loeb 13'08"2

SS16 Ouninpohja 1 31,11 km
1.Rovanpera 16'29"9; 2.Gronholm 16'38"2; 3.McRae 16'41"9; 4.Gardemeister 16'43"1; 5.Delecour 16'44"6; 6.Sainz 16'45"0; Gr.N Sohlberg 17'23"9; S16 Duval 18'20"3

SS17 Vaheri 25,42 km
1.McRae 12'20"6; 2.Gronholm 12'21"7; 3.Sainz 12'23"0; 4.Delecour 12'23"4; 5.Rovanpera 12'24"2; 6.Lindholm 12'27"4; Gr.N Puhakka 13'09"2; S16 Loeb 13'47"1

SS18 Killeri 2 2,06 km
1.Gronholm 1'20"3; 2.Solberg/Alen 1'21"0; 4.Burns 1'21"2; 5.Sainz 1'21"6; 6.Martin 1'21"7; Gr.N Ligato 1'25"2; S16 Loeb 1'30"9

SS19 Moksi - Leustu 40,84 km
1.Burns 20'52"2; 2.McRae 20'57"7; 3.Gronholm 21'01"8; 4.Sainz 21'08"8; 5.Rovanpera 21'10"1; 6.Martin 21'10"8; Gr.N Salo 22'53"8; S16 Loeb 23'32"7

SS20 Talviainen 2 30,30 km
1.Rovanpera 14'53"6; 2.McRae 14'57"2; 3.Solberg 14'57"6; 4.Burns 14'59"7; 5.Martin 15'01"5; 6.Gronholm/Sainz 15'01"5; Gr.N Pozzo 16'24"2; S16 Dallavilla 16'52"8

SS21 Ouninpohja 2 25,20 km
1.Burns 11'43"6; 2.McRae 11'44"2; 3.Gronholm 11'45"5; 4.Solberg 11'45"9; 5.Martin 11'47"3; 6.Lindholm 11'48"0; Gr.N Kuistila 13'04"8; S16 Cols 13'29"7

Results — WRC

	Driver/Navigator	Car	Gr.	Time
1	Gronholm - Rautiainen	Peugeot 206 WRC	A	3h22'21"8
2	Burns - Reid	Subaru Impreza WRC 2001		+ 25"0
3	McRae - Grist	Ford Focus RS WRC 01		+ 32"3
4	Rovanpera - Pietilainen	Peugeot 206 WRC		+ 33"9
5	Martin - Park	Subaru Impreza WRC 2001		+ 1'17"9
6	Sainz - Moya	Ford Focus RS WRC 01		+ 1'40"5
7	Solberg - Mills	Subaru Impreza WRC		+ 2'39"6
8	Lindholm - Hantunen	Peugeot 206 WRC		+ 2'44"6
9	Hagstrom - Gardemeister	Toyota Corolla WRC		+ 5'01"2
10	Loix - Smeets	Mitsubishi Carisma GT		+ 5'05"4
25	Ligato - Garcia	Mitsubishi Lancer Evo 6	N	+21'23"4

Leading Retirements

SS 21	Gardemeister - Lukander	Mitsubishi Carisma GT	Accident
SS.19	Pykalisto - Mertsalmi	Toyota Corolla WRC	Accident
SS.19	Sperrer - Carlsson	Peugeot 206 WRC	Accident
SS.19	Delecour - Grataloup	Ford Focus RS WRC 01	Fuel pump
SS.16	Kankkunen - Repo	Hyundai Accent WRC2	Brakes on fire
SS.14	Paasonen - Kapanen	Ford Focus WRC	Accident
SS.13	Auriol - Giraudet	Peugeot 206 WRC	Suspension
SS.8	Kangas - Ovaskainen	Toyota Corolla WRC	Transmission
SS.1	Makinen - Mannisenmaki	Mitsubishi Lancer Evolution	Accident

Championship Classifications

Drivers
1. Makinen 40; 2. C. McRae 34; 3. Sainz 27; 4. Rovanpera 23; 5. Burns 21; 6. Gronholm, Delecour 14; 8. Auriol 10; 9. Solberg, Loix 9; 11. Schwarz 7; 12. Radstrom, Panizzi 6; 14. Gardemeister 5; 15. Arai 3; 16. Martin 2; 17. A. McRea, Hagstrom, Bugalski, Pozzo 1

Constructors
1. Mitsubishi, Ford 66; 3. Peugeot 39; 4. Subaru 35; 5. Skoda 15; 6. Hyundai 10

Group N
1. Pozzo 53; 2. Trelles 26; 3. Ligato 22; 4. Stohl 12; 5. Gillet, Walfridsson, Da Silva 10; 8.Blomqvist 8...

Team's Cup
1. Toyota Castrol Team Finland (Hagstrom), Toyota Castrol Team Denmark (Lundgaard) 20; 3. Toyota Team Saudi Arabia (Bakashab) 15...

FIA Super 1600
1. Loeb 30; 2. Dallavilla 14; 3. Stenshorne 7; 4. Basso, Fontana 6...

Performers

	1	2	3	4	5	6
Gronholm	6	5	3	2	1	2
Rovanpera	6	5	-	2	3	1
Burns	4	1	2	5	1	2
C. McRae	2	4	5	1	-	1
Sainz	2	-	2	3	2	4
Solberg	1	3	1	2	-	1
Martin	1	-	4	1	6	4
Auriol	-	1	1	2	2	-
Delecour	-	1	-	2	2	-
Alen	-	1	-	-	-	-
Paasonen	-	-	1	2	-	2
Lindholm	-	-	1	-	1	4
Gardemeister	-	-	-	1	-	-
Pykalisto	-	-	-	-	1	-
Kankkunen	-	-	-	-	-	1

Event Leaders

SS.1 > SS.2	Rovanpera
SS.3 > SS.7	Gronholm
SS.8 > SS.9	Burns
SS.10 > SS.21	Gronholm

Previous winners

1973	Makinen - Liddon Ford Escort RS 1600	1987	Alen - Kivimaki Lancia Delta HF Turbo
1974	Mikkola - Davenport Ford Escort RS 1600	1988	Alen - Kivimaki Lancia Delta Integrale
1975	Mikkola - Aho Toyota Corolla	1989	Ericsson - Billstam Mitsubishi Galant VR4
1976	Alen - Kivimaki Fiat 131 Abarth	1990	Sainz - Moya Toyota Celica GT-Four
1977	Hamalainen - Tiukkanen Ford Escort RS	1991	Kankkunen - Piironen Lancia Delta Integrale 16v
1978	Alen - Kivimaki Fiat 131 Abarth	1992	Auriol - Occelli Lancia Delta Integrale
1979	Alen - Kivimaki Fiat 131 Abarth	1993	Kankkunen - Giraudet Toyota Celica Turbo 4WD
1980	Alen - Kivimaki Fiat 131 Abarth	1994	Makinen - Harjanne Ford Escort RS Cosworth
1981	Vatanen - Richards Ford Escort RS	1995	Makinen - Harjanne Mitsubishi Lancer Ev.3
1982	Mikkola - Hertz Audi Quattro	1996	Makinen - Harjanne Mitsubishi Lancer Ev.3
1983	Mikkola - Hertz Audi Quattro	1997	Makinen - Harjanne Mitsubishi Lancer Ev.4
1984	Vatanen - Harryman Peugeot 205 T16	1998	Makinen - Mannisenmaki Mitsubishi Lancer Ev.5
1985	Salonen - Harjanne Peugeot 205 T16	1999	Kankkunen - Repo Subaru Impreza WRC
1986	Salonen - Harjanne Peugeot 205 T16	2000	Gronholm - Rautiainen Peugeot 206 WRC

New Zealand

This rally was characterised by the infuriating problem of the running order on loose surface stages. In the end, it was won quite logically by Richard Burns, thanks to a mix of astute tactics and a big heart. However, a clumsy Peugeot made a pig's ear of it

Remembering Victims & Families September 11, 2001

(top) Thanks to his second place, Colin McRae caught up with Tommi Makinen in the drivers' classification.

(bottom) A talented guy like Burns should not have had to wait until this point in the season to take his first win of the year. At last, he made amends in the Antipodes.

THE RALLY
BURNS, CHECK MATE

There would be no hay-making on the New Zealand Rally, as it had moved from its traditional July date to mid-September. This meant that the antipodean event was taking place at the very end of winter rather than the middle. The change had been brought about primarily by David Richards, the Mr. Fixit for the sport's television coverage, who wanted viewers to see pretty blue skies instead of sheets of rain. That goal was certainly achieved and the setting looked even more spectacular than usual. The stages on the first leg, run alongside the Tasman Sea are reckoned to be the most beautiful in the world, but this year, the tracks were very dry. On top of that, they had become excessively slippery because of a thin layer of gravel tossed over them by the local authorities. What should have been a contest all about speed, ended up being run at a relative snail's pace. Therefore the first leg turned into one of those terribly tedious and depressing affairs where the main theme was the handicap involved in running with an early start number. The disadvantage was patently obvious right from the start. Makinen was first off and immediately suffered the consequences. "There is no grip with this layer of gravel. As there are no lines, I am struggling to keep control of the car. I have to brake very early for all the corners. It's incredibly difficult....and frustrating!"

Naturally, with every passing car, the grip level improved and it was not until cars 6 and 7 that the tracks were really suitable for a true competition. Running sixth in fact, was Gronholm, who immediately took the lead, despite the fact his 206 was struggling in the handling department, with incorrect settings on his electronic differentials; a problem which also affected Auriol. But the two men were dealing with their difficulties in fine style. The situation was even more favourable for Hyundai, who were starting from 13th and 14th place. As the kilometres

Another no-score for Makinen, who suffered excessively from running first on the road on the first day.

Rovanpera was third, making it to the podium for the fourth time this season.

rolled by, the major players were not only slowed by the conditions, but also of their own volition, in order to avoid the purgatory of leading on the road for the second leg. The running order for this would be based on the classification after the first six stages. McRae, Sainz, Rovanpera and Burns all set their speedos to "cruise." In fact, only Gronholm, Solberg, Auriol and the two Hyundais seemed prepared to make a fight of it, waiting to play their own tactical game at the end of stage six. Each team posted a crew at its finish line to inform their drivers how long to sit at the final control, in order to drop down the overall order! Ford pulled it off very well, as did Subaru. Their drivers all

"Loss of concentration" admitted Delecour after rolling at the start of the second leg.

seemed capable of scoring twenty out of twenty in the reading test, whereas the brains at Peugeot only managed nought out of twenty in maths. The Peugeot bosses got their sums wrong, not delaying Gronholm by enough and slowing Auriol too much.

When he realised what had happened, the reigning world champion was furious. "Well done everybody, the whole team. A great job! I am sure Didier appreciates it just as much as I do!" Later, he tried to make light of it. "We have a tactic at Peugeot that is... special. As strategy Number One hasn't worked, we'll try Number Two tomorrow. Maybe that will work better!" Jean-Pierre Nicholas admitted the mistake in the number crunching

department, but added in his defence: "it is very difficult to react from the moment you know what time the leaders are doing and the point at which you give out the orders."

Only one team was revelling in the situation and that was Hyundai. For the first time in its history, it won a leg, thanks to Eriksson, who made the most of his lowly position in the running order. Having been remarkably consistent when it came to driving like a novice, all on purpose of course, Burns changed his spots completely for the second leg, driving like a madman.

The first stage on day two was 59 kilometres in length, the longest stage in the entire world

Burns can smile: in New Zealand he was untouchable, including for Sainz (seen right).

Eriksson won the first leg, which was a nice boost for Hyundai.

championship, outside the Safari. It soon became apparent that starting at Number 8, Burns was ideally placed. The rally would come down to a duel between the Englishman and Rovanpera, with Auriol trying desperately to keep in touch in third spot.

The Finnish driver and his Peugeot came out on top with a time of 33'59"9, just three tenths up on Burns, but no one was reading too much into this. On the next three stages, the Englishman was quickest, moving up from seventh to first. He was relaxed and surprisingly happy to chat, claiming to have but one goal in mind. "I want to have the biggest lead possible at the end of the second leg, in order to have an easy time controlling those behind me on the final one." With that game plan, he was taking all sorts of risks. Flat out in sixth gear, in a right hander, the car slid too wide towards the outside and landed in a ditch. "It bounced back onto its wheels and I accelerated like mad to get it back on the road. Honestly, I was at 110% at the time!" His excessive courage was rewarded with a lead of 42.6 seconds over second placed McRae.

"With this sort of lead, he can drive without worrying too much," reckoned the Scotsman's co-driver, Nicky Grist. "That means from now on, we will be concentrating more on fighting off Rovanpera for second place, rather than chasing Richard."

As for the reigning world champion, he was having a day he described as "terrible. I am fighting, but I can't do anything. I'm running second on the road and I've got absolutely no grip at all. It's frustrating, because the 206 is capable of winning here." He was down in the dumps and totally out of character, he was not being particularly cooperative towards his team. Slightly down on Burns and Rovanpera, Didier Auriol was nevertheless making a huge leap forward, but it was not enough.

Luckily for the sake of adding some much needed interest to the event, the final leg was a gem. Right from the first stage, Otorhea Trig, Burns lost 4.4 seconds over the 4.62 kilometres covered. At the end of the next one, Te Akau South, his initial lead over McRae had been cut in half. Watching the Subaru repeating the previous day's show by Eriksson's Hyundai and Makinen on the first day, as the car kicked up a wave of gravel as it struggled through this obstacle like a drowning man, there was something almost pathetic about the frustration Burns must have felt. With two stages to go and 21.20 kilometres in prospect, to end what had finally turned into a thrilling battle, Burns was now only 14.7 seconds ahead. At the death, he took his and Subaru's first win of the season by a margin of 44.6 seconds. Colin McRae filled us in on the final act. "I had a half-spin in Fyfe, the engine stalled and it was very difficult to fire it up again. That's all." From then on, Burns only had to cruise to the finish, with none of the pressure

If Peugeot had not got their wires crossed with driver orders, Auriol would have finished on the podium.

that he so often finds hard to deal with. But the rally was by no means over, because three men - Rovanpera, Sainz and Gronholm - were still thrashing it out for third place on the podium, leaving Auriol trailing far behind. The Frenchman had been incapable of pulling off the sort of performance on the final leg, that he had managed on the previous two. The world champion got the better of his three way battle to take third, ahead of Rovanpera and Sainz. But the giant Finn had only just stepped onto the podium, when he was given a ten-second penalty for a false start on the final stage, which dropped him to fifth. "I complained about my team

glory for the squad to bask in, while his Scottish team-mate was instructed to back off, finally ending the first day in eighth place. In the end, all these machinations came to little, as neither Hyundai was capable of fighting off a major offensive from the big guns. But they had enjoyed their moment of glory and hoped it would not be the last. Alister McRae summed up their situation. "Yes, it's a bit disappointing to finish only 9th (McRae) and 10th (Eriksson.) "But when you consider the fact that not one factory car retired on this event – which must be a first of sorts – our results are actually excellent." ■

Another lacklustre rally for Japanese driver Arai.

on Friday. But this time, they can blame me. We are equal!" he said, laughing off his misfortune. ■

THE STAR TURN
HYUNDAI IS REASSURED

In the World Rally Championship, there are the great, the rich, the strong, the Fords, the Peugeots, the Subarus and Mitsubishis. Alongside them are the triers, who often end up with nothing to show for their efforts: Skoda and Hyundai. In the absence of the Czech cars, the role of leading those who play the game of who loses wins, fell to the Korean firm. Starting

13th and 14th, the two Accent WRC drivers brought their cars front of house on the first leg. Of course, they were making the most of their running order, established by the regulations. But they also benefited from the fact that several of their colleagues, such as Burns and Rovanpera, were not too inclined to press the loud pedal. This meant that Kenneth Eriksson and Alister McRae shot to the top of the time sheets. Both these cars were handily placed towards the end of the first leg. The team bosses therefore decided not to put all their eggs in one basket. Eriksson was asked not to slow down, in order to win the leg and bring some television coverage and a bit of

31st NEW ZEALAND RALLY

10th leg of the 2001 World Rally championship for constructors and drivers. **10th** leg of the Group N World Championship.

Date 20th to 23rd September 2001

Route
1690,39 km divided into 3 legs
24 special stages on dirt roads
(382,46 km)

Start
Thursday 20th September: Auckland
1st leg
Friday 21st September: Auckland - Raglan - Auckland, 8 stages
(117,17 km)
2nd leg
Saturday 22nd September: Auckland - Ruawai - Auckland, 8 stages
(176,29 km)
3rd leg
Sunday 23rd September: Auckland- Manukau, 8 stages (89 km)

Starters - Finishers: 68 - 49

Conditions: dirt roads covered with a layer of gravel and pebbles.

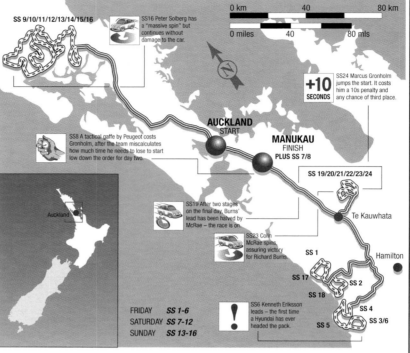

SS 9/10/11/12/13/14/15/16

SS16 Peter Solberg has a "massive spin" but continues without damage to the car.

0 km   40   80 km
0 miles   40   80 mls

+10 SECONDS

SS24 Marcus Gronholm jumps the start. It costs him a 10s penalty and any chance of third place.

AUCKLAND START

MANUKAU FINISH PLUS SS 7/8

SS8 A tactical gaffe by Peugeot costs Gronholm, after the team miscalculates how much time he needs to lose to start low down the order for day two.

SS 19/20/21/22/23/24

Auckland

SS19 After two stages on the final day, Burns' lead has been halved by McRae – the race is on.

Te Kauwhata

SS23 Colin McRae spins, assuring victory for Richard Burns.

SS 1

Hamilton

SS 17

SS 2

SS 18

SS 4

SS6 Kenneth Eriksson leads – the first time a Hyundai has ever headed the pack.

SS 3/6

SS 5

FRIDAY   SS 1-6
SATURDAY   SS 7-12
SUNDAY   SS 13-16

TOP ENTRIES

1 Marcus Gronholm - Timo Rautiainen
   Peugeot 206 WRC
2 Didier Auriol - Denis Giraudet
   Peugeot 206 WRC
3 Carlos Sainz - Luis Moya
   Ford Focus RS WRC
4 Colin McRae - Nicky Grist
   Ford Focus RS WRC
5 Richard Burns - Robert Reid
   Subaru Impreza WRC
6 Petter Solberg - Philip Mills
   Subaru Impreza WRC
7 Tommi Makinen - Risto Mannisenmaki
   Mitsubishi Lancer Evo 6
8 Freddy Loix - Sven Smeets
   Mitsubishi Carisma GT
9 Kenneth Eriksson - Staffan Parmander
   Hyundai Accent WRC
10 Alister McRae - David Senior
    Hyundai Accent WRC
16 Harri Rovanpera - Risto Pietilainen
    Peugeot 206 WRC
17 Francois Delecour - Daniel Grataloup
    Ford Focus RS WRC
18 Toshihiro Arai - Glenn MacNeall
    Subaru Impreza WRC
19 Toni Gardemeister - Paavo Lukander
    Mitsubishi Carisma GT
20 Possum Bourne - Craig Vincent
    Subaru Impreza WRC
21 Neil Wearden - Trevor Agnew
    Peugeot 206 WRC
22 Manfred Stohl - Peter Muller
    Mitsubishi Lancer Evo 6
23 Gabriel Pozzo - Daniel Luis Stillo
    Mitsubishi Lancer Evo 6
25 Marcos Ligato - Ruben Garcia
    Mitsubishi Lancer Evo 6
26 Stig Blomqvist - Ana Goni
    Mitsubishi Lancer Evo 6

Special Stage Times

SS1 Te Akau North 32,37 km
1.Gronholm 18'04"6; 2.A. McRae 18'07"4; 3.McRae 18'07"8; 4.Solberg 18'09"0; 5.Auriol 18'11"3; 6.Eriksson 18'15"5; Gr.N Stohl 18'51"5

SS2 Maungatawhiri 6,52 km
1.Solberg 3'39"8; 2.Gronholm 3'40"0; 3.Auriol 3'41"4; 4.Eriksson 3'41"6; 5.A. McRae 3'41"8; 6.Sainz 3'42"4; Gr.N Stohl 3'51"6

SS3 Te Papatapu 1 16,62 km
1.Solberg 11'00"2; 2.Eriksson 11'02"2; 3.Sainz 11'02"9; 4.Gronholm 11'03"1; 5.Delecour-Wearden 11'03"9; Gr.N Stohl 11'25"1

SS4 Te Hutewai 11,32 km
1.Gronholm 8'03"7; 2.Delecour 8'07"0; 3.Solberg 8'08"2; 4.Auriol 8'09"5; 5.Eriksson 8'11"3; 6.Burns 8'11"5; Gr.N Crocker 8'21"8

SS5 Whaanga Coast 29,52 km
1.Auriol-Eriksson 21'28"2; 3.A. McRae 21'37"0; 4.Gronholm 21'37"4; 5.Solberg 21'38"9; 6.Loix 21'41"3; Gr.N Crocker 22'01"0

SS6 Te Papatapu 2 16,62 km
1.McRae 10'49"1; 2.Sainz 10'53"2; 3.Eriksson 10'53"9; 4.Burns 10'57"4; 5.Loix 10'58"7; 6.Bourne 11'01"2; Gr.N Crocker 11'14"6

SS7 Manukau Super 1 2,10 km
1.Sainz 1'21"6; 2.Solberg 1'21"8; 3.McRae 1'22"4; 4.Rovanpera 1'22"9; 5.Gronholm 1'23"4; 6.Auriol-Loix 1'23"5; Gr.N Stohl/Crocker 1'27"7

SS8 Manukau Super 2 2,10 km
1.Sainz 1'20"1; 2.Solberg 1'20"6; 3.McRae 1'20"7; 4.Auriol 1'21"3; 5.Gronholm 1'21"4; 6.Loix 1'21"8; Gr.N Stohl 1'26"2

SS9 Parahi – Ararua 59 km
1.Rovanpera 33'59"9; 2.Burns 34'00"2; 3.McRae 34'20"7; 4.Makinen 34'20"7; 5.Auriol 34'28"1; 6.Sainz 34'45"0; Gr.N Stohl 35'48"

SS10 Batley 19,82 km
1.Burns 10'55"9; 2.Rovanpera 10'57"3; 3.Auriol 11'01"1; 4.Delecour 11'02"4; 5.McRae 11'03"6; 6.Makinen 11'03"9; Gr.N Stohl 11'32"4

SS11 Waipu Gorge 11,24 km
1.Burns 6'31"2; 2.Rovanpera 6'31"6; 3.Auriol 6'33"9; 4.McRae 6'34"2; 5.Makinen 6'34"4; 6.Delecour 6'37"4; Gr.N Stohl 6'49"9

SS12 Brooks 16,03 km
1.Burns 9'44"6; 2.Rovanpera 9'47"3; 3.Makinen 9'50"7; 4.McRae 9'51"1; 5.Sainz 9'52"0; 6.Gronholm 9'53"6; Gr.N Stohl 10'15"7

SS13 Paparoa Station 11,64 km
1.Burns 6'17"9; 2.Rovanpera 6'19"7; 3.Auriol 6'21"4; 4.Makinen 6'21"6; 5.Delecour 6'22"5; 6.McRae 6'23"3; Gr.N Stohl/Crocker 6'38"0

SS14 Cassidy 21,64 km
1.Auriol 12'23"9; 2.Burns 12'25"0; 3.Delecour 12'26"5; 4.Rovanpera 12'27"5; 5.McRae 12'31"7; 6.Makinen 12'33"1; Gr.N Stohl 13'15"4

SS15 Mititai 26,77 km
1.Burns 13'42"3; 2.McRae 13'50"6; 3.Delecour 13'52"9; 4.Rovanpera 13'54"3; 5.Auriol 13'59"0; 6.Makinen 13'59"6; Gr.N Stohl 14'39"5

SS16 Tokatoka 10,15 km
1.Burns 5'19"3; 2.Rovanpera 5'20"2; 3.McRae 5'21"6; 4.Delecour 5'21"8; 5.Makinen 5'24"6; 6.Auriol-Sainz 5'25"0; Gr.N Stohl 5'42"9

SS17 Otorohea Trig 4,62 km
1.Gronholm 3'06"0; 2.Delecour 3'07"0; 3.Solberg 3'07"1; 4.Gardemeister 3'07"9; 5.Eriksson 3'08"4; 6.Sainz 3'08"8; Gr.N Nutahara 3'16"9

SS18 Te Akau South 31,24 km
1.Sainz 18'45"0; 2.Gronholm 18'45"1; 3.Solberg 18'48"5; 4.Auriol 18'50"8; 5.Eriksson 18'51"1; 6.A. McRae 18'52"2; Gr.N Stohl 19'45"6

SS19 Ridge 1 8,53 km
1.Gronholm 4'47"1; 2.McRae 4'48"0; 3.Delecour 4'48"7; 4.Sainz 4'49"0; 5.Rovanpera 4'49"8; 6.Auriol 4'51"2; Gr.N Holmes 5'06"6

SS20 Campbell 1 7,44 km
1.Solberg 3'55"7; 2.McRae 3'57"4; 3.Delecour 3'58"3; 4.Gronholm 3'58"7; 5.Burns 3'58"9; 6.Sainz 3'59"4; Gr.N Holmes 4'14"7

SS21 Ridge 2 8,53 km
1.Gronholm 4'41"4; 2.McRae 4'43"4; 3.Auriol 4'43"7; 4.Sainz 4'43"8; 5.Delecour 4'43"9; 6.Burns-Solberg 4'44"0; Gr.N Nutahara 5'08"3

SS22 Campbell 2 7,44 km
1.Solberg 3'50"9; 2.McRae 3'51"5; 3.Delecour 3'52"0; 4.Gronholm 3'52"1; 5.Burns 3'52"1; 6.Sainz 3'52"6; Gr.N Blomqvist 4'16"9

SS23 Fyfe 1 10,60 km
1.Solberg 5'42"6; 2.Gronholm 5'43"0; 3.Delecour 5'45"3; 4.Auriol 5'45"7; 5.Sainz-Makinen 5'45"8; Gr.N Nutahara 6'08"3

SS24 Fyfe 2 10,60 km
1.Solberg 5'32"6; 2.Gronholm 5'34"3; 3.Rovanpera 5'36"7; 4.Auriol 5'38"3; 5.Makinen 5'39"3; 6.Delecour 5'39"5; Gr.N Nutahara 6'05"6

Results — WRC

	Driver/Navigator	Car	Gr.	Time
1	Burns - Reid	Subaru Impreza WRC 2001	A	3h47'28"0
2	C. McRae - Grist	Ford Focus RS WRC 01		+ 44"6
3	Rovanpera - Pietilainen	Peugeot 206 WRC		+ 50"1
4	Sainz - Moya	Ford Focus RS WRC 01		+ 50"2
5	Gronholm - Rautiainen	Peugeot 206 WRC		+ 55"8
6	Auriol - Giraudet	Peugeot 206 WRC		+ 1'11"3
7	Solberg - Mills	Subaru Impreza WRC 2001		+ 2'15"8
8	Makinen - Mannisenmaki	Mitsubishi Lancer Evo		+ 2'21"0
9	A. McRae - Senior	Hyundai Accent WRC 2		+ 3'33"8
10	Eriksson - Parmander	Hyundai Accent WRC 2		+ 4'21"9
16	Stohl - Müller	Mitsubishi Lancer Evo 6	N	+ 11'05"1

Leading Retirements

SS.14	Crocker - Foletta	Subaru Impreza WRX	Accident
SS.5	Ligato - Garcia	Mitsubishi Lancer Evo	Accident
SS.5	Manfrinato - Condotta	Mitsubishi Lancer Evo	Engine
SS.4	Wearden - Agnew	Peugeot 206 WRC	Fuel feed

Championship Classifications

Drivers
1. Makinen, C. McRae 40; 3. Burns 31; 4. Sainz 30; 5. Rovanpera 27; 6. Gronholm 16; 7. Delecour 14; 8. Auriol 11; 9. Solberg, Loix 9; 11. Schwarz 7; 12. Radstrom, Panizzi 6; 14. Gardemeister 5; 15. Arai 3; 16. Martin 2; 17. A. McRae, Hagstrom, Bugalski, Pozzo 1

Constructors
1. Ford 76; 2. Mitsubishi 66; 3. Subaru 46; 4. Peugeot 44; 5. Skoda 15; 6. Hyundai 10

Group N
1. Pozzo 59; 2. Trelles 26; 3. Ligato, Stohl 22; 5. Gillet, Walfridsson, Da Silva 10; 9. Backlund, Pascoal, Feghali, Baldacci 6...

Team's Cup
1. Toyota Castrol Team Finland (Hagstrom), Toyota Castrol Team Denmark (Lundgaard) 20; 3. Toyota Team Saudi Arabia (Bakashab) 15...

FIA Super 1600
1. Loeb 30; 2. Dallavilla 14; 3. Stenshorne 7; 4. Basso, Fontana 6...

Performers

	1	2	3	4	5	6
Solberg	6	2	3	1	1	1
Burns	6	2	-	1	2	2
Gronholm	5	4	-	4	2	1
Sainz	3	1	1	2	2	5
Auriol	2	-	5	5	3	3
C. McRae	1	5	5	2	2	1
Rovanpera	1	5	1	3	1	-
Eriksson	1	1	1	1	3	1
Delecour	-	2	6	2	3	2
A. McRae	-	1	1	-	1	1
Makinen	-	-	1	2	4	4
Gardemeister	-	-	-	1	-	-
Loix	-	-	-	-	1	3
Wearden	-	-	-	-	1	-
Bourne	-	-	-	-	-	1

Event Leaders

SS.1 > SS.5	Gronholm
SS.6 > SS.8	Eriksson
SS.9 > SS.24	Burns

Previous winners

1977	Bacchelli - Rosetti Fiat 131 Abarth	1991	Sainz - Moya Toyota Celica GT-Four
1978	Brookes - Porter Ford Escort RS	1992	Sainz - Moya Toyota Celica Turbo 4WD
1979	Mikkola - Hertz Ford Escort RS	1993	McRae - Ringer Subaru Legacy RS
1980	Salonen - Harjanne Datsun 160J	1994	McRae - Ringer Subaru Impreza
1982	Waldegaard - Thorzelius Toyota Celica GT	1995	McRae - Ringer Subaru Impreza
1983	Rohrl - Geistdorfer Opel Ascona 400	1996	Burns - Reid Mitsubishi Lancer Ev.3
1984	Blomqvist - Cederberg Audi Quattro A2	1997	Eriksson - Parmander Subaru Impreza WRC
1985	Salonen - Harjanne Peugeot 205 T16	1998	Sainz - Moya Toyota Corolla WRC
1986	Kankkunen - Piironen Peugeot 205 T16	1999	Makinen - Mannisenmaki Mitsubishi Lancer Evo 6
1987	Wittmann - Patermann Lancia Delta HF 4WD	2000	Gronholm - Rautainen Peugeot 206 WRC
1988	Haider - Hinterleitner Opel Kadett GSI		
1989	Carlsson - Carlsson Mazda 323 Turbo		
1990	Sainz - Moya Toyota Celica GT-Four		

Italy

San Remo

Citroen, whose appearance had been eagerly awaited, saw its chances reduced to almost nothing, after Puras and Bugalski had crashed off the road, even though Loeb valiantly picked up the standard. Right to the bitter end, he posed a threat to a remarkable Panizzi, who along with Auriol, gave Peugeot's championship aspirations a great boost at just the right moment.

WRC
WORLD RALLY
CHAMPIONSHIP

A tricky debut for the Mitsubishi Lancer WRC (here with Makinen) as it suffered recurring electrical bothers.

After a good start to the rally, Marcus Gronholm was delayed by power steering problems.

Loeb finished second to Panizzi, making the most of his first rally in a factory WRC.

THE RALLY
PANIZZI DESPITE CITROEN

It's "funny" how, over the past few years, the tarmac rallies have kicked off with some major damage. If there was an award for a Captain Damage on the San Remo, it would have gone to Richard Burns who, just four kilometres after the start, visited a precipice, luckily without injury to the crew. It happened at the exit to a left-hander and his Subaru ended up three metres over the edge.

"We slid. I lacked grip. I couldn't catch the car. It's as simple as that," he explained laconically, not looking too bothered by his error. The young man took comfort from the fact that, throughout the rally, his main rivals for the Drivers' title were languishing unusually far down the order. "It doesn't seem to be going too well for Colin (McRae) and Tommi (Makinen)." Those he mentioned could hardly deny the Englishman's claim. Both the Scotsman and the Finn had a desperate start, both of them suffering electronic maladies associated with the differentials. While eyeing up his Lancer WRC, which was having its maiden outing, Makinen was furious. "The car was working well in testing on Wednesday, but it's a disaster now," he moaned, before threatening to head home if the team did not find a solution to his problems. At the end of the first leg, these two title candidates rolled into the overnight halt in lowly 13th and 14th positions. Meanwhile, those who had no hope of featuring in the championship fight, were busy setting

the Italian tarmac alight. As expected, driving a French car fitted with Michelin tyres was going to be a winning formula. With three Peugeots and the same number of Citroens, that made a total of six works cars representing the PSA group. They occupied all the top six places, alternating from one marque to the other in perfect symmetry. It was total commitment, as underlined by Bugalski. "They should widen the tunnels! Seriously, I lost the car in the first stage when it understeered. The right rear hit, then the front. I found myself stuck at the entrance to a tunnel with the engine stalled. Luckily, I didn't break anything important." The match had barely begun, but several cars already bore the scars of over-enthusiasm.

Puras' Xsara was running late, but still going strong enough to sneak the lead away from Panizzi at the end of the second stage. But the Peugeot man stole it back again in no time at all. It seemed that Citroen was getting on terms with Peugeot better than in Catalunya six months earlier. Panizzi was out in front and Gronholm looked menacing. In the Peugeot camp, only Auriol was off form, blaming the five-speed gearbox the team had lumbered him with, much to his annoyance. "I can't get on with it. I'm losing about two or three seconds a kilometre just because of this box. I am losing time in the quick bits, partly because my notes are not adapted to the five-speed, but also because once I am in fourth, or even worse, fifth, I've got no torque to hold the car on line."

He would have to put up with this handicap for the entire event and worse

Like his team-mates, Sainz had to make the best of the Pirellis to finish fourth.

If he had not been struggling with a five-speed box, instead of a six, Auriol could certainly have taken the fight to Panizzi and Loeb.

David Richards congratulates Guy Frequelin after a great showing from Citroen.

still, next time out in Corsica as well. Having been so dominant and so spectacular, the Xsaras were the big losers in the second leg. And it did not take long for them to be left by the side of the road. Right from the second stage, Puras was leading, until he ripped a wheel off. Bugalski had been third

until he decided to remodel the appearance of his Xsara, scrunching the front end up against a wall. Running very late, he had the beast put down on the very next stage. This time he hit something again, braking a suspension arm at the rear, which chopped through the wiring loom.

This way please, all those of you who are retiring. Later, once they had made their way back to the service area, the two men, hanging their heads in defeat, tried to explain the error of their ways. "I had decided to increase my lead over Panizzi," related the Spaniard. "I took a lot of risks, driving really on the limit. I

came up to a corner too quickly and the car hit at the back on the left and unfortunately, it ripped the wheel off." Bugalski also had something to say on the subject and had an interesting take on the feverish pace of events. "The lack of competitivity this year, the end of the season approaching and no

Relations had strained to breaking point. In San Remo, Auriol announced he was leaving Peugeot at the end of the season.

McRae no longer seems on the pace on tarmac. Is it because of his terrible accident in Corsica in 2000?

contracts signed for next year, gives you an urge to do well. And sometimes you can do a bit too much."
Gillies Panizzi, who had been aggressive, without going over the limit, now took a comfortable lead over Auriol, who was under attack from Loeb's Xsara, which had escaped the slaughter. "Puras gave us a hell of a fight," puffed the Frenchman. "Now the battle is over, or almost."
This called for an immediate briefing from the driver's boss, Guy Frequelin. "I told him to drive his own rally and not to get swallowed up by the others."
It seemed that Guy's young protégé misunderstood, thinking he had been told to eat up the others.
Because, right from the second run through Molini, he pulled off an incredible run, "pasting" his mentor Auriol by almost nine seconds, ending up 34.5 seconds down on Panizzi, with a comfortable 7.3 bonus over his frantic pursuer.
The best was yet to come. On the morning of the final run out, fog slowly moved in over the hills of the Italian Riviera. After two very tense stages, the man from Alsace went for it in the third, holding nothing back. It was the longest stage and heavy rain had brought the leaves down from the trees. The fog was heavy in some parts and would throw its blanket over the traps in the road. "I was in first gear,"

explained Panizzi. "The leaf cover was so thick that the road looked to be that colour. As I kept aquaplaning, I decided to back off and that meant I immediately lost my rhythm." He handed the Citroen driver, who was in full attack mode, a handy 21 seconds. "I think I caught him off-guard," laughed Loeb.
At this point, there were still another 15.19 timed kilometres to the end of the rally. It seemed as though, once again, Panizzi had thrown away his chances and the Citroen looked like pulling it off. But Panizzi woke up and retook the initiative, finally winning without any more dramas, ahead of Loeb, who had been the revelation of the rally. Next up was Auriol. Once they had crossed the finish line, Didier was delighted for his young pupil, greeting him with a warmly felt, "you'll go far!"
The Lion had been hungry when it arrived in the Italian arena and, as expected, it had gorged itself. The Citroen marque failed to score a single point in the Championship. Auriol's third place brought Peugeot a further six points, making a San Remo total of sixteen, including those Panizzi picked up for the win. That meant the French constructor had jumped to third in the championship, seven points down on second-placed Mitsubishi, but 23 points down on Ford, who had added a further seven points here. However, nothing much changed in the

Sebastien Loeb's performance was breathtaking. He made the most of Citroen handing him a Xsara WRC which he took to his first podium finish, having harried Panizzi all the way for the win!

Drivers' classification. With Makinen and McRae out of the running and Burns off the road, Sainz was the only front runner to add to his total, picking up three points for fourth place. He had been incapable of standing up to the onslaught of Peugeot and Citroen. ■

THE REVELATION
LOEB, THE RIGHT NUMBER

Gilles Panizzi might have been the winner and a remarkable one at that, especially as he had to fight off the pacey Puras and Bugalski. But he also had to deal with the man who was the undoubted revelation of this Italian round of the World Championship, Loeb. Guy Frequelin had promised him a drive in the Xsara WRC during the course of the season and it was up to the driver to make the best of it. He did not have to be asked twice to make his mark. He started steadily enough, playing himself in. But then he became Citroen's final hope when Puras and Bugalski went off the road, shortly after the start of the second leg.
Understandably, he lost concentration for a moment, passing the two stricken cars of his team leaders. But after that, he set off to besiege fortress Auriol, setting his first ever world championship fastest stage time. In the end, he would notch up four of them; the same number as the winner. "It feels good," he said, unable to hide a huge

smile. "Now I am the last Citroen still running, which to be honest is a bit of a shame. The pressure I felt at the start had gone, but I think it might come back now." He would go on to prove that, not only did he have the driving skill, but that he also had a wise head on his shoulders, whatever the circumstances. In the final leg, which was run in terrible weather, with poor grip, he even managed to set a mind-blowing time to put himself in a position where Panizzi was seriously worried. It would have been too much of a fairytale and despite his pace, he decided to settle for second, rather than risk sticking his Xsara in a tree. His final result did not really matter. He was almost as much of a winner as Panizzi. No sooner was the rally over, than the recruiting sergeants from other teams gathered like vultures around the Citroen encampment. Instantly the rumours began to fly. There was talk of him going to Subaru or even to Mitsubishi, on the basis of a temporary swop with Citroen, or to Hyundai. Everyone was being most complimentary, although in the case of some admirers, it was for reasons of self-interest. However, you did not need to have psychic powers to realise that his future was already assured with Citroen, even if they only had half a world championship programme on offer. Guy Frequelin was unwilling to say anything about his 2002 driver line-up, but he did rather give the game away after the finish. "If Sebastien wants to stay with us, I would be more than happy. He has proved he's got the

potential to compete at world level." It was an inevitable statement."He certainly seems to want to stay with us!" "Yes, but blast, I didn't want to say it yet," came back the reply. Loeb was not quite the same man as he left San Remo. He was full of confidence and the future was smiling at him. The following weekend, he cruised to the title in the French Rally Championship. A fortnight later, he added another crown in the shape of the Super 1600 title. By relegating Auriol to third in Italy, in the wake of his Xsara, many observers saw it as something of a changing of the guard. ■

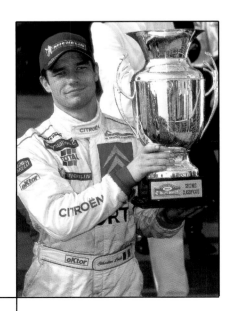

43rd SANREMO RALLY

11th leg of the 2001 World Rally championship for constructors and drivers. 11th leg of the Group N World Championship. 5th leg of the Team's cup. 4th leg of FIA Super 1600 Championship

Date 4th to 7th October 2001

Route
1425,97 km divided into 3 legs
20 special stages on tarmac roads
(368,12 km)

Start
Thursday 4th October: Piazza Mamelli, Sanremo (2,58 km)
1st leg
Friday 5th October: Sanremo-Imperia-Sanremo, 8 stages (138,45 km)
2nd leg
Saturday 6th October: Sanremo-Imperia-Sanremo, 8 stages (142,01 km)
3rd leg
Sunday 7th October: Sanremo-Imperia-Sanremo, 4 stages (87,66 km)

Starters - Finishers: 73 - 37

Conditions: good weather, dry roads.

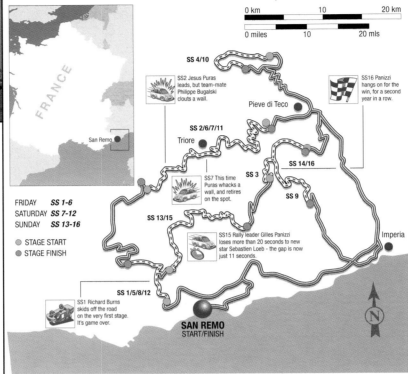

0 km 10 20 km
0 miles 10 20 mls

SS 4/10

SS2 Jesus Puras leads, but team-mate Philippe Bugalski clouts a wall.

Pieve di Teco

SS16 Panizzi hangs on for the win, for a second year in a row.

SS 2/6/7/11
Triore

SS 14/16

SS 3

SS7 This time Puras whacks a wall, and retires on the spot.

SS 9

SS 13/15

Imperia

SS15 Rally leader Gilles Panizzi loses more than 20 seconds to new star Sebastien Loeb - the gap is now just 11 seconds.

FRIDAY **SS 1-6**
SATURDAY **SS 7-12**
SUNDAY **SS 13-16**

● STAGE START
● STAGE FINISH

SS 1/5/8/12

SS1 Richard Burns skids off the road on the very first stage. It's game over.

SAN REMO
START/FINISH

N

TOP ENTRIES

1   Marcus Gronholm - Timo Rautiainen
    Peugeot 206 WRC

2   Didier Auriol - Denis Giraudet
    Peugeot 206 WRC

3   Carlos Sainz - Luis Moya
    Ford Focus RS WRC

4   Colin McRae - Nicky Grist
    Ford Focus RS WRC

5   Richard Burns - Robert Reid
    Subaru Impreza WRC

6   Petter Solberg - Philip Mills
    Subaru Impreza WRC

7   Tommi Makinen - Risto Mannisenmaki
    Mitsubishi Lancer WRC

8   Freddy Loix - Sven Smeets
    Mitsubishi Lancer WRC

9   Piero Liatti - Carlo Cassina
    Hyundai Accent WRC

10 Alister McRae - David Senior
    Hyundai Accent WRC

11 Armin Schwarz - Manfred Hiemer
    Skoda Octavia WRC

12 Bruno Thiry - Stephane Prevot
    Skoda Octavia WRC

14 Philippe Bugalski - Jean-Paul Chiaroni
    Citroen Xsara WRC

15 Jesus Puras - Marc Marti
    Citroen Xsara WRC

16 Gilles Panizzi - Herve Panizzi
    Peugeot 206 WRC

17 Francois Delecour - Daniel Grataloup
    Ford Focus RS WRC

18 Markko Martin - Michael Park
    Subaru Impreza WRC

19 Toshihiro Arai - Glenn MacNeall
    Subaru Impreza WRC

20 Sebastien Loeb - Daniel Elena
    Citroen Xsara WRC

21 Paolo Andreucci - Alessandro Ford
    Focus RS WRC

22 Roman Kresta - Jan Tomanek
    Skoda Octavia WRC

23 Pasi Hagstrom - Tero Gardemeister
    Toyota Corolla WRC

24 Henrik Lundgaard - Jens-Christian
    Anker Toyota Corolla WRC

25 Harri Rovanpera - Risto Pietilainen
    Peugeot 206 WRC

26 Renato Travaglia - Flavio Zanella
    Peugeot 206 WRC

31 Simon Jean-Joseph - Jacques Boyere
    Peugeot 206 WRC

38 Gabriel Pozzo - Daniel Luis Stillo
    Mitsubishi Lancer Evo 6

39 Marcos Ligato - Ruben Garcia
    Mitsubishi Lancer Evo 6

40 Gustavo Trelles - Jorge Del Buono
    Mitsubishi Lancer Evo 6

41 Stig Blomqvist - Ana Goni
    Mitsubishi Lancer Evo 6

Special Stage Times

SS1 Coldirodi 1 12,41 km
1.Panizzi 7'55"7; 2.Gronholm 7'57"3; 3.Sainz 7'58"0; 4.Puras 7'58"2; 5.Auriol 8'01"6; 6.Delecour 8'01"8; Gr.N Stagni 8'41"5; S16 Dallavilla 8'32"8

SS2 Langan 1 25,29 km
1.Puras 16'48"2; 2.Bugalski 16'49"7; 3.Panizzi 16'56"6; 4.Gronholm 16'59"0; 5.Loeb 16'59"8; 6.Jean-Joseph 17'00"0; Gr.N Ligato 18'35"2; S16 Dallavilla 18'13"8

SS2B Rezzo 1 12,29 km
1.Panizzi 9'12"4; 2.Gronholm 9'14"2; 3.Auriol 9'14"5; 4.Bugalski 9'15"7; 5.Puras 9'16"4; 6.Delecour 9'17"3; Gr.N Stagni 10'10"0; S16 Dallavilla 9'56"9

SS3 San Bernardo 1 19,44 km
1.Puras 11'34"8; 2.Panizzi 11'36"8; 3.Bugalski 11'37"7; 4.Auriol 11'40"4; 5.Loeb 11'41"0; 6.Solberg 11'42"2; Gr.N Trelles 12'47"1; S16 Dallavilla 12'33"9

SS4 Nava 1 19,03 km
1.Bugalski 12'00"5; 2.Gronholm 12'03"5; 3.Panizzi 12'03"6; 4.Loeb 12'06"0; 5.Auriol 12'07"0; 6.Sainz 12'07"7; Gr.N Stagni 13'15"8; S16 Robert 12'56"1

SS5 Coldirodi 2 12,41 km
1.Bugalski 7'53"5; 2.Panizzi 7'53"6; 3.Solberg 7'57"1; 4.Puras 7'57"3; 5.Auriol 7'57"9; 6.Gronholm 7'58"2; Gr.N Trelles 8'41"9; S16 Dallavilla 8'31"8

SS6 Langan 2 25,29 km
1.Puras 16'41"9; 2.Bugalski 16'46"1; 3.Panizzi 16'47"5; 4.Loeb 16'47"9; 5.Auriol 16'48"8; 6.Travaglia 16'53"6; Gr.N Pozzo 18'33"9; S16 Robert 18'08"9

SS6B Rezzo 2 12,19 km
1.Bugalski 9'11"2; 2.Puras 9'16"6; 3.Panizzi 9'16"7; 4.Auriol-Loeb 9'17"1; 6.Sainz 9'21"1; Gr.N Pozzo 10'27"3; S16 Dallavilla 10'05"5

SS7 Passo Teglia 1 14,32 km
1.Puras 10'25"6; 2.Panizzi 10'26"8; 3.Gronholm 10'28"7; 4.Travaglia 10'28"9; 5.Bugalski 10'29"7; 6.Sainz 10'29"9; Gr.N Ligato 11'24"2; S16 Dallavilla 11'17"8

SS7B Molini 1 25,29 km
1.Loeb 16'52"6; 2.Panizzi 16'55"1; 3.Delecour 16'59"0; 4.Solberg 17'00"7; 5.Auriol 17'01"1; 6.Sainz 17'01"2; Gr.N Stagni 18'29"0; S16 Robert 18'01"7

SS8 Perinaldo 1 12,16 km
1.Auriol 7'43"9; 2.Panizzi 7'44"6; 3.Solberg 7'45"6; 4.Travaglia 7'47"8; 5.Loeb 7'48"6; 6.Gronholm 7'49"5; Gr.N Stagni 8'24"6; S16 Dallavilla 8'18"5

SS9 San Bernardo 2 19,44 km
1.Solberg 11'35"9; 2.Gronholm 11'35"9; 3.Panizzi 11'36"8; 4.Loeb 11'36"9; 5.Travaglia 11'39"2; 6.Auriol 11'39"9; Gr.N/S16 SS stopped - accident

SS10 Nava 2 19,03 km
1.Panizzi 11'58"0; 2.Gronholm 11'59"4; 3.Loeb 12'01"5; 4.Auriol 12'02"1; 5.Travaglia 12'02"2; 6.Solberg 12'02"4; Gr.N/S16 SS stopped - delay

SS11 Passo Teglia 2 14,32 km
1.Auriol 10'23"0; 2.Travaglia 10'23"2; 3.Panizzi 10'23"4; 4.Loeb 10'26"6; 5.Gronholm 10'27"6; 6.McRae 10'27"9; Gr.N Stagni 11'21"2; S16 Robert 11'17"0

SS11B Molini 2 25,29 km
1.Loeb 16'43"7; 2.Gronholm 16'51"4; 3.Auriol 16'52"3; 4.Solberg 16'53"3; 5.Panizzi 16'53"6; 6.Travaglia 16'57"6; Gr.N Trelles 18'28"3; S16 Robert 18'03"8

SS12 Perinaldo 2 12,16 km
1.Panizzi 7'41"6; 2.Auriol 7'42"7; 3.Loeb 7'43"1; 4.Gronholm 7'43"7; 5.Sainz 7'45"3; 6.Travaglia 7'48"4; Gr.N Trelles 11'22"9; S16 Dallavilla 8'15"7

SS13 San Romolo 1 28,64 km
1.Loeb 19'04"7; 2.Travaglia 19'06"2; 3.Auriol 19'10"3; 4.Panizzi 19'12"4; 5.Makinen 19'15"6; 6.Delecour 19'16"2; Gr.N Trelles 20'43"9; S16 Dallavilla 20'27"9

SS14 Colle d'Oggia 1 15,19 km
1.Sainz 10'04"3; 2.Panizzi 10'04"9; 3.Martin 10'05"3; 4.Loeb 10'11"6; 5.Travaglia 10'15"5; 6.Delecour 10'18"1; Gr.N Trelles 10'29"2; S16 Robert 10'46"3

SS15 San Romolo 2 28,64 km
1.Loeb 20'20"6; 2.Sainz 20'21"1; 3.Gronholm 20'27"4; 4.Travaglia 20'30"7; 5.Auriol 20'35"8; 6.Panizzi 20'42"3; Gr.N De Dominicis 24'12"6; S16 Dallavilla 22'51"4

SS16 Colle d'Oggia 2 15,19 km
1.Delecour 10'13"0; 2.McRae 10'13"4; 3.Jean-Joseph 10'20"3; 4.Thiry 10'20"4; 5.Sainz 10'20"5; 6.Rovanpera 10'24"4; Gr.N Pozzo 11'13"9; S16 Duval 10'37"3

Results — WRC

	Driver/Navigator	Car	Gr.	Time
1	Panizzi - Panizzi	Peugeot 206 WRC	A	4h05'49"5
2	Loeb - Elena	Citroen Xsara WRC		+ 11"4
3	Auriol - Giraudet	Peugeot 206 WRC		+ 54"9
4	Sainz - Moya	Ford Focus RS WRC 01		+ 1'11"9
5	Travaglia - Zanella	Peugeot 206 WRC		+ 1'32"1
6	Delecour - Grataloup	Ford Focus RS WRC 01		+ 2'28"6
7	Gronholm - Rautiainen	Peugeot 206 WRC		+ 2'47"3
8	McRae - Grist	Ford Focus RS WRC 01		+ 3'53"7
9	Solberg - Mills	Subaru Impreza WRC 2001		+ 3'59'
10	Jean-Joseph - Broyere	Peugeot 206 WRC		+ 4'01"5
15	Lundgaard - Anker	Toyota Corolla WRC	Team's Cup	+ 8'54"7
16	Dallavilla - Bernacchini	Fiat Punto	Super 1600	+ 18'25"3
17	Fiorio - Cantoni	Mitsubishi Lancer Evo 6	N	+ 22'30"8

Leading Retirements

SS.15	Makinen - Mannisenmaki	Mitsubishi Lancer Evo WRC	Accident
SS.15	Martin - Park	Subaru Impreza WRC 2001	Accident
SS.11	A. McRae - Senior	Hyundai Accent WRC	Brakes
SS.8	Bugalski - Chiaroni	Citroen Xsara WRC	Accident
SS.7	Arai - McNeal	Subaru Impreza WRC 2001	Accident
SS.7	Puras - Marti	Citroen Xsara WRC	Accident
SS.1	Schwarz - Hiemer	Skoda Octavia WRC	Alternator
SS.1	Liatti - Cassima	Hyundai Accent WRC	Accident
SS.1	Burns - Reid	Subaru Impreza WRC 2001	Accident

Championship Classifications

Drivers
1. Makinen, C. McRae 40; 3. Sainz 33; 4. Burns 31; 5. Rovanpera 27; 6. Panizzi, Gronholm 16; 8. Delecour, Auriol 15; 10. Solberg, Loix 9; 12. Schwarz 7; 13. Radstrom, Loeb 6; 15. Gardemeister 5; 16. Arai 3; 17. Martin, Travaglia 2; 19. A. McRae, Hagstrom, Bugalski, Pozzo 1

Constructors
1. Ford 83; 2. Mitsubishi 67; 3. Peugeot 60; 4. Subaru 48; 5. Skoda 15; 6. Hyundai 10

Group N
1. Pozzo 65; 2. Trelles 26; 3. Ligato, Stohl 22; 5. Blomqvist 14; 6. Gillet, Walfridsson, Da Silva, Fiorio 10...

Team's Cup
1. Toyota Castrol Team Denmark (Lundgaard) 30; 2. Toyota Castrol Team Finland (Hagstrom) 20; 3. Toyota Team Saudi Arabia (Bakashab) 15...

FIA Super 1600
1. Loeb 30; 2. Dallavilla 24; 3. Stenshorne 7; 4. Basso, Fontana, Duval 6...

Performers

	1	2	3	4	5	6
Panizzi	4	6	6	1	1	1
Puras	4	1	-	2	1	-
Loeb	4	-	2	6	3	-
Bugalski	3	2	1	1	1	-
Auriol	2	1	3	3	5	1
Sainz	1	1	1	-	2	4
Solberg	1	-	2	2	1	2
Delecour	1	-	1	-	-	4
Gronholm	-	6	2	2	1	2
Travaglia	-	2	-	3	3	3
C. McRae	-	1	-	-	-	1
Jean-Joseph	-	-	1	-	-	1
Martin	-	-	1	-	-	-
Thiry	-	-	-	1	-	-
Makinen	-	-	-	-	1	-
Rovanpera	-	-	-	-	-	1

Event Leaders

SS.1	Panizzi
SS.2 > SS.4	Puras
SS.5 > SS.6	Panizzi
SS.7 > SS.8	Puras
SS.9 > SS.20	Panizzi

Previous winners

Corsica

France

In Corsica, Jesus Puras scored his first ever win in a World Championship rally and, at the same time, bestowed the same honour on the Xsara WRC. This victory suited Peugeot perfectly well, as Panizzi and Auriol finished second and third respectively

THE RALLY
JESUS BRINGS A GIFT FOR CITROEN

It was the last chance saloon for Citroen in Corsica. It was the final bullet in the barrel with which to hit its target of securing at least one win from the four world championship events on its programme for the year. The Circuit of Ajaccio was a far better name for the island rally, than the rather presumptuous Tour of Corsica. It got underway right from the start with nothing in the way of a prologue and thankfully there were no major dramas,

Solberg is making promising progress on tarmac and finished fifth.

although it came close, very close in fact. Crashes, anger, bent bodywork, wheels torn off, rolls, fires, dead engines, shredded tyres, sweat, tears, fear and effort: all of these featured on the first leg which was fascinating from the sporting perspective, if occasionally frightening from the human one. Despite his best efforts, it was Bugalski who set the ball rolling, smashing his Xsara into a rather too solid wall. Next up it was Arai, the professional kamikaze, as well as Sainz, McRae and Burns, ending with a roll from Makinen. One by one they lost any chance of doing something on this rally, either by

visiting ditches, or by collecting a rock or heading for a stone wall.
Until then, the rally had been as thrilling as expected, living up to its promise. Peugeot and Citroen had immediately moved to the head of the leaderboard. First it was Panizzi and then Puras took over from the second stage, with the two men having a right old ding-dong. Just behind them came Auriol, driving with all the passion of the past, proving over and over again that he was still one of the very best, despite an imminent divorce from his team. His Corsican credo seemed to be "win it or bin it." It was a high-octane Auriol performance.
Despite this, the Spanish Xsara driver was managing to pull out a fragile lead over Panizzi, which eventually stretched to 10.5 seconds; the gap to Auriol being 11.3 and to Gronholm, 38 seconds. "The car is going very well," he explained. "It's just on the really bumpy bits that it's getting a bit loose. I am trying to concentrate and drive carefully." There was little sign of that on the second leg, as he picked up five fastest times, one of them shared with Gilles Panizzi, out of the seven on the menu. The Citroen driver did not seem too keen on sharing. "I can do what I like with this car and there are absolutely no problems with it," he announced, delighted with himself. "Puras has done what we would have all liked to do," was Panizzi's analysis of his rival. "He has built up his lead by attacking all the time. He wants to be in control for the final leg. That's understandable and I would say he now

has a big enough lead to do that."
"I certainly can't catch him," added a philosophical Auriol in third place. Indeed it was not Didier's day, the sun literally shining on Jesus and Gilles. Just as the whistle blew at Carbuccia station to signal the start of stage seven, the rains arrived. But while Puras and

Didier Auriol was a bit more effective in Corsica than in San Remo, despite not getting on with his gearbox.

McRae did not have an enjoyable time, slowed at the end by a faulty power steering.

A frightening and painful time for Makinen and especially for co-driver Mannisenmaki, who had to be airlifted to hospital in Marseille for a back operation.

realistic. Peugeot needs the points, but for us to have a chance now, it would have to snow." This meant that Puras thus picked up the second leg as well, with a comfortable 23"5 second lead over Panizzi and a gap of 49"9 to Auriol.

Behind this trio, it was all going wrong. Gronholm had been going great guns up until then, but he ripped a wheel off, half-way through the leg. As for Ford, the team was running out of luck. It had lost Sainz the previous day, with a blown engine and now McRae had been seriously delayed with a faulty power steering system.

During the last stages on the final leg, Panizzi, despite dropping back, made one last attempt to push the lead Citroen into making a mistake. "The surface in the first stage was slippery," he explained. "In these conditions, I knew I could be quicker than Puras. So I attacked."

He regained six seconds over 24 kilometres. Sadly, brake problems in the next stage meant he could not get the most out of his machine. The first Tour

of Corsica of the new millennium thus drew to a close, while more heavy rain fell on the cliff tops of the tough Coti-Chiavari section.

Jesus Puras was overwhelmed by it all, almost in tears as he became the 62nd driver to win a world championship rally. "I am very relieved," he gasped. "I have been trying for so long. Maybe this will be a turning point in my life." For his part, Guy Frequelin was delighted for his driver and also for his team. "It has worked so hard that this result is an enormous satisfaction."

Finally, a Citroen WRC had taken a win this season and a very convincing one at that. It was the icing on the cake for the red team as, a week earlier, Loeb had won the French title and on the very same day as the Corsican success in the overall classification, he had also added the world title for the Super 1600 class!

The other PSA marque had to admit that Citroen was totally dominant, but Peugeot had also been successful to a lesser degree. Second and third places for Panizzi and Auriol meant it added

Panizzi escaped when just a few drops were falling, Auriol, who was third away and the rest of the field, all got caught in the downpour. With the tarmac soaking wet, he somehow and miraculously managed to stay on the road, despite having tyres totally unsuited to the conditions. But he had

to give away 29"6 to his team-mate, who set the quickest time. Before this stage, the two Peugeot men were level pegging in second place, equal to the nearest tenth of a second! "It was after this stage that we lost touch," related Auriol. "Then, looking at the gap, I knew it was over for me. You have to be

Marcus Gronholm tried a bit too hard and tore a wheel off in the second leg.

Burns brought along a lucky charm – his girlfriend Zoe.

Even McRae struggled with the Pirellis on the Corsican tarmac.

another sixteen points to its championship tally, so that it was now just seven points behind Ford, who had failed to score.

In the Drivers' Championship, the Blue Oval suffered a similar fate. McRae and Sainz picking up zero points. The only one of the four top men to come away from Corsica with something was Burns, who finished fourth thanks to the compliant efforts of his team-mates, Martin and Solberg, who let him get ahead of them in the closing stages. He now had 34 points compared with 40 for the joint leaders, Makinen and McRae. "I've come out of it well," he admitted at the finish. "The start of the rally was difficult as I hit something. The end of the season will be very exciting." He wasn't joking. ■

THE FIRST
LOEB TAKES THE TITLE

Arriving in Corsica, Sebastien Loeb was on cloud nine. A fortnight earlier he had put on a breathtaking display in San Remo and a week after that, he took the French Rally Championship crown. All that was left was the Super 1600 title. He was leading the championship with three wins from as many starts, as he was at the wheel of a Xsara WRC in San Remo. But Andrea Dallavilla, the other pretender to the crown, who had won a fortnight earlier, had full support from Fiat and was not about to roll over and let the title go without a fight. The opening leg seemed to go pretty well for the Frenchman, despite a brake problem in the third stage, with the pedal only coming back right at the end.

Having led until then, he handed over the top slot to the Italian, finishing a mere seven seconds behind him. "But the car and the crew are fine and it's going to be flat out all the way, as Dallavilla is really quick," predicted the man from Alsace. It was all change on the second leg, as the Citroen man retook the lead, as Dallavilla was slowed with gremlins attacking his power steering, giving away 18 seconds. "I must admit that sometimes I am hard pressed to match Andrea's pace, even though I am driving flat out," puffed Loeb. "Compared with Catalunya in March (the first tarmac round of the junior series), the Punto has made a lot of progress. The Citroen Saxo does not seem to have been affected by the changes made to its injection, as required by the rules, but it's the others who have made a big step forward." As expected, the final day provided the backdrop for a fascinating duel between the two men, who both drove absolutely to the limit. In the penultimate stage, Dallavilla clawed back nine seconds in one go. Loeb was not on the right tyres, as he tackled the soaked roads on slicks. This meant his lead had now been cut to a meagre 5.7 seconds, with just 31.97 kilometres of competitive motoring remaining. At the finish, the Frenchman could hardly contain his excitement, when it came to describing events on the final stage. "Some sections were completely crazy, because the slick tyres had absolutely no grip whatsoever on the wet. I didn't scare myself, but I had some pretty big slides which were right on the very limit, as I couldn't get the tyres up to temperature. It would just get away from me in the quick bits. It was

Like Solberg, Martin also proved that tarmac held no fears for him anymore.

First win for Puras and the Xsara WRX: the podium was an all-Michelin, all-French affair with Peugeot picking up a further 16 points. The cockerel had reason to crow with pride.

stressful all the way to the end. In fact, we beat him by two seconds."

Victory and the title: he could not have asked for more. The final round of the Super 1600 would take place in Great Britain, but the outcome would not be that vital and it would be a rally for the simple matter of the honour of winning. The car was very well developed and prepared and the driver was as good on the loose as on tarmac and he was a cool customer. Seb' justified his role as favourite. "In fact, I only really had to fight for the French Championship title," he said after the rally. "This title is really great. In the space of three weekends, I switched from the Xsara WRC to the Xsara Kit-Car to the Saxo vts. It meant I was under a lot of pressure. No sooner was one rally over, that the following day, I was recceing for the next one." In the end, this year without any serious mistakes, apart from two off-track excursions which did not do too much damage, in the Limousin and Le Touquet events, would reap its own reward. Loeb would be at the wheel of a Xsara WRC in 2002 and 2003. In 2001, it seemed as though the Loeb saga had only just begun. ■

45th RALLY OF FRANCE

12th leg of the 2001 World Rally championship for constructors and drivers. **12th** leg of the Group N World Championship. **5th** leg of FIA Super 1600 Championship

Date 19th to 21st October 2001

Parcours
891,59 km divided into 3 legs
16 special stages on tarmac roads
(394,04 km)

1st leg
Friday 19th October: Ajaccio-Ajaccio, 5 stages (126,81 km)
2nd leg
Saturday 20th October: Ajaccio-Ajaccio, 7 stages (155,55 km)
3rd leg
Sunday 21st October: Ajaccio-Ajaccio, 4 stages (111,68 km)

Starters - Finishers: 84 - 50

Conditions: good weather, dry roads.

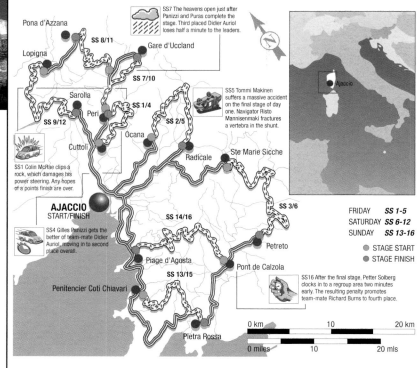

Pona d'Azzana
Lopigna
Gare d'Uccland
SS 8/11
SS7 The heavens open just after Panizzi and Puras complete the stage. Third placed Didier Auriol loses half a minute to the leaders.
Sarolla
SS 7/10
SS5 Tommi Makinen suffers a massive accident on the final stage of day one. Navigator Risto Mannisenmaki fractures a vertebra in the shunt.
Peri
SS 1/4
SS 9/12
SS 2/5
Ocana
Cuttoli
Radicale
Ste Marie Sicche
SS1 Colin McRae clips a rock, which damages his power steering. Any hopes of a points finish are over.
AJACCIO START/FINISH
SS 3/6
SS 14/16
SS4 Gilles Panizzi gets the better of team-mate Didier Auriol, moving in to second place overall.
Petreto
Piage d'Agosta
Pont de Calzola
SS 13/15
Penitencier Coti Chiavari
SS16 After the final stage, Petter Solberg clocks in to a regroup area two minutes early. The resulting penalty promotes team-mate Richard Burns to fourth place.
Pietra Rossa

Ajaccio

FRIDAY SS 1-5
SATURDAY SS 6-12
SUNDAY SS 13-16
● STAGE START
● STAGE FINISH

0 km 10 20 km
0 miles 10 20 mls

TOP ENTRIES

1 Marcus Gronholm - Timo Rautiainen
Peugeot 206 WRC

2 Didier Auriol - Denis Giraudet
Peugeot 206 WRC

3 Carlos Sainz - Luis Moya
Ford Focus RS WRC

4 Colin McRae - Nicky Grist
Ford Focus RS WRC

5 Richard Burns - Robert Reid
Subaru Impreza WRC

6 Petter Solberg - Philip Mills
Subaru Impreza WRC

7 Tommi Makinen - Risto Mannisenmaki
Mitsubishi Lancer WRC

8 Freddy Loix - Sven Smeets
Mitsubishi Lancer WRC

9 Piero Liatti - Carlo Cassina
Hyundai Accent WRC

10 Alister McRae - David Senior
Hyundai Accent WRC

11 Armin Schwarz - Manfred Hiemer
Skoda Octavia WRC

12 Bruno Thiry - Stephane Prevot
Skoda Octavia WRC

14 Philippe Bugalski - Jean-Paul Chiaroni
Citroen Xsara WRC

15 Jesus Puras - Marc Marti
Citroen Xsara WRC

16 Gilles Panizzi - Herve Panizzi
Peugeot 206 WRC

17 Francois Delecour - Daniel Grataloup
Ford Focus RS WRC

18 Markko Martin - Michael Park
Subaru Impreza WRC

24 Toshihiro Arai - Glenn Mac Neall
Subaru Impreza WRC

28 Gustavo Trelles - Jorge Del Buono
Mitsubishi Lancer Evo 6

29 Harri Rovanpera - Risto Pietilainen
Peugeot 206 WRC

38 Neil Wearden - Trevor Agnew
Peugeot 206 WRC

50 Manfred Stohl - Ilka Petrasko
Fiat Punto

51 Patrick Magaud - Guylene Brun
Ford Puma

52 Andrea Dallavilla - Giovanni Bernacchini Fiat Punto

53 Sebastien Loeb - Daniel Elena
Citroen Saxo

54 Larry Cols - Yasmine Gerard
Peugeot 206

55 Niall McShea - Michael Orr
Citroen Saxo

57 Cedric Robert - Marie-Pierre Billoux
Peugeot 206

63 Martin Stenshorne - Clive Jenkins
Ford Puma

71 Francois Duval - Jean-Marc Fortin
Ford Puma

Special Stage Times

SS1 Cuttoli – Peri 1 17,40 km
1.Panizzi 11'24"6; 2.Gronholm 11'26"9; 3.Puras 11'27"3; 4.Delecour 11'29"9; 5.Auriol 11'30"2; 6.Burns 11'31"4; Gr.N Trelles 12'40"0; S16 Duval 12'15"1

SS2 Ocana – Radicale 1 27,64 km
1.Puras 17'17"5; 2.Auriol 17'23"0; 3.Gronholm 17'28"7; 4.Panizzi 17'28"9; 5.Martin 17'33"6; 6.Solberg 17'36"0; Gr.N Santoni 19'11"9; S16 Loeb 18'36"9

SS3 Ste Marie Sicche – Petreto 1 36,73 km
1.Puras 23'49"7; 2.Auriol 23'51"7; 3.Panizzi 23'52"1; 4.Solberg 24'07"8; 5.Makinen-Burns 24'08"5; Gr.N Manfrinato 26'05"8; S16 Dallavilla 25'31"0

SS4 Cuttoli – Peri 2 17,40 km
1.Panizzi 11'21"8; 2.Puras 11'22"4; 3.Auriol 11'23"3; 4.Gronholm 11'28"1; 5 Delecour 11'30"5; 6.Burns 11'31"2; Gr.N Santoni 12'35"5; S16 Dallavilla 12'14"2

SS5 Ocana – Radicale 2 27,64 km
Cancelled – Tommi Makinen's accident

SS6 Ste Marie Sicche – Petreto 2 36,73 km
1.Puras 23'38"2; 2.Auriol 23'41"1; 3.Panizzi 23'41"9; 4.Solberg 23'41"0; 5.Gronholm 23'54"8; 6.Delecour 23'57"2; Gr.N Manfrinato 25'51"6; S16 Loeb 25'26"7

SS7 Gare de Carbuccia – Gare d'Ucciani 1 10,66 km
1.Panizzi 7'14"3; 2.Puras 7'16"4; 3.McRae 7'40"0; 4.Delecour 7'41"0; 5.Auriol 7'41"2; 6.Gronholm 7'48"7; Gr.N Manfrinato 8'12"3; S16 Dallavilla 8'17"0

SS8 Vero – Pont d'Azzana 1 18,28 km
1.McRae 13'06"0; 2.Auriol 13'16"9; 3.Delecour 13'17"2; 4.Liatti 13'26"1; 5.Panizzi/Wearden 13'26"7; Gr.N Manfrinato 14'11"5; S16 Dallavilla 14'07"0

SS9 Lopigna – Sarrola 1 30,11 km
1.Puras 19'33"8; 2.Panizzi 19'41"0; 3.Auriol 19'41"8; 4 Delecour 19'54"8; 5.Burns 19'59"9; 6.Solberg 20'00"0; Gr.N Trelles 21'30"5; S16 Dallavilla 21'01"4

SS10 Gare de Carbuccia – Gare d'Ucciani 2 10,66 km
1.Puras-Panizzi 7'17"8; 3.Auriol 7'19"2; 4.Delecour 7'21"8; 5.Loix 7'23"6; 6.Solberg 7'23"9; Gr.N Trelles 7'58"3; S16 Dallavilla 7'45"0

SS11 Vero – Pont d'Azzana 2 18,28 km
1.Puras 12'48"1; 2.Panizzi 12'49"4; 3.Auriol 12'53"4; 4.Solberg 12'59"7; 5.Burns 13'02"5; 6.Delecour 13'03"6; Gr.N Trelles 14'02"7; S16 Dallavilla 13'42"8

SS12 Lopigna – Sarrola 2 30,11 km
1.Puras 19'23"4; 2.Panizzi 19'29"7; 3.Auriol 19'32"8; 4.Burns 19'40"3; 5.Solberg 19'45"8; 6.Martin 19'47"7; Gr.N Trelles 21'29"5; S16 Loeb 20'44"4

SS13 Penitencier Coti – Pietra Rossa 1 24,05 km
1.Panizzi 15'10"6; 2.Puras 15'10"6; 3.Auriol 15'23"3; 4.Burns 15'24"2; 5.Rovanpera 15'32"3; 6.Loix 15'35"1; Gr.N Sanchez 16'53"1; S16 Dallavilla 16'19"2

SS14 Pont de Calzola – Agosta Plage 1 31,79 km
1.Panizzi 19'10"4; 2.Panizzi 19'26"4; 3.Burns 19'37"2; 4.Solberg 19'40"5; 5.Martin 19'42"5; 6.Rovanpera 19'48"4; Gr.N Sanchez 21'25"0; S16 Dallavilla 20'37"8

SS15 Penitencier Coti – Pietra Rossa 2 24,05 km
1.Panizzi 15'08"2; 2.Puras 15'10"5; 3.Auriol 15'10"7; 4.Solberg 15'16"1; 5.Delecour 15'38"0; 6.Burns 16'10"5; Gr.N Sanchez 17'16"3; S16 Dallavilla 17'13"9

SS16 Pont de Calzola – Agosta Plage 2 31,79 km
1.Burns 20'32"8; 2.McRae 20'42"4; 3.Liatti 20'50"3; 4.Rovanpera 20'52"2; 5.Solberg 20'54"3; 6.A. McRae 21'07"6; Gr.N Trelles 22'13"6; S16 Loeb 21'33"0

Results — WRC

	Driver/Navigator	Car	Gr.	Time
1	Puras – Marti	Citroen Xsara WRC	A	3h58'35"5
2	Panizzi – Panizzi	Peugeot 206 WRC		+ 17"5
3	Auriol – Giraudet	Peugeot 206 WRC		+ 1'11"9
4	Burns – Reid	Subaru Impreza WRC 2001		+ 4'53"1
5	Solberg – Mills	Subaru Impreza WRC 2001		+ 4'53"9
6	Martin – Park	Subaru Impreza WRC 2001		+ 5'21"6
7	Rovanpera – Pietilainen	Peugeot 206 WRC		+ 7'26"9
8	Liatti – Cassina	Hyundai Accent WRC		+ 8'09"2
9	A. McRae – Senior	Hyundai Accent WRC		+ 8'52"07
10	Delecour – Grataloup	Ford Focus RS WRC 01		+ 10'06"1
13	Loeb – Elena	Citroen Saxo	Team's Cup	+ 17'40"9
17	Trelles – Del Buono	Mitsubishi Lancer Evo 6	N	+ 24'15"8

Leading Retirements

SS.9	Schwarz – Hiemer	Skoda Octavia WRC	Power steering
SS.8	Gronholm – Rautiainen	Peugeot 206 WRC	Accident
SS.5	Makinen – Mannisenmaki	Mitsubishi Lancer Evo WRC	Accident
SS.4	Thiry – Prévot	Skoda Octavia WRC	Power steering
SS.3	Duval – Forti	Ford Puma	Engine
SS.2	Tirabassi – Le Gars	Citroen Saxo Kitcar	Accident
SS.2	Sainz – Moya	Ford Focus RS WRC 01	Engine
SS.1	Arai – McNeall	Subaru Impreza WRC 2001	Accident
SS.1	Bugalski – Chiaroni	Citroen Xsara WRC	Accident

Championship Classifications

Drivers
1. Makinen, C. McRae 40; 3. Burns 34; 4. Sainz 33; 5. Rovanpera 27; 6. Panizzi 22; 7. Auriol 19; 8. Gronholm 16; 9. Delecour 15; 10. Solberg 11; 11. Puras 10; 12. Loix 9; 13. Schwarz 7; 14. Radstrom, Loeb 6; 16. Gardemeister 5; 17. Arai, Martin 3; 19. Travaglia 2; 20. A. McRae, Hagstrom, Bugalski, Pozzo 1

Constructors
1. Ford 83; 2. Peugeot 76; 3. Mitsubishi 67; 4. Subaru 55; 5. Skoda 15; 6. Hyundai 13

Group N
1. (CHAMPION) Pozzo 65; 2. Trelles 26; 3. Ligato, Stohl 22; 5. Blomqvist 14; 6. Gillet, Walfridsson, Da Silva, Fiorio 10...

Team's Cup
1. Toyota Castrol Team Denmark (Lundgaard) 30; 2. Toyota Castrol Team Finland (Hagstrom) 20; 3. Toyota Team Saudi Arabia (Bakashab) 15...

FIA Super 1600
1. Loeb (CHAMPION) 40; 2. Dallavilla 30; 3. Basso 10...

Performers

	1	2	3	4	5	6
Puras	8	4	1	–	–	–
Panizzi	6	4	2	1	1	–
C. McRae	1	1	1	–	–	–
Burns	1	–	1	2	3	3
Auriol	–	4	7	–	2	–
Gronholm	–	1	1	1	1	–
Delecour	–	–	1	4	2	2
Liatti	–	–	1	1	–	–
Solberg	–	–	–	5	2	4
Rovanpera	–	–	–	1	1	1
Martin	–	–	–	–	2	1
Loix	–	–	–	–	1	1
Makinen	–	–	–	–	1	–
Wearden	–	–	–	–	1	–
A. McRae	–	–	–	–	–	1

Event Leaders

SS.1	Panizzi
SS.2 > SS.16	Puras

Previous winners

1973	Nicolas – Vial Alpine Renault A 110	1987	Béguin – Lenne BMW m3
1974	Andruet – "Biche" Lancia Stratos	1988	Auriol – Occelli Ford Sierra RS Cosworth
1975	Darniche – Mahé Lancia Stratos	1989	Auriol – Occelli Lancia Delta Integrale
1976	Munari – Maiga Lancia Stratos	1990	Auriol – Occelli Lancia Delta Integrale
1977	Darniche – Mahé Fiat 131 Abarth	1991	Sainz – Moya Toyota Celica GT-Four
1978	Darniche Mahé Fiat 131 Abarth	1992	Auriol – Occelli Lancia Delta HF Integrale
1979	Darniche – Mahé Lancia Stratos	1993	Delecour – Grataloup Ford Escort RS Cosworth
1980	Thérier – Vial Porsche 911SC	1994	Auriol – Occelli Toyota Celica Turbo 4WD
1981	Darniche – Mahé Lancia Stratos	1995	Auriol – Giraudet Toyota Celica GT-Four
1982	Ragnotti – Andrié Renault 5 Turbo	1996	Bugalski – Chiaroni Renault Maxi Megane
1983	Alen – Kivimaki Lancia Rally 037	1997	McRae – Grist Subaru Impreza WRC
1984	Alen – Kivimaki Lancia Rally 037	1998	McRae – Grist Subaru Impreza WRC
1985	Ragnotti – Andrié Renault 5 Turbo	1999	Bugalski – Chiaroni Citroen Xsara Kit Car
1986	Saby – Fauchille Peugeot 205 T16	2000	Bugalski – Chiaroni Peugeot 206 WRC

Australia

When he is at the wheel of a car worthy of his talent, then Gronholm is a giant. On the roads around Perth, he was in a league of his own, and his fine performance allowed Peugeot to take the lead in the championship.

WRC WORLD RALLY

First event for the Lancer WRC on the loose, but both Loix (seen here) and Makinen admitted there was still plenty of development work to be done.

THE RALLY
SUPER MARCUS

The tarmac intermission provided by San Remo and Corsica had long gone, as had the ephemeral Citroen presence. Here in the Antipodes, the world rally championship returned to the warm familiarity of its regular habits, for the penultimate round which would prove interesting, given how close things were getting. In fact, it was entirely possible for both major world titles, the Drivers' and Constructors' to be decided at the end of this event, as both McRae and Ford were in a position to wrap them up. In order to avoid the sort of shenanigans which had upset the 2000 running of this rally, with the usual and delicate problem of sorting out the running order, because the tracks were covered in ball bearing gravel, the rules regarding start numbers had been modified. Thus, each driver was able to request a start position, starting with the current leader of the championship for the first leg and then the leader of the rally at the end of the first and second legs. Naturally, this meant that the Hyundai drivers were inevitably made to open the stages by

the others, but for the six drivers who were still in with a chance of winning the title, the start system seemed to spread the load quite well.
This system meant there was none of the usual jockeying for positions on the road, with the consequence that everyone was going hell for leather right from the very start.
Gronholm took the lead on the opening stage, chased by Rovanpera, McRae, Sainz, Burns and Auriol. This round half-dozen were playing in a different ball park to the rest of the pack, who just could not keep up. The leaders scrapped amongst themselves, trading fastest times for second places, with much cut and thrust thankfully in evidence. Half-way through the leg, the magnificent six were covered by just eleven seconds. Although he was leading, the reigning world champion was a bit out of sorts. "I don't know what's wrong with my steering and I'm finding it hard to control my 206." For his part, Rovanpera was struggling to pick the most suitable rubber out of the range on offer from Michelin, gradually dropping back.
Sainz had a more disastrous spiral down the order. He had an off, broke the right

A driver is a jack of all trades: Delecour, Gronholm and Rovanpera do a spot of wheel-changing between stages.

The second half of the season saw Burns back in contention in the championship and after this event, he would pose a threat to the leaders.

rear suspension, pulled a wheel off and finally had a small fire on the run into the service area. He was 1 minute 40 down on the leader, but then had to add a 1 minute 30 penalty. He could kiss his hopes goodbye. "I've made one mistake all season, but I've done it at the worst possible moment," lamented the Spaniard. Makinen was having an even more fraught time. Leading the drivers' classification jointly with McRae, he was punished with inadequate tyres, an overheating engine and dodgy handling from the Lancer WRC. Added to that catalogue of disasters, Mannisenmaki's replacement, Hantunen, was unable to cope with the pace and the final straw was that Tommi's back was once again causing him a great deal of pain.

This meant that only four drivers were now left fighting for the lead. They were all posting good times, but it was an on-form Auriol who took control at the end of the leg, over some vicious stages; narrow and dangerous with eucalyptus trees seemingly crossing the road. He was doing a great job, but it was not enough to wrest the lead off Gronholm. Third, he had only given away 3"8 and in fact, the top five were separated by just 5"3, after 150 timed kilometres! Ironic therefore that such a magnificent first day's rallying should end with many of the combatants rolling around laughing, while others were left despondent. As planned, the drivers were all summoned ten minutes before the start of the final super-special to chose their start number for the following day. All the drivers turned up, with the notable exception of one: Colin McRae! Where was he? No. one knew. One thing was certain, he was late. But time waits for no man and all the

drivers picked a start number, except the absent Scot, which meant McRae found himself with the unpalatable job of leading the field away. It was the worst position possible. He would be a big loser, but maybe his team would lose even more.

Because the next day, slipping on his 206, Gronholm swallowed up the stages like an ogre. The super-special went to Auriol, but the other five on difficult and demanding terrain, all fell to the Finn. Nothing escaped him and his appetite was evidently insatiable that day. Having fixed the rather vague steering from the previous day, he gave free rein to his talent. "The car is ideal," he kept repeating. "I've got an incredible feeling with it. It's better than in New Zealand in September, because, with my engineer, Francois-Xavier Demaison, we have sorted out the electronic mapping." Burns, Auriol and Rovanpera all tried to hang on, but they all had to admit they were powerless against Marcus. "I had some gearbox problems," offered the Englishman as some sort of excuse. "But even if I had not, I could not have matched Marcus." He had just seen the Finn take 7.4 seconds off him in the space of 15 kilometres.

With this brilliant performance, his attackers dropped by the wayside one by one. On the Friday, the four leaders had finished within five seconds after ten stages. On Saturday, after six timed sections, Gronholm had a 34.3 advantage over a defeated Burns and 54.2 over Auriol. "I am quicker than Richard," said the leader, trying out his new found grasp of the French language. That day, he had learned a new word, an adverb, "beaucoup," (a lot) and it seemed to keep him amused.

In Australia, Gronholm was in a class of his own. No one could match the world champion and his win propelled Peugeot into the lead in the Constructors' Championship.

The cohabitation between these two men at Peugeot in 2002 should be more than interesting!

The final leg was almost a formality for the big Finn. All through the weekend, he gave a real demonstration of top line driving and professionalism – wouldn't you agree Mr. McRae? He also proved to be a strong on the human side. Wouldn't you agree Mr. Burns? And it made it him untouchable. "It all came down to the second leg," he commented. "I think without a doubt it was the best day of my career."

The effects of this event on the world championship were multiple. Second placed Burns now had a total of forty points, which was two less than Colin McRae and just one behind Makinen, as these two had carried out an effective damage limitation exercise at the end of the rally. There was one rally to go: three drivers within two points and a fourth one giving chase. Sainz was limping a bit further back, nine points behind. "It looks like being fun in Great Britain. It's simple; whoever wins, will get the title," explained McRae.

In the constructors' classification, Gronholm and Rovanpera brought home fourteen points for Peugeot, which instantly put the Lion ahead of Ford by four points. Corrado Provera's prophecy from a few rallies ago was seemingly uncannily accurate. "I dream that it will all be fought out on the final stage of the final rally." ∎

ATMOSPHERE
THE HOLIDAYS BECKON!

There,s a whiff of end of season about Australia. The sunshine, blue skies and the beach... Even in early November, it makes one think of holidays. Maybe the season should end in Perth and the Rally of Great Britain moved to the summer.

In the land of the kangaroos, Sainz tried to emulate them, but with little success. He ripped the rear axle out of his Focus.

Showing one another no mercy on the road, the McRae boys
never forget they are first and foremost brothers.

Solberg will turn his hand to anything.

But that would not do really. From a purist point of view, the Welsh campaign, swathed in fog and rain, when it,s not snowing, is as enticing as the heat of these early summer days in the Antipodes. It is part of the rich tapestry which makes up the world rally championship.

A journalist covering a full season of Formula 1 might find it difficult to work out where he was, if he was simply dropped into a grand prix circuit, without any other points of reference. But for the rally reporter, each event, apart from the sporting contest itself, brings with it a whole new set of experiences depending on the course tackled by the competitors, which is different every time, with its own unique atmosphere.

The decor changes as do the seasons, the weather and the culture. If this is the case for those merely there to watch, imagine what it feels like for the team members, especially the drivers. Remember, that until 2000 when the Safari moved to July, Sweden and Kenya followed one another just a fortnight apart, which is no time at all when one consider that the crews have to be at a

Despite his best efforts, Makinen could do no better than sixth with Hantunen standing in for Mannisenmaki.

venue at least one week before the start. From a thermal and cultural point of view, the shock was considerable.Of course, the calendar, as it can be in other disciplines, is subject to the vagaries of the different seasons in the four corners of the globe. The last two New Zealand rallies have now been moved from July, which is winter time over there to September, the start of spring. Which means one is heading to the Antipodes once a year for heavy rain to fall on the green hills as sure as the earth is round.

The Monte Carlo on the other hand, deserves to remain a winter event, preceded by lengthy test sessions with everyone kitted out in woolly hats and collars turned up against the elements as far as the eye can see. Without all this, the earthly paradise that is Australia would not hold the same charm.

Come on, it,s time to go now. The Rally of Great Britain awaits. The good thing is that, as has often been the case, it will decide the outcome of the championships, somewhere amidst the rain and the fog. ∎

14ᵗʰ RALLY AUSTRALIA

14ᵉ leg of the 2001 World Rally championship for constructors and drivers. 14ᵗʰ leg of the Group N World Championship. 6ᵗʰ leg of the Team's cup.

Date 1ˢᵗ to 4ᵗʰ november 2001

Route
1403,12 km divided into 3 legs
21 special stages on dirt roads
(380,62 km), but 20 ran
(351,35 km)

Prologue
Thursday 1ˢᵗ november: Langley Park-Perth, 1 stage (2,20 km)
1ˢᵗ leg
Friday 2 november: Perth-Mundaring-Perth, 9 stages (147,76 km)
2ⁿᵈ leg
Saturday 3 november: Perth-Collie-Perth, 7 legs but 6 ran (95,70 km)
3ʳᵈ leg
Sunday 4 november: Perth-Bunnings (Sotico)-Perth, 4 legs (105,69 km)

Starters - Finishers: 73 - 52

Conditions: Good weather, hot.

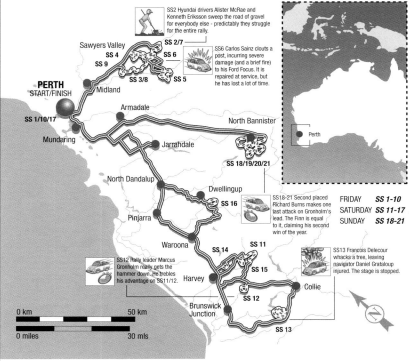

SS2 Hyundai drivers Alister McRae and Kenneth Eriksson sweep the road of gravel for everybody else - predictably they struggle for the entire rally.

SS6 Carlos Sainz clouts a post, incurring severe damage (and a brief fire) to his Ford Focus. It is repaired at service, but he has lost a lot of time.

SS18-21 Second placed Richard Burns makes one last attack on Gronholm's lead. The Finn is equal to it, claiming his second win of the year.

SS13 Francois Delecour whacks a tree, leaving navigator Daniel Grataloup injured. The stage is stopped.

SS12 Rally leader Marcus Gronholm really gets the hammer down. He trebles his advantage on SS11/12.

FRIDAY *SS 1-10*
SATURDAY *SS 11-17*
SUNDAY *SS 18-21*

TOP ENTRIES

1 Marcus Gronholm - Timo Rautiainen
Peugeot 206 WRC

2 Didier Auriol - Denis Giraudet
Peugeot 206 WRC

3 Carlos Sainz - Luis Moya
Ford Focus RS WRC

4 Colin McRae - Nicky Grist
Ford Focus RS WRC

5 Richard Burns - Robert Reid
Subaru Impreza WRC

6 Petter Solberg - Philip Mills
Subaru Impreza WRC

7 Tommi Makinen - Timo Hantunen
Mitsubishi Lancer WRC

8 Freddy Loix - Sven Smeets
Mitsubishi Lancer WRC

9 Kenneth Eriksson - Staffan Parmander
Hyundai Accent WRC

10 Alister McRae - David Senior
Hyundai Accent WRC

16 Harri Rovanpera - Risto Pietilainen
Peugeot 206 WRC

17 Francois Delecour - Daniel Grataloup
Ford Focus RS WRC

18 Toshihiro Arai - Glenn MacNeall
Subaru Impreza WRC

19 Gilles Panizzi - Herve Panizzi
Peugeot 206 WRC

20 Possum Bourne - Mark Stacey
Subaru Impreza WRC

21 Pasi Hagstrom - Tero Gardemeister
Toyota Corolla WRC

22 Henrik Lundgaard - Jens Christian Anker
Toyota Corolla WRC

23 Neal Bates - Coral Taylor
Toyota Corolla WRC

24 Hamed Al Wahaibi - Tony Sircombe
Subaru Impreza WRC

25 Abdullah Bakhashab - Bobby Willis
Toyota Corolla WRC

26 Cody Crocker - Greg Foletta
Subaru Impreza

27 Juha Kangas - Mika Ovaskainen
Mitsubishi Lancer Evo 6

28 Ed Ordynski - Ian Stewart
Mitusbishi Lancer Evo 6

29 Marko Ipatti - Karri Marttila
Subaru Impreza

30 Achim Mortl - Stefan Eichorner
Subaru Impreza WRC

31 Manfred Stohl - Peter Muller
Mitsubishi Lancer Evo 6

32 Gabriel Pozzo - Daniel Luis Stillo
Mitsubishi Lancer Evo 6

33 Marcos Ligato - Ruben Garcia
Mitsubishi Lancer Evo 6

34 Stig Blomqvist - Ana Goni
Mitsubishi Lancer Evo 6

37 Natalie Baratt - Chris Patterson
Mitsubishi Lancer Evo 6

Special Stage Times

SS1 Langley Park Super 1 2,20 km
1.Sainz/Auriol 1'30"7; 3.Delecour 1'31"3; 4.Hagstrom 1'31"5; 5.Rovanperä 1'31"7; 6.Grönholm 1'31"8; Gr.N Stohl 1'35"8

SS2 Helena North 1 24,14 km
1.Grönholm 13'43"6; 2.McRae 13'48"6; 3.Rovanperä 13'48"8; 4.Burns 13'52"0; 5.Sainz 15'52"2; 6.Auriol 13'53"8; Gr.N Stohl 14'46"6

SS3 Helena South 1 18,43 km
1.Grönholm 9'42"7; 3.Burns 9'43"0; 4.McRae 9'44"2; 5.Sainz 9'45"7; 6.Auriol 9'46"8; Gr.N Ordynski 10'29"2

SS4 Kev's 9,56 km
1.Sainz 6'01"5; 2.Burns 6'02"8; 3.McRae 6'03"4; 4.Rovanperä 6'04"5; 5.Grönholm 6'04"7; 6.Auriol 6'05"3; Gr.N Nutahara 6'28"4

SS5 Beraking 26,46 km
1.Burns 14'52"2; 2.McRae 14'53"7; 3.Auriol 14'56"3; 4.Sainz 14'56"4; 5.Grönholm 14'59"1; 6.Rovanperä 15'01"0; Gr.N Crocker 16'06"1

SS6 Flynns Short 19,98 km
1.Auriol 12'08"7; 2.McRae 12'09"0; 3.Burns 12'09"8; 4.Grönholm 12'10"0; 5.Rovanperä 12'11"5; 6.Solberg 12'16"3; Gr.N Ordynski 13'00"0

SS7 Helena North 2 24,14 km
1.Auriol 13'29"4; 2.Sainz 13'29"8; 3.Grönholm 13'31"6; 4.Burns 13'35"2; 5.McRae 13'37"3; 6.Rovanperä 13'38"4; Gr.N Ordynski 14'39"1

SS8 Helena South 2 18,43 km
1.Sainz/Burns 9'34"2; 3.Auriol 9'35"5; 4.McRae 9'35"7; 5.Grönholm 9'35"9; 6.Rovanperä 9'38"3; Gr.N Ordynski 10'29"9

SS9 Atkins 4,42 km
1.Sainz 3'01"3; 2.Auriol 3'02"8; 3.Rovanperä 3'03"7; 4.Burns 3'04"5; 5.McRae 3'05"0; 6.Grönholm/Bourne 3'05"7; Gr.N Ordynski 3'14"3

SS10 Langley Park Super 2 2,20 km
1.Auriol/Solberg 1'30"8; 3.Sainz 1'31"1; 4.Grönholm 1'31"2; 5.Delecour 1'31"5; 6.Rovanperä 1'31"6; Gr.N Stohl 1'35"4

SS11 Stirling East 35,48 km
1.Grönholm 19'38"8; 2.Burns 19'46"7; 3.Auriol 19'53"2; 4.Rovanperä 19'54"7; 5.Solberg 20'06"6; 6.Sainz 20'08"5; Gr.N Stohl 20'54"0

SS12 Brunswick 16,63 km
1.Grönholm 9'08"5; 2.Burns 9'13"2; 3.Solberg 9'17"4; 4.Mäkinen 9'19"9; 5.Rovanperä 9'21"4; 6.Sainz/McRae 9'23"5; Gr.N Stohl 9'57"4

SS13 Wellington Dam 45,42 km
Cancelled -Francois Delecour' Accident.

SS14 Harvey Weir 6,97 km
1.Grönholm 3'47"8; 2.Burns 3'48"6; 3.Rovanperä 3'50"7; 4.Mäkinen 3'51"2; 5.Sainz/Solberg 3'51"4; Gr.N Stohl 4'08"0

SS15 Stirling West 15,89 km
1.Grönholm 9'20"0; 2.Auriol 9'26"2; 3.Burns 9'27"4; 4.Rovanperä 9'29"9; 5.Sainz 9'31"3; 6.Solberg 9'32"9; Gr.N Stohl 9'57"3

SS16 Murray Pines 18,53 km
1.Grönholm 10'40"4; 2.Burns 10'48"8; 3.Auriol 10'51"3; 4.Sainz 10'55"0; 5.Loix 10'55"9; 6.Mäkinen 10'56"7; Gr.N Stohl 11'24"9

SS17 Langley Park Super 3 2,20 km
1.Auriol 1'29"7; 2.Grönholm 1'30"0; 3.Solberg 1'30"1; 4.Sainz 1'30"2; 5.McRae 1'30"9; 6.Rovanperä 1'31"1; Gr.N Pozzo 1'35"1

SS18 Bannister West Reverse 34,57 km
1.Burns 17'22"7; 2.Grönholm 17'23"1; 3.Rovanperä 17'24"9; 4.McRae 17'27"7; 5.Mäkinen 17'28"7; 6.Auriol 17'33"7; Gr.N Stohl 18'35"3

SS19 Bannister North 36,84 km
1.McRae 19'26"6; 2.Grönholm 19'27"0; 3.Burns 19'29"2; 4.Mäkinen 19'31"8; 5.Rovanperä 19'39"5; 6.Auriol 19'40"1; Gr.N Kangas 21'09"3

SS20 Bannister South Reserve 28,65 km
1.McRae 16'32"1; 2.Grönholm 16'39"2; 3.Auriol 16'39"4; 4.Rovanperä 16'40"2; 5.Sainz 16'43"3; 6.Burns 16'44"1; Gr.N Duval 17'52"2

SS21 Michelin TV Stage 5,63 km
1.McRae 3'28"1; 2.Mäkinen 3'29"2; 3.Burns/Rovanperä 3'29"6; 5.Grönholm 3'30"2; 6.Sainz/Solberg 3'31"3; Gr.N Stohl 3'44"7

Results WRC

	Driver/Navigator	Car	Gr.	Time
1	Grönholm - Rautiainen	Peugeot 206 WRC	A	3h17'01"3
2	Burns - Reid	Subaru Impreza WRC 2001		+ 40"4
3	Auriol - Giraudet	Peugeot 206 WRC		+ 1'20"1
4	Rovanperä - Pietilainen	Peugeot 206 WRC		+ 1'30"9
5	C. McRae - Grist	Ford Focus RS WRC 01		+ 1'40"0
6	Mäkinen - Hantunen	Mitsubishi Lancer WRC		+ 3'02"7
7	Solberg - Mills	Subaru Impreza WRC 2001		+ 3'41"2
8	Sainz - Moya	Ford Focus RS WRC		+ 4'59"2
9	Panizzi - Panizzi	Peugeot 206 WRC		+ 5'09"0
10	A. McRae - Senior	Hyundai Accent WRC 2		+ 7'31"7
17	Ordynski - Stewart	Mitsubishi Lancer Evo 6	N	+ 17'25"9

Leading retirements

SS.13	Delecour - Grataloup	Ford Focus RS WRC 01	Accident
SS.11	Bates - Taylor	Toyota Corolla WRC	Accident
SS.11	Arai - McNeall	Subaru Impreza WRC 2001	Engine
SS.10	Bourne - Stacey	Subaru Impreza WRC 2001	Engine
SS.6	Bakashab - Willis	Toyota Corolla WRC	Wheel torn off

Performers

	1	2	3	4	5	6
Gronholm	7	4	1	2	4	2
Auriol	5	2	5	-	-	5
Sainz	4	1	1	3	5	3
Burns	3	5	5	3	-	1
C. McRae	3	3	1	3	3	-
Rovanpera	1	-	5	4	4	5
Solberg	1	-	2	-	2	2
Makinen	-	1	-	3	1	1
Delecour	-	-	1	-	1	-
Hagstrom	-	-	-	-	1	-
Loix	-	-	-	-	1	-

Leaders

SS.1	Auriol / Sainz
SS.2 > SS.5	Gronholm
SS.6	McRae
SS.7 > ES.21	Gronholm

Championship Classifications

Drivers
1. C. McRae 42; 2. Mäkinen 41; 3. Burns 40; 4. Sainz 33; 5. Rovanperä 30; 6. Grönholm 26; 7. Auriol 23; 8. Panizzi 22; 9. Delecour 15; 10. Solberg 11; 11. Puras 10; 12. Loix 9; 13. Schwarz 7; 14. Rådström, Loeb 6; 16. Gardemeister 5; 17. Arai, Märtin 3; 19. Travaglia 2; 20. A. McRae, Hagström, Bugalski, Pozzo, 1

Constructors
1. Peugeot 90; 2. Ford 86; 3. Mitsubishi 69; 4. Subaru 62; 5. Skoda 15; 6. Hyundai 13

Group N
1. (CHAMPION) Pozzo 71; 2. Trelles 36; 3. Stohl 23...

Team's Cup
1. Toyota Castrol Team Denmark (Lundgaard) 36; 2. Team Toyota Castrol Finland (Hagström) 24; 3. Oman Arab World Rally Team (Al Wahaibi) 16...

FIA Super 1600
1. (CHAMPION) Loeb 40; 2. Dallavilla 30; 3. Basso 10...

Previous winners

1989	Kankkunen - Piironen Toyota Celica GT-Four		1995	Eriksson - Parmander Mitsubishi Lancer Ev.2
1990	Kankkunen - Piironen Lancia Delta Integrale		1996	Mäkinen - Harjanne Mitsubishi Lancer Ev.3
1991	Kankkunen - Piironen Lancia Delta Integrale		1997	McRae - Grist Subaru Impreza WRC
1992	Auriol - Occelli Lancia Delta HF Integrale		1998	Mäkinen - Mannisenmäki Mitsubishi Lancer Ev.5
1993	Kankkunen - Grist Toyota Celica Turbo 4WD		1999	Burns - Reid Subaru Impreza WRC
1994	McRae - Ringer Subaru Impreza		2000	Grönholm - Rautiainen Peugeot 206 WRC

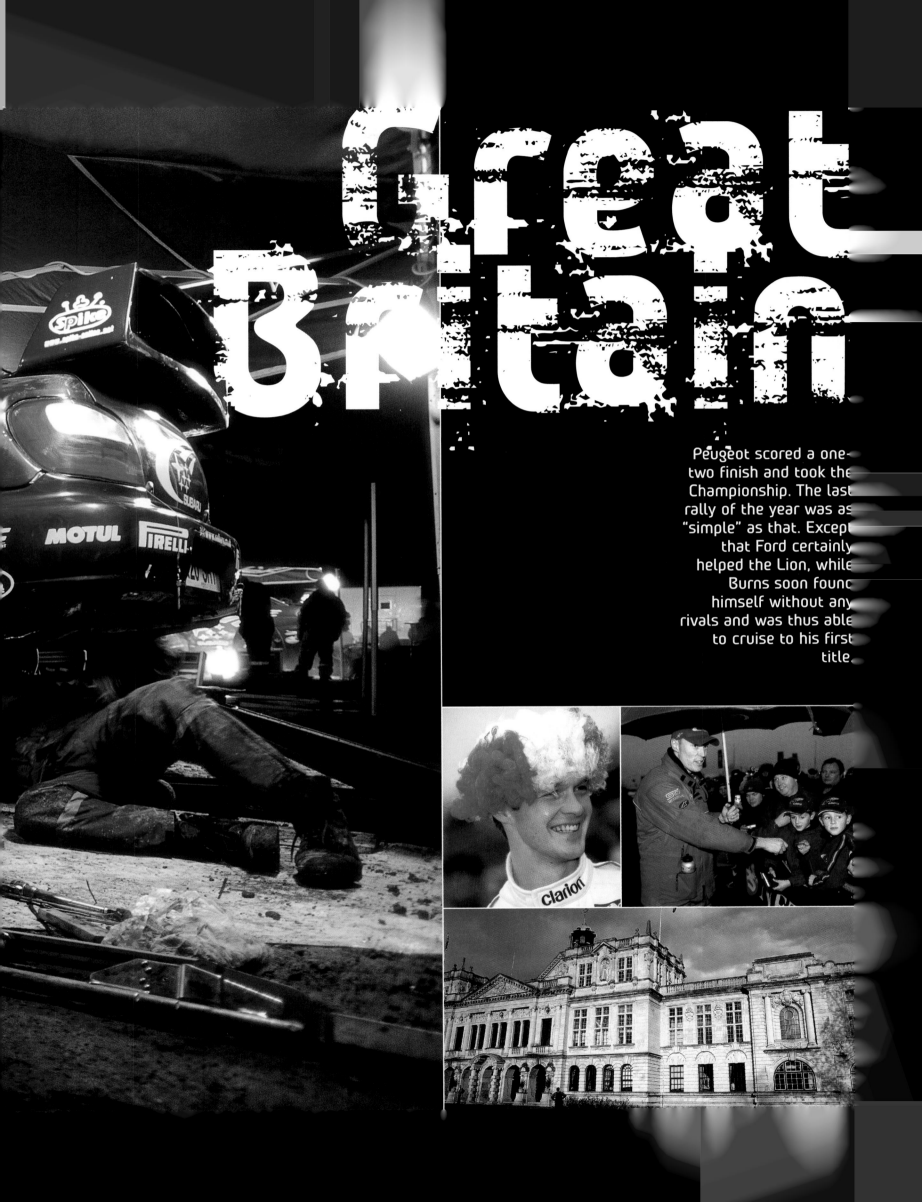

Great Britain

Peugeot scored a one-two finish and took the Championship. The last rally of the year was as "simple" as that. Except that Ford certainly helped the Lion, while Burns soon found himself without any rivals and was thus able to cruise to his first title.

One stage and that's your lot. Makinen's hopes went out the window with broken suspension.

Fifth rally in the Super 1600 class and fifth win for Loeb. Impressive!

Colin McRae went too far: according to his rivals, there was no way the corner he crashed out on was flat in sixth, trying to hook it one metre inside the corner.

fourth place and the crown was his. Unfortunately, for the Englishman,s nerves, strength was not his Subaru,s strong point. Both his team-mates, Solberg, then Martin retired in rapid succession with mechanical woes. "I am driving carefully," he admitted at the end of the leg. "Marcus is first and I am second. It,s not worth trying to do too much."

In the Ford camp, the ill fortune for Sainz and the excessive attacks of McRae had left the personnel in a mood of deep and dark despair.

Thanks to Gronholm and Rovanpera, Peugeot could legitimately hope to keep its Constructors, trophy. The world champion, still reigning for these final three legs, was in scintillating form, taking the lead handed him by McRae, while setting fastest times along the way. "The car is remarkable, but having said that, I am not driving at a hundred percent. You have to be careful. There are still two long and difficult days to go."

THE RALLY
GRONHOLM OUT ON HIS OWN

A sparkling sun rose above the hills, bathing the fields in shafts of light and sent a ray of hope that the first day would be a good one. It would be a close fought combat with the four key players, McRae, Makinen, Burns and Sainz, the last ones in the running to be champion, able to give us their best shot. It was all to take place against the magnificent backdrop of the Welsh mountains, on roads that were greasy of course, but not too muddy.

Up against Burns the Englishman, it was Scotland,s McRae who fired the first salvo. Highlander was quite simply magnificent, seemingly flying his Ford gracefully through the forests. The only one who could hang on to his exhaust pipe was Gronholm. Surprisingly, the Subaru driver was unable to lift his game enough and was even out-shone by an extravagant Auriol, looking to be the quickest in the world until slowed by mechanical bothers and driver error. More surprising still, Makinen and Sainz

both abdicated shortly after curtain-up. Three kilometres into the first stage of the day, the former destroyed the front left suspension on his Mitsubishi, going through a hole. "Yes, I was attacking," explained the Finn, "but I had to. It is hard to have to face up to the fact I am no longer in the running! One down. On the same stage, Sainz,s front right tyre exploded with a puncture, the Spaniard running on the rim and damaging the brakes. He somehow attempted a makeshift repair, but arriving late at the start of the next stage, he was saddled with a forty-second penalty, dropping down the order like a stone. That made two.

On the Rhondda stage, Colin McRae took one risk too many, cutting a corner excessively, pitching the Focus and its crew into "four or five rolls." The Scotsman likes to do these things in style and could not be bothered to count accurately. "That,s rallying for you." That was number three.

That meant, with only fifteen percent of the mileage covered, Richard Burns was the only serious championship contender still on four wheels. "When I

saw Colin,s tyre marks, I realised that objectively, he must have been taking huge risks," he commented calmly. "Now it was up to me to score three points." All he had to do was finish the rally in

Armin Schwarz did well, ending his Skoda days with a fine fifth place.

A runaway end to the season saw Peugeot hang onto its Constructors' crown. A win, a one-two finish and the title! It would all be celebrated in style!

Thanks to McRae (seen here) who finished fourth and Eriksson, sixth, Hyundai added a further four points to its total.

Difficult for everyone, especially Ford as the Blue Oval,s season came to its end. Certainly after Colin McRae,s disaster, which left his Focus looking "like a slightly damaged coupe," according to Gronholm as he drove past the wreck, and after Carlos Sainz was seriously delayed by brake problems, it was hard to imagine that things could get worse for Ford.

But they did. On the second leg, the Spaniard, in the last surviving Ford, set off along with the rest of the field, to tackle stage 12. Trawscoed, which runs through the darkness of Brechfa forest. Fifteen kilometres in on a muddy track covered in mist, the driver was tackling a left hand corner, hiding a fork. But he missed his braking point and hit several

spectators. The crew was able to keep going, getting to the end of the stage. But the team decided to retire them. Of course, the Trawscoed stage was cancelled as was the following one, which meant the second leg came down to just three stages, one of them a super-stage.

Then Gronholm set two fastest times out of three, extending his lead to 1'35"4 over Burns. "Richard won,t try anything now," commented the Finn. "Let,s wait for the finish."

The finish changed nothing. It all took place on a day when Great Britain seemed so over-populated that one wonders why it has not sunk. Water around it, water on top, water inside. Luckily, the front-runners opted for a

A sad end for Ford and Sainz. The Spaniard went off the road, halfway through the second leg, hitting thirteen spectators, luckily without serious injury. The team decided to throw in the towel.

sensible pace. Gronholm set a further three fastest times out of four, allowing Rovanpera to take one stage, which lifted him to second place, before getting him back in line. Alistair McRae, Schwarz and Eriksson did not try anything stupid, thus letting their "little" teams pick up a few useful end of term positions. Burns trundled along steadily to the finish, to take third place and pick up four points. This meant he now had forty-four, which was two more than McRae. The Englishman thus took the 23rd World Rally Championship title. The incontestable crowning of Richard Burns was similar to Keke Rosberg,s top honours in Formula 1 back in 1981. For the first time in the history of the championship, the winning driver was only victorious on one rally and had scored just 44 points.

These were just statistics and the ambitious young lad,s happiness was a pleasure to see, as he stood under the shadow of Margram castle, with the fog swirling and its towers. Only his pretty girlfriend Zoe will ever know if those were ears or rain on his cheeks, once he crossed the finish line. Salt always adds something to the emotions. ∎

THE CHAMPIONS
PEUGEOT PULLS IT OFF

From now on we are the champions," announced Peugeot Sport boss Claudio Provera calmly, once the Fords had retired. The party came the next day with tricolor wigs and all the usual nonsense,

accompanied by much horn blowing. The target had been reached before the final rally. Even if Peugeot had not done as well as in 2000, when they picked up the drivers, title to go with the constructors, the French team had won the only trophy it was really interested in. That is because this title is built over fourteen rounds in eleven months and while the 206 WRC got off to an erratic start, it was undoubtedly the best car of the 2001 pack.
"Jean Pierre Nicolas and I never doubted for a moment that we could succeed," continued Provera, recalling those difficult times. "We had to count on our ability to bounce back." It was a searing comeback at that. "After New Zealand, when all the Peugeot Sport staff got together," related rally department chief Jean-Pierre Nicolas, "I explained that so

He can wrap himself up in the Union Jack: Burns is the first ever Englishman to win the world rally championship.

Freddy Loix had another rather anonymous season. The Belgian hopes to bounce back with Hyundai in 2002.

The worthy little Tom Thumb of the Skoda family will try and do better in 2002, with Eriksson and Gardemeister replacing Schwarz (seen here) and Thiry.

With McRae and
Makinen out of the way,
Burns took no risks at
the wheel of his Subaru,
bringing it home safely
in third place, enough to
take the title.

A remarkable end to his time with
Peugeot for Didier Auriol and
possibly the end of a career as well.

The handing over of the
title from the 2000
world champion to his
successor. Nest year,
they will be Peugeot
team-mates.

far, we had picked up forty four points in
ten rallies and we had four rallies
remaining to pick up slightly over fifty,
which would guarantee us the title. A lot
of people laughed, but we did it last
year." The French team did even better,
scoring 62 out of a possible 64. Adding
a touch of style to proceedings, the
whole thing ended with a one-two
finish, the third of the year, which was
also its fifth win. No one else had done
better this year. It was a worthy title.
Finally, the irony of the situation was
that the Lion would keep the Number
One, as Burns was joining the team. "I
plan to take it with me to Peugeot in
2002," he had explained back in
Corsica, shortly after signing his
contract with the French constructor. He
kept his word. ■

57th RALLY OF GREAT BRITAIN

14th leg of the 2001 World Rally championship for constructors and drivers. **14th leg** of the Group N World Championship. **6th leg** of FIA Super 1600 Championship

Date 22th to 25th november 2001

Route
1714,77 km divided into 3 legs
17 special stages on dirt roads
(380,86 km)

Prologue
Thursday 22 november: Cardiff - Cardiff, 1 stage (2,45 km)
1st leg
Friday 23 november: Cardiff - Felindre - Cardiff, 7 stages (137,26 km)
2nd leg
Saturday 24 november: Cardiff - Felindre - Cardiff, 5 stages (132,89 km)
3rd leg
Sunday 25 november: Cardiff - Felindre - Cardiff, 4 stages (108,26 km)

Starters - Finishers: 121 - 51

Conditions: rain and heavy winds. Very muddy and slippery forest roads.

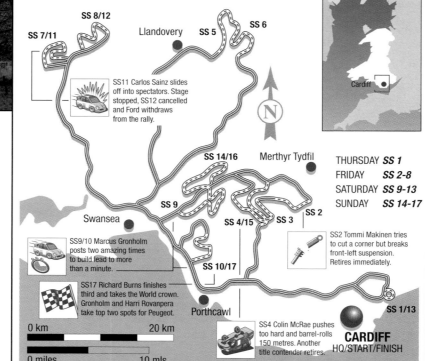

SS 8/12
SS 7/11
Llandovery
SS 5
SS 6

SS11 Carlos Sainz slides off into spectators. Stage stopped, SS12 cancelled and Ford withdraws from the rally.

Cardiff

THURSDAY *SS 1*
FRIDAY *SS 2-8*
SATURDAY *SS 9-13*
SUNDAY *SS 14-17*

SS 14/16
Merthyr Tydfil

SS 9

Swansea

SS 4/15
SS 3
SS 2

SS9/10 Marcus Gronholm posts two amazing times to build lead to more than a minute.

SS2 Tommi Makinen tries to cut a corner but breaks front-left suspension. Retires immediately.

SS10/17

SS17 Richard Burns finishes third and takes the World crown. Gronholm and Harri Rovanpera take top two spots for Peugeot.

Porthcawl

0 km   20 km
0 miles   10 mls

SS4 Colin McRae pushes too hard and barrel-rolls 150 metres. Another title contender retires.

CARDIFF
HQ/START/FINISH

SS 1/13

TOP ENTRIES

1 Marcus Gronholm - Timo Rautiainen
   Peugeot 206 WRC

2 Didier Auriol - Denis Giraudet
   Peugeot 206 WRC

3 Carlos Sainz - Luis Moya
   Ford Focus RS WRC

4 Colin McRae - Nicky Grist
   Ford Focus RS WRC

5 Richard Burns - Robert Reid
   Subaru Impreza WRC

6 Petter Solberg - Philip Mills
   Subaru Impreza WRC

7 Tommi Makinen - Kaj Lindstrom
   Mitsubishi Lancer WRC

8 Freddy Loix - Sven Smeets
   Mitsubishi Lancer WRC

9 Kenneth Eriksson - Staffan Parmander
   Hyundai Accent WRC

10 Alister McRae - David Senior
   Hyundai Accent WRC

11 Armin Schwarz - Manfred Hiemer
   Skoda Octavia WRC

12 Bruno Thiry - Stephane Prevot
   Skoda Octavia WRC

16 Harri Rovanpera - Risto Pietilainen
   Peugeot 206 WRC

17 Mark Higgins - Bryan Thomas
   Ford Focus RS WRC

18 Markko Martin - Michael Park
   Subaru Impreza WRC

19 Piero Liatti - Carlo Cassina
   Hyundai Accent WRC

20 Roman Kresta - Jan Tomanek
   Skoda Octavia WRC

21 Toshihiro Arai - Tony Sircombe
   Subaru Impreza WRC

22 Gilles Panizzi - Herve Panizzi
   Peugeot 206 WRC

23 Janne Tuohino - Petri Vihavainen
   Toyota Corolla WRC

24 Gwyndaf Evans - Chris Patterson
   Seat Cordoba WRC

26 Gregoire de Mevius - Jack Boyere
   Peugeot 206 WRC

28 Kenneth Backlund - Tord Andersson
   Mitsubishi Lancer Evo 6

29 Neil Wearden - Trevor Agnew
   Subaru Impreza WRC

31 Stig Blomqvist - Ana Goni
   Mitsubishi Lancer Evo 6

50 Manfred Stohl - Ilka Petrasko
   Fiat Punto

51 Patrick Magaud - Guylene Brun
   Ford Puma

52 Andrea Dallavilla - Giovanni Bernacchini
   Fiat Punto

53 Sebastien Loeb - Daniel Elena
   Citroen Saxo

54 Larry Cols - Dany Colebunders
   Peugeot 206

Special Stage Times

SS1 Cardiff Super 1 2,45 km
1.McRae 2'10''1; 2.Solberg 2'10''2; 3.Sainz 2'10''8; 4.Grönholm 2'11''2; 5.Panizzi 2'11''5; 6.Auriol 2'11''8; Gr.N Backlund 2'17''6; S16 Loeb 2'24''0

SS2 St. Gwynno 13,67 km
1.McRae 6'34''7; 2.Grönholm 6'36''5; 3.Auriol 6'37''8; 4.Burns 6'39''6; 5.A. McRae 6'43''4; 6.Martin 6'44''2; Gr.N Ferreyros 7'19''2 S16 Duval 7'22''9

SS3 Tyle 10,55 km
1.Grönholm 5'41''9; 2.Auriol 5'44''2; 3.Burns 5'44''5; 4.McRae 5'44''6; 5.Rovanperä 5'49''7; 6.Sainz 5'50''0; Gr.N D. Higgins 6'19''4; S16 Duval 6'24''8

SS4 Rhondda 1 26,47 km
1.Grönholm 14'09''3; 2.Auriol 14'17''0; 3.Burns 14'21''6; 4.Rovanperä 14'21''6; 5.Sainz 14'22''5; 6.Schwarz 14'33''4; Gr.N Backlund 15'38''0; S16 Loeb 16'00''0

SS5 Crychan 13,06 km
1.Grönholm 7'17''2; 2.Sainz 7'24''8;

3.Rovanperä 7'28''3; 4.Auriol 7'28''5; 5.Burns 7'29''6; 6.A.McRae 7'34''0; Gr.N D. Higgins 8'14''3; S16 Dallavilla 8'25''7

SS6 Halfway 17,45 km
1.Grönholm 10'00''1; 2.Auriol 10'02''3; 3.Burns/Rovanperä 10'04''8; 5.Sainz 10'05''1; 6.A. McRae 10'15''9; Gr.N Ferreyros 11'08''9; S16 Dallavilla 11'31''7

SS7 Brechfa 1 29,80 km
1.Grönholm 17'23''0; 2.Burns 17'23''9; 3.Sainz 17'25''3; 4.Rovanperä 17'31''0; 5.Auriol 17'41''8; 6.Loix 18'01''5; Gr.N Backlund 20'10''3; S16 Loeb 20'21''2

SS8 Trawscoed 1 26,26 km
1.Rovanperä 16'51''9; 2.Burns 16'55''0; 3.Grönholm 16'55''8; 4.A. McRae 17'24''8; 5.Higgins 17'45''3; 6.Eriksson 17'46''4; Gr.N Ferreyros 18'38''9; S16 Loeb 18'48''1

SS9 Resolfen 46,45 km
1.Grönholm 25'28''1; 2.Rovanperä 25'35''0; 3.Sainz 25'46''7; 4.Burns 25'48''8; 5.Loix 25'56''9; 6.A. McRae

25'59''6; Gr.N D. Higgins 28'03''3; S16 Loeb 28'31''1

SS10 Margam 1 27,93 km
1.Grönholm 16'26''2; 2.Burns 16'38''5; 3.Sainz 16'40''5; 4.A. McRae 16'50''8; 5.Higgins 16'52''4; 6.Rovanperä 16'53''1; Gr.N D. Higgins 18'17''7; S16 Loeb 18'59''9

SS11 Brechfa 2 29,80 km
1.Grönholm 17'12''1; 2.Burns 17'27''6; 3.Rovanperä 17'28''9; 4.Higgins 17'41''7; 5.A. McRae 17'54''6; 6.Auriol 18'08''9; Gr.N/S16 SS neutralised

SS12 Trawscoed 2 26,26 km
Cancelled

SS13 Cardiff Super 2 2,45 km
1.A. McRae 2'11''3; 2.Schwarz 2'12''0; 3.Eriksson 2'12''3; 4.Grönholm/Auriol 2'12''8; 6.Burns 2'13''1; Gr.N Backlund 2'18''4; S16 Cols 2'25''2

SS14 Rheola 1 26,93 km
1.Rovanperä 15'36''8; 2.Grönholm 15'45''4; 3.Auriol 16'08''4; 4.Schwarz 16'10''8; 5.Burns 16'12''7; 6.Thiry

16'27''1; Gr.N D. Higgins 16'49''9; S16 Dallavilla 17'24''5

SS15 Rhondda 2 26,47 km
1.Grönholm 14'31''6; 2.Rovanperä 14'42''3; 3.Burns 14'51''8; 4.Schwarz 14'56''2; 5.Eriksson 14'56''3; 6.Auriol 15'04''3; Gr.N D. Higgins 15'47''9; S16 McShea 16'10''5

SS16 Rheola 2 26,93 km
1.Grönholm 15'23''6; 2.Auriol 15'36''7; 3.Schwarz 15'42''9; 4.Eriksson 15'45''4; 5.Rovanperä 15'45''9; 6.Burns 15'47''5; Gr.N D. Higgins 16'38''3; S16 Dallavilla 17'19''7

SS17 Margam 2 27,93 km
1.Grönholm 16'30''0; 2.Auriol 16'44''4; 3.Rovanperä 16'48''1; 4.Schwarz 16'55''3; 5.A. McRae 16'56''8; 6.Burns 16'58''6; Gr.N D. Higgins 17'53''4; S16 McShea 18'33''6

Results WRC

	Driver/Navigator	Car	Gr.	Time
1	Gronholm - Rautiainen	Peugeot 206 WRC	A	3h23'44''8
2	Rovanpera - Pietilainen	Peugeot 206 WRC		+ 2'27''1
3	Burns - Reid	Subaru Impreza WRC 2001		+ 3'15''4
4	A. McRae - Senior	Hyundai Accent WRC 2		+ 3'33''4
5	Schwarz - Hiemer	Skoda Octavia WRC		+ 7'31''3
6	Eriksson - Parmander	Hyundai Accent WRC 2		+ 8'11''0
7	Auriol - Giraudet	Peugeot 206 WRC		+ 8'21''1
8	Thiry - Prevot	Skoda Octavia WRC		+ 10'55''6
9	De Mevius - Boyere	Peugeot 206 WRC		+ 14'17''7
10	Arai - Sircombe	Subaru Impreza WRC 2001		+ 15'06''4
11	Higgins - Thorley	Subaru Impreza WRC 2001 N		+ 21'11''9
15	Loeb - Elena	Citroen Saxo VTS Super 1600		+ 26'52''5

Leading Retirements

SS.12	Higgins - Thomas	Ford Focus RS WRC 01	Withdraw
SS.11	Sainz - Moya	Ford Focus RS WRC 01	Withdraw
SS.11	Loix - Smeets	Mitsubishi Lancer WRC	Gearbox
SS.5	Märtin - Park	Subaru Impreza WRC 2001	Engine
SS.4	C. McRae - Grist	Ford Focus RS WRC 01	Accident
SS.2	Solberg - Mills	Subaru Impreza WRC 2001	Fuel pressure
SS.2	Mäkinen - Lindström	Mitsubishi Lancer Evo. WRC	Suspension

Championship Classifications

Drivers
1. Burns 44; 2. C. McRae 42; 3. Makinen 41; 4. Rovanpera, Gronholm 36; 6. Sainz 33; 7. Auriol 23; 8. Panizzi 22; 9. Delecour 15; 10. Solberg 11; 11. Puras 10; 12. Loix, Schwarz 9; 14. Loeb, Radstrom 6; 16. Gardemeister 5; 17. A. McRae 4; 18. Märtin, Arai 3; 20. Travaglia 2; 21. Bugalski, Eriksson, Pozzo, Hagstrom 1

Constructors
1. Peugeot 106; 2. Ford 86; 3. Mitsubishi 69; 4; Subaru 66; 5. Skoda, Hyundai 17

Group N
1. Pozzo 71; 2. Trelles 36; 3. Stohl 23...

Team's Cup
1. Toyota Castrol Team Denmark (Lundgaard) 36; 2. Team Toyota Castrol Finland (Hagstrom) 24; 3. Oman Arab World Rally Team (Al Wahaibi) 16...

FIA Super 1600
1. Loeb 50; 2. Dallavilla 30; 3. McShea 12...

Performers

	1	2	3	4	5	6
Gronholm	11	2	1	2	-	-
Rovanpera	2	2	4	2	2	1
C. McRae	2	-	-	1	-	-
A. McRae	1	-	-	2	3	3
Burns	-	4	4	2	2	3
Sainz	-	1	4	-	2	1
Schwarz	-	1	1	3	-	1
Solberg	-	1	-	-	-	-
Eriksson	-	-	1	1	1	1
Loix	-	-	-	-	1	1
Panizzi	-	-	-	-	1	-
Martin	-	-	-	-	-	1
Thiry	-	-	-	-	-	1

Leaders

SS.1 > SS.3	McRae
SS.4 > SS.17	Gronholm

Previous winners

1974	Makinen - Liddon Ford Escort RS 1600		1988	Alen - Kivimaki Lancia Delta Integrale
1975	Makinen - Liddon Ford Escort RS		1989	Airikkala - McNamee Mitsubishi Galant VR4
1976	Clark - Pegg Ford Escort RS		1990	Sainz - Moya Toyota Celica GT-Four
1977	Waldegaard - Thorszelius Ford Escort RS		1991	Kankkunen - Piironen Lancia Delta Integrale
1978	Mikkola - Hertz Ford Escort RS		1992	Sainz - Moya Toyota Celica Turbo 4WD
1979	Mikkola - Hertz Ford Escort RS		1993	Kankkunen - Piironen Toyota Celica Turbo 4WD
1980	Toivonen - White Talbot Sunbeam Lotus		1994	McRae - Ringer Subaru Impreza
1981	Mikkola - Hertz Audi Quattro		1995	McRae - Ringer Subaru Impreza
1982	Mikkola - Hertz Audi Quattro		1996	Schwarz - Giraudet Toyota Celica GT-Four
1983	Blomqvist - Cederberg Audi Quattro		1997	McRae - Grist Subaru Impreza WRC
1984	Vatanen - Harryman Peugeot 205 T16		1998	Burns - Reid Mitsubishi Carisma GT
1985	Toivonen - Wilson Lancia Delta S4		1999	Burns - Reid Subaru Impreza WRC
1986	Salonen - Harjanne Peugeot 205 T16		2000	Burns - Reid Subaru ImprezaWRC 2000
1987	Kankkunen - Piironen Lancia Delta HF			

2001 World Championship for Drivers

Drivers	Monte-Carlo	Sweden	Portugal	Spain	Argentina	Cyprus	Greece	Safari	Finland	New Zealand	Italy	France	Australia	Great Britain	TOTAL
1 Burns	-	-	3	-	6	6	-	-	6	10	-	3	6	4	44
2. C. Mc Rae	-	-	-	-	10	10	10	-	4	6	-	-	2	-	42
3. Makinen	10	-	10	4	3	-	3	10	-	-	-	-	1	-	41
4. Gronholm	-	-	4	-	-	-	-	-	10	2	-	-	10	10	36
= Rovanpera	-	10	-	-	-	-	4	6	3	4	-	-	3	6	36
5. Sainz	6	4	6	2	4	4	-	-	1	3	3	-	-	-	33
6. Auriol	-	-	-	10	-	-	-	-	-	1	4	4	4	-	23
7. Panizzi	-	-	-	6	-	-	-	-	-	-	10	6	-	-	22
8. Delecour	4	2	2	1	-	-	2	3	-	-	1	-	-	-	15
9. Solberg	-	1	-	-	2	6	-	-	-	-	-	2	-	-	11
10. Puras	-	-	-	-	-	-	-	-	-	-	-	10	-	-	10
11. Loix	1	-	-	3	1	2	-	2	-	-	-	-	-	-	9
= Schwartz	3	-	-	-	-	4	-	-	-	-	-	-	2	-	9
13. Radstrom	-	6	-	-	-	-	-	-	-	-	-	-	-	-	6
= Loeb	-	-	-	-	-	-	-	-	-	-	-	6	-	-	6
15. Gardemeister	2	3	-	-	-	-	-	-	-	-	-	-	-	-	5
16. A. McRae	-	-	1	-	-	-	-	-	-	-	-	-	-	3	4
17. Arai	-	-	-	-	-	3	-	-	-	-	-	-	-	-	3
= Martin	-	-	-	-	-	-	-	-	2	-	-	1	-	-	3
19. Tavaglia	-	-	-	-	-	-	-	-	-	-	2	-	-	-	2
20. Eriksson	-	-	-	-	-	-	-	-	-	-	-	-	1	-	1
= Bugalski	-	-	-	-	-	1	-	-	-	-	-	-	-	-	1
= Pozzo	-	-	-	-	-	-	1	-	-	-	-	-	-	-	1
= Hagstrom	-	-	-	-	1	-	-	-	-	-	-	-	-	-	1

2001 World Championship for Constructors

Constructors	Monte-Carlo	Sweden	Portugal	Spain	Argentina	Cyprus	Greece	Safari	Finland	New Zealand	Italy	France	Australia	Great Britain	TOTAL
1. Peugeot	-	-	4	16	-	-	-	6	13	5	16	16	14	16	106
2. Ford	6	8	6	2	14	14	10	-	6	10	7	-	3	-	86
3. Mitsubishi	13	10	10	7	4	3	6	13	-	-	1	-	2	-	69
4. Subaru	-	4	3	1	8	6	6	-	7	11	2	7	7	4	66
5. Skoda	5	1	-	-	-	1	4	4	-	-	-	-	2	-	17
= Hyundai	2	3	3	-	-	2	-	-	-	-	-	3	-	4	17

REGULATIONS: DRIVERS'CHAMPIONSHIP: All result count. 1st - 10 points, 2nd - 6 points, 3rd - 4 points, 4th - 3points, 5th - 2 points, 6th - 1 point.
CONSTRUTORS'CHAMPIONSHIP: To be eligible, the constructors who have registered with FIA, must take part in all the events with a minimum of two cars.
The first two cars score the points according to their finishing position. All results are taken into consideration. Points scale is the same as for the drivers

World Championship for Constructors

1973 Alpine-Renault
1974 Lancia
1975 Lancia
1976 Lancia
1977 Fiat
1978 Fiat
1979 Ford
1980 Fiat
1981 Talbot
1982 Audi
1983 Lancia
1984 Audi
1985 Peugeot
1986 Peugeot

1987 Lancia
1988 Lancia
1989 Lancia
1990 Lancia
1991 Lancia
1992 Lancia
1993 Toyota
1994 Toyota
1995 Subaru
1996 Subaru
1997 Subaru
1998 Mitsubishi
1999 Toyota
2000 Peugeot
2001 Peugeot

World Championship for drivers

1977 Sandro Munari (I)
1978 Markku Alen (SF)
1979 Bjorn Waldegaard (S)
1980 Walter Rohrl (D)
1981 Ari Vatanen (SF)
1982 Walter Rohrl (D)
1983 Hannu Mikkola (SF)
1984 Stig Blomqvist (S)
1985 Timo Salonen (SF)
1986 Juha Kankkunen (SF)
1987 Juha Kankkunen (SF)
1988 Miki Biasion (I)

1989 Miki Biasion (I)
1990 Carlos Sainz (E)
1991 Juha Kankkunen (SF)
1992 Carlos Sainz (E)
1993 Juha Kankkunen (SF)
1994 Didier Auriol (F)
1995 Colin McRae (GB)
1996 Tommi Makinen (SF)
1997 Tommi Makinen (SF)
1998 Tommi Makinen (SF)
1999 Tommi Makinen (SF)
2000 Marcus Grönholm (SF)
2001 Richard Burns (GB)

1977-1978: FIA cup for Drivers

2001 Productions car Championship for Drivers (Group N)

Drivers	Monte-Carlo	Sweden	Portugal	Spain	Argentina	Cyprus	Greece	Safari	Finland	New Zealand	Italy	France	Australia	Great Britain	TOTAL
1. Pozzo	3	-	-	10	10	4	10	10	6	6	6	-	6	-	71
2. Trelles	4	-	-	-	6	10	6	-	-	-	-	10	-	-	36
3. Stohl	6	-	-	-	-	6	-	4	-	10	-	-	1	-	27
4. Ligato	2	-	-	-	-	4	6	10	-	-	-	-	-	-	22
5. Blomqvist	-	4	-	4	-	-	-	-	-	3	3	-	-	3	17
= Sanchez	-	-	-	4	-	-	-	-	-	-	-	6	-	-	10
8. Duval	-	-	-	-	-	-	-	-	-	-	-	-	4	-	4
= Nutahara	-	-	-	-	-	-	-	-	-	-	4	-	-	-	4
10. Latvala	-	-	-	-	-	-	3	-	-	-	-	-	-	-	3
= Hugo	-	-	-	-	3	-	-	-	-	-	-	-	-	-	3
12. Crocker	-	-	-	-	-	-	-	-	-	-	-	-	2	-	2
= Holmes	-	-	-	-	-	-	-	-	-	-	2	-	-	-	2
= Baratten	-	-	-	-	2	-	-	-	-	-	-	-	-	-	2
= Smith	-	-	-	-	-	-	-	2	-	-	-	-	-	-	2
15. Jones	-	-	-	-	-	-	-	-	-	-	1	-	-	-	1
= Kayser	-	-	-	-	-	-	1	-	-	-	-	-	-	-	1
= Villagra	-	-	-	1	-	-	-	-	-	-	-	-	-	-	1

REGULATIONS: The classification is based on the total number of rallies minuus one. At least one rally outside Europe has to be entered. Points scored as follows; 1st – 10 points, 2nd – 6 points, 3rd – 4 points, 4th – 3points, 5th – 2 points, 6th – 1 point. The points are added with those scored in the different capacity classes (up to 1300cc; 1301-2000cc; over2000cc) on the following scale: 1st – 3 points, 2nd – 2 points, 3rd – 1 point; Class points are only attributed to drivers finishing in the top six of the production car classification

Group N Cup Winners

1987	Alex Fiorio (I)	1994	Jesus Puras (E)
1988	Pascal Gaban (B)	1995	Rui Madeira (P)
1989	Alain Oreille (F)	1996	Gustavo Trelles (ROU)
1990	Alain Oreille (F)	1997	Gustavo Trelles (ROU)
1991	Grégoire de Mevius (B)	1998	Gustavo Trelles (ROU)
1992	Grégoire de Mevius (B)	1999	Gustavo Trelles (ROU)
1993	Alex Fassina (I)	2000	Manfred Stohl (D)
		2001	Gabriel Pozzo (RA)

FIA Team's Cup

1998	H.F. Grifone
1999	Valencia Terra Mar – Luis Climent
2000	Spike Subaru Team – Toshihiro Arai
2001	Toyota Team Denmark – Lundgaard

2001 FIA Team's Cup

Teams	Sweden	Portugal	Cyprus	Greece	Italy	Australia	TOTAL	
1. Toyota Castrol Team Denmark	10	-	-	10	10	6	36	Lundgaard
2. Toyota Castrol Team Finland	-	10	10	-	-	4	24	Hagstrom
3. Toyota Team Saudi Arabia	3	-	6	6	-	-	15	Bakashab
4. Oman Arab World Rally Team	-	6	-	-	-	10	16	Al Wahaibi
5. David Sutton Cars LTD	6	-	-	-	4	-	10	Blomquist
6. Natalie Barratt Rallysport	-	-	4	3	-	2	9	Barratt
7. World Rally Hire	1	3	-	-	-	1	5	Heath

REGULATIONS: To be eligible to score points each team must take part in 7 Cup Rallies with at least one outside Europe, with a maximum of two cars (Group A or Group N) per team. Only the best placed car score points according to its position relative to the other cup competitors, on the same scale of points as the FIA world rally championship.

FIA Super 1600 Championship

Drivers	Spain	Greece	Finland	Italy	France	Great Britain	TOTAL
1. Loeb	10	10	10	-	10	10	50
2. Dallavila	2	6	6	10	6	-	30
3. McShea	-	-	-	3	3	6	12
4. Cols	-	-	3	4	-	4	11
5. Basso	6	-	-	-	4	-	10
6. Stenshorne	3	4	-	-	1	-	8
7. Duval	-	-	-	6	-	-	6
= Fontana	4	-	2	-	-	-	6
9. Valimaki	-	-	4	-	-	-	4
= Galanti	-	-	1	-	-	3	4
= Magaud	-	2	-	2	-	-	4
12. Robert	-	3	-	-	-	-	3
= Vallejo	-	-	-	1	2	-	3
14. Malzan	-	-	1	-	-	1	2
= Ceccato	-	1	-	-	-	1	2
16. Chemin	1	-	-	-	-	-	1

DRIVERS WHO HAVE WON WORLD CHAMPIONSHIP RALLIES FROM 1973 TO 2001

DRIVERS	Number of WINS	RALLIES
Andrea Aghini (I)	1	1992 I
Pentti Airikkala (SF)	1	1989 GB
Markku Alen (SF)	20	1975 P • 1976 SF • 1977 P • **1978** P-SF-I • 1979 SF • 1980 SF • 1981 P • 1983 F-I • 1984 F • 1986 I-USA • 1987 P-GR-SF • 1988 S-SF-GB
Alain Ambrosino (F)	1	1988 CI
Ove Andersson (S)	1	1975 EAK
Jean-Claude Andruet (F)	3	1973 MC • 1974 F • 1977 I
Didier Auriol (F)	20	1988 F • 1989 F • 1990 MC-F-I • 1991 I • 1992 MC-F-GR-RA-SF-AUS • 1993 MC • 1994 F-RA-I • 1995 F • 1998 E • 1999 C • 2001 E
Fulvio Bacchelli (I)	1	1977 NZ
Bernard Beguin (F)	1	1987 F
Miki Biasion (I)	17	1986 RA • 1987 MC-RA-I • **1988** P-EAK-GR-USA-I • **1989** MC-P-EAK-GR-I • 1990 P-RA • 1993 GR
Stig Blomqvist (S)	11	1973 S • 1977 S • 1979 S • 1982 S-I • 1983 GB • **1984** S-GR-NZ-RA-CI
Walter Boyce (CDN)	1	1973 USA
Philippe Bugalski (F)	2	1999 E-F
Richard Burns (GB)	9	1998 EAK • 1999 Gr-AUS-GB • 2000 EAK-P-RA-GB • 2001 NZ
Ingvar Carlsson (S)	2	1989 S-NZ
Roger Clark (GB)	1	1976 GB
Gianfranco Cunico (I)	1	1993 I
Bernard Darniche (F)	7	1973 MA • 1975 F • 1977 F • 1978 F • 1979 MC-F • 1981 F
François Delecour (F)	4	1993 P-F-E • 1994 MC
Ian Duncan (EAK)	1	1994 EAK
Per Eklund (S)	1	1976 S
Mikael Ericsson (S)	2	1989 RA-SF
Kenneth Eriksson (S)	6	1987 CI 1991 S • 1995 S-AUS 1997 S-NZ
Tony Fassina (I)	1	1979 I
Guy Frequelin (F)	1	1981 RA
Marcus Gronholm (SF)	7	**2000** S-NZ-F-AUS • 2001 FIN-AUS-GB
Sepp Haider (A)	1	1988 NZ
Kyosti Hamalainen (SF)	1	1977 SF
Mats Jonsson (S)	2	1992 S • 1993 S
Harry Kallstom (S)	1	1976 GR
Juha Kankkunen (SF)	23	1985 EAK-CI • **1986** S-GR-NZ • **1987** USA-GB • 1989 AUS • 1990 AUS 1991 EAK-GR-SF-AUS-GB 1992 P • **1993** EAK-RA-SF-AUS-GB • 1994 P 1999RA-SF
Anders Kullang (S)	1	1980 S
Piero Liatti (I)	1	1997 MC
Colin McRae (GB)	23	1993 NZ • 1994 NZ-GB • **1995** NZ-GB • 1996 GR-I-E • 1997 EAK-F-I-AUS-GB 1998 P-F-GR 1999 EAK-P • 2000 E-GR • 2001 RA-CY-GR
Timo Makinen (SF)	4	1973 SF-GB • 1974 GB • 1975 GB
Tommi Makinen (SF)	23	1994 SF • **1996** S-EAK-RA-SF-AUS • **1997** P-E-RA-SF **1998** S-RA-NZ-SF-I-AUS **1999** Mc-S-NZ-I 2000 Mc • 2001 MC-POR-EAK
Shekhar Mehta (EAK)	5	1973 EAK • 1979 EAK • 1980 EAK • 1981 EAK • 1982 EAK
Hannu Mikkola (SF)	18	1974 SF • 1975 MA-SF • 1978 GB • 1979 P-NZ-GB-CI • 1981 S-GB • 1982 SF-GB **1983** S-P-RA-SF • 1984 P • 1987 EAK
Joaquim Moutinho (P)	1	1986 P
Michèle Mouton (F)	4	1981 I • 1982 P-GR-BR
Sandro Munari (I)	7	1974 I-CDN • 1975 MC • 1976 MC-P-F • **1977** MC
Jean-Pierre Nicolas	5	1973 F • 1976 MA • 1978 MC-EAK-CI
Alain Oreille (F)	1	1989 CI
Jesus Puras (E)	1	2001 FR
Gilles Panizzi (F)	2	2000 F-I • 2001 IT
Rafaelle Pinto (P)	1	1974 P
Jean Ragnotti (F)	3	1981 MC • 1982 F • 1985 F
Jorge Recalde (RA)	1	1988 RA
Walter Rôhrl (D)	14	1975 GR • 1978 GR-CDN **1980** MC-P-RA-I • **1982** MC-CI • 1983 MC-GR-NZ 1984 MC • 1985 I
Harri Rovanpera (SF)	1	2001 S
Bruno Saby (F)	2	1986 F • 1988 MC
Carlos Sainz (E)	23	**1990** GR-NZ-SF-GB • 1991 MC-P-F-NZ-RA • **1992** EAK-NZ-E-GB • 1994 GR 1995 MC-P-E • 1996 RI • 1997 GR-RI 1998 MC-NZ 2000 CY
Timo Salonen (SF)	11	1977 CDN • 1980 NZ • 1981 CI • **1985** P-GR-NZ-RA-SF • 1986 SF-GB • 1987 S
Armin Schwarz (D)	1	1991 E
Kenjiro Shinozuka (J)	2	1991 CI • 1992 CI
Joginder Singh (EAK)	2	1974 EAK • 1976 EAK
Patrick Tauziac (F)	1	1990 CI
Jean-Luc Thèrier (F)	5	1973 P-GR-I • 1974 USA • 1980 F
Henri Toivonen (SF)	3	1980 GB • 1985 GB • 1986 MC
Ari Vatanen (SF)	10	1980 GR • **1981** GR-BR-SF • 1983 EAK • 1984 SF-I-GB • 1985 MC-S
Bjorn Waldegaard (S)	16	1975 S-I • 1976 I • 1977 EAK-GR-GB • 1978 S • **1979** GR-CDN • 1980 CI • 1982 NZ 1983 CI • 1984 EAK • 1986 EAK-CI • 1990 EAK
Achim Warmbold (D)	2	1973 PL-A
Franz Wittmann (A)	1	1987 NZ

A: Austria – AUS: Australia – BR: Brazil – C : China – CDN: Canada – CI: Ivory Coast – CY : Cyprus – E: Spain – EAK : Kenya – F: France – GB: Great Britain– GR: Greece – I: Italia – MA: Marocco – MC: Monte-Carlo – NZ: New Zealand – P: Portugal – PL: Poland – RA: Argentina – RI: Indonésia – S: Sweden – SF: Finland – USA : United States of America

World Rally Championship
From the 4,000 corners of the earth

PlayStation.2

14 countries. Hundreds of miles. Thousands of different corners.